How Professors Think

HOW PROFESSORS THINK

INSIDE THE CURIOUS WORLD OF ACADEMIC JUDGMENT

Michèle Lamont

HARVARD UNIVERSITY PRESS
Cambridge, Massachusetts / London, England / 2009

TO FRANK, AVEC AMOUR

Copyright © 2009 by the President and Fellows of Harvard College
All rights reserved
Printed in the United States of America

Library of Congress Cataloging-in-Publication Data

Lamont, Michèle, 1957–
    How professors think : inside the curious world of academic judgment /
Michèle Lamont.
        p.   cm.
    Includes bibliographical references and index.
    ISBN 978-0-674-03266-8 (cloth : alk. paper)
        1. College teachers—Rating of.   2. Peer review.   3. Teacher effectiveness.
4. Portfolios in education.   I. Title.
    LB2333.L36   2009
    378.1'2—dc22   2008031423

Contents

1/Opening the Black Box of Peer Review

There are competing narratives about what passes for being good. There are different standards of excellence, different kinds of excellence, and I'm certainly willing to entertain somebody else's standard of excellence up to a point. I'm not sure that I could articulate what that point is, but I'm pretty confident that I'd know it when I see it. You develop a little bit of a nose for it. Particularly for what's bad.

Sociologist

Definitions of excellence come up every time. [My colleagues] feel perfectly comfortable saying, "I didn't think this was a terribly good book," as if what they mean by a good book is self-apparent . . . What they mean seems really sort of ephemeral or elusive.

English professor

I felt like we were sitting on the top of a pyramid where people had been selected out at various stages of their lives and we were getting people who had demonstrated a fair amount of confidence and were sorting between kind of B, B+, and A scholars, and we all thought we were A's.

Political scientist

"Excellence" is the holy grail of academic life. Scholars strive to produce research that will influence the direction of their field. Universities compete to improve their relative rankings. Students seek inspiring mentors. But if excellence is ubiqui-tously evoked, there is little cross-disciplinary consensus about what it means and how it is achieved, especially in the world of research. "The cream of the crop" in an English or anthropology department has little in common with "the best and the brightest" in an econom-ics department. This disparity does not occur because the academic enterprise is bankrupt or meaningless. It happens because disciplines shine under varying lights and because their members define quality in various ways. Moreover, criteria for assessing quality or excellence can be differently weighted and are the object of intense conflicts. Making sense of standards and the meanings given to them is the ob-ject of this book.

The Latin word *academia* refers to a community dedicated to higher learning. At its center are colleagues who are defined as "peers" or "equals," and whose opinions shape shared definitions of quality. In the omnipresent academic evaluation system known as peer re-view, peers pass judgment, usually confidentially, on the quality of the work of other community members. Thus they determine the al-location of scarce resources, whether these be prestige and honors, fellowships and grants to support research, tenured positions that provide identifiable status and job security, or access to high-status publications. Peers monitor the flow of people and ideas through the various gates of the academic community. But because academia is not democratic, some peers are given more of a voice than others and serve as gatekeepers more often than others. Still, different peo-ple guard different gates, so gatekeepers are themselves subject to evaluation at various times.[1]

Peer review is secretive. Only those present in the deliberative chambers know exactly what happens there. In this book I report what I have learned about this peculiar world. I studied humanists and social scientists serving on multidisciplinary panels that had been charged with distributing prestigious fellowships and grants in support of scholarly research. I conducted in-depth interviews with these experts and also observed their deliberations. During their face-to-face discussions, panelists make their criteria of evaluation explicit to one another as they weigh the merits of individual proposals and try to align their own standards with those of the applicants' disciplines. Hence, grant review panels offer an ideal setting for observing competing academic definitions of excellence. That peer evaluation consumes what for many academics seems like an ever-growing portion of their time is an additional reason to give it a close look.

Academic excellence is produced and defined in a multitude of sites and by an array of actors. It may look different when observed through the lenses of editorial peer review, books that are read by generations of students, current articles published by top journals, elections at national academies, or appointments at elite institutions. American higher education also has in place elaborate processes for hiring, promoting, and firing academics. Systematically examining parts of this machinery is an essential step in assessing the extent to which this system is harmonized by a shared evaluative culture.

Evaluations of fellowship programs typically seek answers to such questions as: Are these programs successful in identifying talent? Do awardees live up to their promise? The tacit assumption is that these programs give awards to talented people with the hope that the fellowship will help them become "all they can be."[2] Examining how the worth of academic work is ascertained is a more counterintuitive, but I think ultimately more intriguing, undertaking. Rather than focusing on the trajectory of the brilliant individual or the outstanding oeuvre, I approach the riddle of success by analyzing the context of evaluation—including which standards define and constrain what we see as excellent.[3]

By way of introduction, I pose and answer the same kinds of questions that are typically asked in peer review of completed or proposed research proposals.

What do you study? I study evaluative cultures.[4] This broad term includes many components: cultural scripts that panelists employ when discussing their assessments (is the process meritocratic?);[5] the meaning that panelists give to criteria (for instance, how do you recognize originality?); the weight they attribute to various standards (for example, "quality" versus "diversity"); and how they understand excellence. Do they believe excellence has an objective reality? If so, where is it located—in the proposal (as economists generally believe) or in the eye of the beholder (as English scholars claim)?

Evaluative cultures also include how reviewers conceive of the relationship between evaluation and power dynamics, their ability to judge and reach consensus, and their views on disciplinary boundaries and the worth and fate of various academic fields. Finally, evaluative cultures include whether panelists think that subjectivity has a corrupting influence on evaluation (the caricatured view of those in the harder social sciences) or is intrinsic to appreciation and connoisseurship (the view of those in the humanities and more interpretive social sciences).[6]

I study shared standards and evaluative disciplinary cultures in six disciplines. Each presents its own characteristics and challenges. In philosophy, members claim a monopoly on the assessment of their disciplinary knowledge. In history, a relatively strong consensus is based on a shared sense of craftsmanship. Anthropologists are preoccupied with defining and maintaining the boundaries of their discipline. English literary scholars experience their field as undergoing a "legitimation crisis," while political scientists experience theirs as divided. In contrast, economists view their own field as consensual and unified by mathematical formalism.

Whom do you study? I study panelists, who are, in principle, highly regarded experts known for their good "people skills" and sound judgments. They have agreed to serve on grant peer review panels for a host of reasons having to do with influence, curiosity, or pleasure. Some say that they are "tremendously delighted" to spend a day or two witnessing brilliant minds at work. Others serve on panels to participate in a context where they can be appreciated, that is, where they can sustain—and ideally, enhance—their identities as highly respected experts whose opinions matter.

Why study peer review? As I write, debates are raging about the relative significance of excellence and diversity in the allocation of resources in American higher education. Are we sacrificing one for the other? Analyzing the wider culture of evaluation helps us understand their relationship. For all but the top winners, decisions to fund are based generally on a delicate combination of considerations that involve both excellence and diversity. Often panelists compete to determine which of several different types of diversity will push an A− or B+ proposal above the line for funding—and very few proposals are pure As. Evaluators are most concerned with disciplinary and institutional diversity, that is, ensuring that funding not be restricted to scholars in only a few fields or at top universities. A few are also concerned with ethnoracial diversity, gender, and geographic diversity. Contra popular debates, in the real world of grant peer review, excellence and diversity are not alternatives; they are additive considerations. The analysis I provide makes clear that having a degree from say, a Midwestern state university, instead of from Yale, is not weighed in a predictable direction in decision-making processes. Similarly, while being a woman or person of color may help in some contexts, it hurts in others.[7]

What kind of approach do you take? I think that as social actors seeking to make sense of our everyday lives, we are guided primarily by pragmatic, problem-solving sorts of concerns. Accordingly, my analysis shows that panelists adopt a pragmatic approach to evaluation. They need to reach a consensus about a certain number of proposals by a predetermined time, a practical concern that shapes what they do as well as how they understand the fairness of the process. They develop a sense of shared criteria as the deliberations proceed, and they self-correct in dialogue with one another, as they "learn by monitoring."[8] Moreover, while the language of excellence presumes a neat hierarchy from the best to the worst proposals, panelists adopt a nonlinear approach to evaluation. They compare proposals according to shared characteristics as varied as topic, method, geographical area, or even alphabetical order. Evaluators are often aware of the inconsistencies imposed by the conditions under which they carry out their task.

What do you find? The actions of panelists are constrained by the mechanics of peer review, with specific procedures (concerning the rules of deliberation, for instance) guiding their work. Their evaluations are shaped by their respective disciplinary evaluative cultures, and by formal criteria (such as originality, significance, feasibility) provided by the funding competition. Reviewers also bring into the mix diversity considerations and more evanescent criteria—elegance, for example. Yet despite this wide array of disciplinary differences, they develop together shared rules of deliberation that facilitate agreement. These rules include respecting the sovereignty of other disciplines and deferring to the expertise of colleagues. They entail bracketing self-interest, idiosyncratic taste, and disciplinary prejudices, and promoting methodological pluralism and cognitive contextualization (that is, the use of discipline-relevant criteria of evaluation). Respect for these rules leads panelists to believe that the peer review process works, because panelists judge each other's standards and behavior just as much as they judge proposals.[9]

Peer review has come under a considerable amount of criticism and scrutiny.[10] Various means—ranging from double-blind reviewing to training and rating—are available to enforce consistency, ensure replicability and stability, and reduce ambiguity. Grant peer review still favors the face-to-face meeting, unlike editorial peer review, where evaluators assess papers and book manuscripts in isolation and make recommendations, usually in writing, to physically distant editors.[11] Debating plays a crucial role in creating trust: fair decisions emerge from a dialogue among various types of experts, a dialogue that leaves room for discretion, uncertainty, and the weighing of a range of factors and competing forms of excellence. It also leaves room for flexibility and for groups to develop their own shared sense of what defines excellence—that is, their own group style, including speech norms and implicit group boundaries.[12] Personal authority does not necessarily corrupt the process: it is constructed by the group as a medium for expertise and as a ground for trust in the quality of decisions made.[13] These are some of the reasons that deliberation is viewed as a better tool for detecting quality than quantitative techniques such as citation counts.

It may be possible to determine the fairness of particular decisions, but it is impossible to reach a definite, evidence-based conclusion concerning the system as a whole. Participants' faith in the system, however, has a tremendous influence on how well it works. Belief in the legitimacy of the system affects individual actions (for instance, the countless hours spent reading applications) as well as evaluators' understanding of what is acceptable behavior (such as whether and how to signal the disregard of personal interest in making awards). Thus embracing the system has important, positive effects on the panelists' behavior.[14]

What is the significance of the study? The literature on peer review has focused almost exclusively on the cognitive dimensions of evaluation and conceives of extracognitive dimensions as corrupting influences.[15] In my view, however, evaluation is a process that is deeply emotional and interactional. It is culturally embedded and influenced by the "social identity" of panelists—that is, their self-concept and how others define them.[16] Reviewers' very real desire to have their opinion respected by their colleagues also plays an important role in deliberations. Consensus formation is fragile and requires considerable emotional work.[17] Maintaining collegiality is crucial. It is also challenging, because the distinctive features of American higher education (spatial dispersion, social and geographic mobility, the sheer size of the field, and so on) increase uncertainty in interaction.

Is higher education really meritocratic? Are academics a self-reproducing elite?[18] These and similar questions are closely tied to issues of biases in evaluation and the trustworthiness of evaluators. Expertise and connoisseurship (or ability to discriminate) can easily slide into homophily (an appreciation for work that most resembles one's own). Evaluators, who are generally senior and established academics, often define excellence as "what speaks most to me," which is often akin to "what is most like me," with the result that the "haves"—anyone associated with a top institution or a dominant paradigm—may receive a disproportionate amount of resources.[19] The tendency toward homophily may explain the perceived conservative bias in funding: it is widely believed that particularly creative and original projects must clear higher hurdles in order to get funded.[20] It would also help explain the Matthew effect (that is, the tendency for resources to go to those who already have them).[21]

But I find a more complex pattern. Evaluators often favor their own type of research while also being firmly committed to rewarding the strongest proposal. Panelists are necessarily situated in particular cognitive and social networks. They all have students, colleagues, and friends with whom they share what is often a fairly small cognitive universe (subfield or subspecialty) and they are frequently asked to adjudicate the work of individuals with whom they have only a few degrees of separation. While their understanding of what defines excellence is contingent on the cultural environment in which they are located, when scholars are called on to act as judges, they are encouraged to step out of their normal milieus to assess quality as defined through absolute and decontextualized standards. Indeed, their own identity is often tied to their self-concept as experts who are able to stand above their personal interest. Thus, evaluators experience contradictory pushes and pulls as they strive to adjudicate quality.[22]

What are the epistemological implications of the study?   Much like the nineteenth-century French social scientist Auguste Comte, some contemporary academics believe that disciplines can be neatly ranked in a single hierarchy (although few follow Comte's lead and place sociology at the top). The matrix of choice is disciplinary "maturity," as measured by consensus and growth, but some also favor scientificity and objectivity.[23] Others firmly believe that the hard sciences should not serve as the aspirational model, especially given that there are multiple models for doing science, including many that do not fit the prevailing archetypical representations.[24] In the social sciences and the humanities, the more scientific and more interpretive disciplines favor very different forms of originality (with a focus on new approaches, new data, or new methods).[25] From a normative standpoint, one leitmotif of my analysis is that disciplines shine under different lights, are good at different things, and are best located on different matrixes of evaluation, precisely because their objects and concerns differ so dramatically. For instance, in some fields knowledge is best approached through questions having to do with "how much"; other fields raise "how" and "why" questions that require the use of alternative approaches, interpretive tools, methods, and data-gathering techniques. These fundamental differences imply that excellence and epistemological diversity are not dichotomous choices. Instead, diversity supports the existence of various types of excellence.

Is the study timely? At the start of the twenty-first century, as I was conducting interviews, market forces had come to favor increasingly the more professional and preprofessional fields, as well as research tied to profit-making.[26] Moreover, the technology of peer review has long been embedded in a vast academic culture that values science. In the public sphere, the social sciences continue to be the terrain for a tug-of-war between neoliberal market explanations for societal or human behavior and other, more institutional and cultural accounts.[27] By illuminating how pluralism factors into evaluation processes, I hope to help maintain a sense of multiple possibilities.

Many factors in American higher education work against disciplinary and epistemological pluralism. Going against the tide in any endeavor is often difficult; it may be even more so in scholarly research, because independence of thinking is not easily maintained in systems where mentorship and sponsored mobility loom large.[28] Innovators are often penalized if they go too far in breaking boundaries, even if by doing so they redefine conventions and pave the way for future changes.[29] In the context of academic evaluation, there does not appear to be a clear alternative to the system of peer review.[30] Moreover, there seems to be agreement among the study's respondents that despite its flaws, overall this system "works." Whether academics who are never asked to evaluate proposals and those who never apply for funds share this opinion remains an open question.

Despite all the uncertainties about academic judgment, I aim to combat intellectual cynicism. Post-structuralism has led large numbers of academics to view notions of truth and reality as highly arbitrary. Yet many still care deeply about "excellence" and remain strongly committed to identifying and rewarding it, though they may not define it the same way.

I also aim to provide a deeper understanding, grounded in solid research, of the competing criteria of evaluation at stake in academic debates. Empirically grounded disciplines, such as political science and sociology, have experienced important conflicts regarding the place of formal theory and quantitative research techniques in disciplinary standards of excellence. In political science, strong tensions have accompanied the growing influence of rational choice theory.[31] In the 1990s, disagreements surrounding the American Sociological Association's choice of an editor for its flagship journal, the *American Sociological Review,* have generated lively discussion about the place of qualitative and quantitative research in the field.[32] In both disciplines, diversity and academic distinction are often perceived as mutually exclusive criteria for selecting leaders of professional associations. My analysis may help move the discussion beyond polemics.

Also, the book examines at the micro level the coproduction of the social and the academic.[33] Since the late 1960s, and based on their understanding of the standards of evaluation used in government organizations, sociologists seeking support from government funding agencies began to incorporate more quantitative techniques in part as a way of legitimizing their work as "scientific."[34] At the same time, government organizations became increasingly dependent on social science knowledge (for example, census information, data pertaining to school achievement, unemployment rates among various groups) as a foundation for social engineering. Thus, knowledge networks and networks of resource distribution have grown in parallel—and this alignment has sustained disciplinary hierarchies. The more a researcher depends on external sources of funding, the less autonomous he or she is when choosing a problem to study.[35] Standards of evaluation that are salient, or that researchers perceive as salient, shape the kind of work that they undertake. These standards also affect the likelihood that scholars will obtain funding and gain status, since receiving fellowships is central to the acquisition of academic prestige.[36] Thus are put in place the conditions for the broader hierarchy of the academic world.

Most of all, I want to open the black box of peer review and make the process of evaluation more transparent, especially for younger academics looking in from the outside.[37] I also want to make the older, established scholars—the gatekeepers—think hard and think again about the limits of what they are doing, particularly when they define "what is exciting" as "what most looks like me (or my work)." Providing a wider perspective may help broaden the disciplinary tunnel vision that afflicts so many. A greater understanding of the differences and similarities across disciplinary cultures may lead academics toward a greater tolerance of, or even an appreciation for, fields outside their own. And coming to see the process as moved by customary rules may help all evaluators view the system in a different and broader perspective as well as develop greater humility and a more realistic sense of their cosmic significance, or lack thereof, in the great contest over excellence.

I now turn to the details of how the research was conducted and to the minutiae of disciplinary positioning. Readers who are not interested in these topics should move directly to Chapter 2, which describes how panels work.

The scholars I talked with served on funding panels that evaluate grant or fellowship proposals submitted by faculty members and graduate students. I interviewed scholars involved in five different national funding competitions and twelve different panels over a two-year period around the turn of the century (for details, see the

Appendix).[38] The individual funding organizations (and the specific competitions studied) are the American Council for Learned Societies (ACLS—the Humanities Fellowship program); a Society of Fellows (an international competition for a residential fellowship sponsored by a top research university); the Social Science Research Council (SSRC—the International Dissertation Field Research program); the Woodrow Wilson National Fellowship Foundation (WWNFF—the Women's Studies program); and an anonymous foundation in the social sciences. In each of these cases, I spoke with panelists, panel chairs, and program officers individually for approximately two hours each. These eighty-one interviews, which include fifteen interviews with program officers and panel chairs, were conducted in absolute confidentiality and occurred within a few hours or a few days of the conclusion of their panel deliberations.

The object of the interviews was to learn about the arguments that panelists had made for and against specific proposals, their views about the outcomes of the competition, and the thinking behind the ranking of proposals both prior to and after the panel meeting. I had both sets of rankings in hand during each interview. Other questions concerned how panelists interpreted the process of selection and its outcome; how they compared their evaluations to those of other panelists; how they recognized excellence in their graduate students, among their colleagues, and in their own work; whether they believed in academic excellence and why; and whether they thought that, in my words, "the cream rises to the top." I also asked interviewees to cite examples of work that they especially appreciated and to explain why they so highly valued this work. My aim here was to locate respondents' framing of excellence within their broader conception of their own scholarly selves.[39] I read a large sample of the finalist proposals before conducting the interviews, to gain background information and prepare targeted questions. In three cases where I was able to observe deliberations firsthand, I used my field notes to probe panelists during the post-deliberation interviews.[40] As a whole, the interviews generated not only information on panelists' understanding of how they assess excellence, but also ethnographic information on the evaluation process itself—from both an organizational and a cultural perspective. I collected several individual accounts about the deliberation and ranking processes to gain complementary and thus more accurate understandings of the types of arguments made by various scholars about a range of proposals.

Most of the literature on peer review tends to neglect the meaning given to criteria of evaluation. To rectify this oversight, I took a different approach. I used an open-ended and inductive interview technique to ask panelists to draw boundaries between what they consider the best and the worst proposals. This made it possible to identify the criteria underpinning their evaluations and to reconstruct the classification system they used. I had found this method effective in my earlier studies of conceptions of worth among middle-class and working-class people. It was particularly fruitful for the study of topics as sensitive as class resentment, racism, and xenophobia in France and the United States.[41] People are less likely to censor themselves when drawing boundaries because they are often unaware that they draw boundaries as they describe the world. Focusing on boundaries in this study was also useful because what the reviewer takes for granted may well drive his boundary work more than his or her explicitly stated beliefs.[42]

All the panels I studied were composed of scholars from different disciplines, but the competitions they judged were open to both disciplinary and interdisciplinary proposals. Panel members were from the social sciences and the humanities, fields often portrayed as less consensual than the pure and applied sciences. The interviewees represent a wide range of disciplines. Some hailed from economics, philosophy, or sociology. Others came from disciplines that have undergone profound epistemological changes over recent decades— such as anthropology, English, history, and political science. And some came from smaller disciplines, such as musicology, geography, and art history. I interviewed scholars about their own disciplines and disciplinary standards as well as about their perceptions of the similarities and differences among fields. Thus my analysis of each discipline draws on multiple accounts. Responses ranged from the highly developed and coherent to the off-the-cuff, unreflective, and inchoate. Participants' frank appraisals of their own and others' fields offer a unique window into what academics—and academia— are all about. My analysis uncovers a world that is understood only partially and generally imperfectly, even by most members of the academic community, let alone the general public.

Grants and fellowships are becoming increasingly important as academic signals of excellence, especially because the proliferation of journals has made the number of publications of academics a less reliable measure of their status.[43] Of the two, fellowships are considered a better measure of excellence than are grants, because across all the social sciences and the humanities, academics are eager to receive fellowships that will support their leaves and allow them to pursue their research. Grants, though valuable and customary in the social sciences where research often requires costly data collection, are less important in the humanities. Prestigious fellowships tell recipients about the quality of their work relative to that of others, and in so doing, they increase motivation and self-confidence.[44] They also provide a public enhancement of status, because a panel of experts has agreed that one's work is superior to that of many other candidates.[45] Indeed, in a recent year, the ratio of awards to applicants was 1:12 for the WWNFF and ACLS competitions; 1:16 for the SSRC competition; and 1:200 for the Society of Fellows. Perhaps less significantly, these competitions also provide material support, which ranges from $3,000 (in the case of WWNFF dissertation grants) to $50,000 (in the case of ACLS fellowships to full professors). These funding panels serve an important role for evaluators as well, providing an instantiation of the esteem that colleagues have for their expertise. In the academic world, being invited to sit on a panel for a prestigious competition can carry a reward that is the symbolic equivalent of the annual bonus bestowed on the senior vice-president of a well-known corporation. The value that evaluators accord such invitations varies greatly with their own position in the academic hierarchy and their degree of seniority, however.

How do I figure in the story? I have a long-standing research interest in the sociology of knowledge and have established expertise in this field.[46] Equally important, I am simultaneously an insider and an outsider to the system I describe.[47] As I note in the acknowledgments, my research was supported by several prestigious grants and fellowship programs, funding sources of the very sort that I analyze in this book. I am also a tenured Harvard professor. Moreover, I have served on a number of funding panels of the same type that I studied (but not the same competitions). These facts alone might seem to make me the consummate insider, a gatekeeper par excellence. And indeed, insiderhood has influenced my analysis in myriad ways—facilitating access to the rather secretive milieus of funding organizations, for instance, and helping me understand these milieus, even as I deliberately made the familiar strange.

Despite my status as an "insider," I am also in some ways an outsider, first because I have had a very unusual professional trajectory. I was socialized in the American higher education system only after having completed my graduate work at the University of Paris. My sense of that distance has always been compounded by my being an ethnographer, a role that provides—indeed, requires—distance if the researcher is to have any hope of deciphering how the natives think, what makes them tick. Moreover, I did not think, socialize, or work in English before coming to the United States at the age of twenty-five. My French-inflected speech cadence and accent continually remind those around me of my otherness.

I also conceive of myself as an outsider because I am a woman, which along with being an immigrant may put me at the margin to some extent, and may help explain why I am not enamored of "insiderism." And it is not irrelevant that most of my past scholarship has concerned racial and class boundaries and social exclusion. This background informs the book's argument that a belief in the relative fairness and openness of the peer review system is crucial to the vitality of American higher education. That belief invites and encourages outsiders to take a gamble and participate in these scholarly competitions, even if they think that the system is only partly meritocratic. Finally, at the center of this book is my own self, and the self-understanding of academics who labor, at least sometimes, to maintain a meaningful life.

The pragmatic approach to evaluation I advocate draws on paradigms from sociology—ethnomethodology and symbolic interactionism (associated with the works of Irving Garfinkel and Erving Goffman, respectively)—that focus attention on the conditions of the collective accomplishment of social life and the social order. These theories have helped me make sense of how social actors (panelists, principally, but also program officers, applicants, and the academic community at large) collaborate to create the conditions necessary for the allocation of awards.[48] My analysis is also informed by the American and European traditions of pragmatic and cultural analysis, because these focus attention on the competing webs of meanings that human beings spin to make sense of their everyday activities—including how people think conflicts should be expressed and conducted, so as not to betray the notion of meritocracy and fair play.[49] Moreover, I build on insights derived from science studies concerning expertise, credibility, the stabilization of facts, and the closure of controversies. Here, studies by Bruno Latour and Steven

Woolgar on circles of credibility and Harry Collins on claims of expertise have been especially helpful.[50] Thus my approach can be contrasted with the views of Robert K. Merton, Richard Whitley, and Pierre Bourdieu, all of whom have addressed academic evaluation.

Most of the research on the topic of how quality is assessed has focused on issues raised by Robert K. Merton's influential work in the sociology of knowledge: consensus in science, issues of universalistic and particularistic evaluation relating to the ethos of science, and the variously construed Matthew and halo effects of reputation and prestige (with halo effect referring to the gain of prestige by association).[51] Researchers working on this topic have addressed whether judgments about "irrelevant," particularistic characteristics, like the age and reputation of the author, affect (or corrupt) the evaluation of his or her work. More recent studies are also concerned with the fairness of the peer review process.[52] Although these studies have made important contributions, their framing of the question implies that a unified process of evaluation can be put in place once particularistic considerations have been eliminated. They tend to overlook that evaluation is not based on stable comparables, and that various competing criteria with multiple meanings are used to assess academic work. These criteria include stylistic virtuosity and the display of cultural capital, empirical soundness, and methodological sophistication.

I build on prior studies by beginning exactly where they leave off: I conduct a detailed examination of neglected aspects of the evaluation process. I analyze situations where the meanings of norms as defined by Merton (for example, about universalism) are created. Using methods similar to those in an earlier study, I undertake a content analysis of grant proposal evaluations, but unlike previous work, I am concerned with disciplinary differences and with criteria of evaluation.[53] For instance, whereas past research found that the significance of a project has a strong influence on funding, I probe what reviewers and panel members from different disciplines mean by "significance." And whereas much of the available literature is concerned with fairness, I examine what is perceived as fair and what panelists do to enact and sustain fairness.[54] I find that between proposals the criteria for comparison and evaluation are continually changing, as different proposals are regrouped based on different principles and compared. Path dependency best explains the definition of the comparables—think of real-estate agents using different comparables across neighborhoods over time, or the "gut feelings" we all experience while making comparative and contextual judgments, feelings that cognitive psychologists inform us are shaped by initial "priming" experiences.[55] Evaluation is by necessity a fragile and uncertain endeavor and one that requires "emotion work" if it is to proceed smoothly. Moreover, the panelists' sense of self and relative positioning cannot be dissociated from the process; it is intrinsic to it. Thus, in contrast to Merton and his associates, I suggest that these extra-cognitive elements do not corrupt the process: evaluation is impossible without them.[56]

Sociologists Richard Whitley and Pierre Bourdieu are among the few scholars who provide systematic bases on which to ground a comparison of disciplines.[57] Whitley focuses on dependency and task uncertainty to predict power relations within fields. He suggests that the greater the need to pool resources within a given discipline or subdiscipline, the greater the competition between scientists over making a reputation and gaining control over material resources. He predicts that in a field characterized by what he calls low functional dependence and high strategic dependence (such as English literature), scholarly contributions will be judged in "relatively diffuse and tacit ways with considerable reliance upon personal contacts and knowledge."[58] Similarly, in *Homo Academicus,* Bourdieu analyzes scientists as people engaged in a struggle to impose as legitimate their vision of the world—and their definition of high-quality scholarly work. Whitley and Bourdieu tell us that scholars compete to define excellence, and then point to the coexistence of alternative criteria of evaluation. Neither author, however, analyzes these criteria inductively. Even in his early work with Monique de St. Martin, where Bourdieu pointed to categories of judgment applied to academic work (such as its excellence or "brilliance"), he did not analyze the meaning of criteria used to place a proposal in a given category.[59] In contrast, this book provides a detailed empirical analysis of the meaning of criteria on which scholars rely to distinguish "excellent" and "promising" research from less stellar work.

My approach differs from Bourdieu's in other ways. Bourdieu argues that the judgments of scholars reflect and serve their position in their academic field, even if they naturalize these judgments and legitimize them in universalistic terms. While he examines the social and economic filtering that lie behind interests, he does not consider whether and how defending excellence is central to the self-concept of many academics and how aspects of disinterestedness, such as pleasure, can be more than a self-serving illusion.[60] In contrast, I factor into the analysis academics' sense of self and their emotions. While Bourdieu suggests that in the competition for distinction, conflicts are strongest among those occupying similar positions in fields, my interviews suggest that actors are motivated by not only the opportunity to maximize their position, but also their pragmatic involvement in collective problem solving.[61] Thus, contra Merton, Bourdieu, and Whitley, I oppose a view of peer review that is driven only or primarily by a competitive logic (or the market) and suggest in addition that peer review is an interactional and an emotional undertaking. In short, building on Goffman, my analysis suggests the importance of considering the self and emotions—in particular pleasure, saving face, and maintaining one's self-concept—as part of the investment that academics make in scholarly evaluation.[62] Contra Whitley, I also argue that homophilic judgments are pervasive across the social sciences and the humanities. How people approach evaluation as problem solving, how they develop evaluative practices and articulate their beliefs, and how they represent the process to themselves are crucial to my analysis.

I also emphasize, in the pragmatist tradition, a pluralism of perspectives and communication styles. New French pragmatism focuses on coordinated action in situations of evaluation.[63] I share with this approach a concern for analyzing the combination of standards of evaluation used and the ways in which panelists make arguments while promoting particular conceptions of fairness. But I do not use predefined logics of justification. Instead, my approach to understanding evaluation criteria is more inductive. It owes much to John Dewey, and to others who are concerned with how trust emerges around problem solving, dialogue, and learning.[64] I am also more concerned with the organizational logic that leads people to "satisfice" (to make "good enough," as opposed to optimal, decisions) given the constraints within which decisions have to be made. Thus my approach is a fairly radical departure from the canonical literature on peer review, which remains concerned primarily with cognitive aspects of evaluation.

2/How Panels Work

I see the need for people to make very careful and [informed] judgments for the academic community to function. It's more as an obligation than an entitlement, and I'm willing to make those judgments because I, on the one hand, have confidence in my own experience, and on the other hand, I defer to people's judgment that would be in a position to make good decisions . . . I think it's experience-based. I would like to think that people have looked at my work and said, "This is good work and he's a very fine scholar himself, and that's why we want him to help us evaluate what's good scholarship."

Political scientist

The institutional framework of evaluation that structures funding decisions in the academic world is not secret. Nevertheless, most of this "nuts and bolts" information—ranging from funding programs' objectives and formal criteria of evaluation to how panels are formed and what panelists are asked to do—is not widely known. In this chapter, then, I describe the objectives of the five funding agencies studied and the formal evaluation criteria associated with those objectives; the structure of the evaluation process, including the role of the program officer, the selection of panelists and screeners, and the pre-deliberation ranking work; and, lastly, the mechanics of the deliberations.

Drawing on the work of Karin Knorr-Cetina, I understand these aspects of panels as a machinery or technology of evaluation around which evaluative cultures are intertwined.[1] This technology defines and constrains possibilities. Together with institutional rules, it sets the context in which selection occurs and interactions happen—the frame and hardware for conversations across disciplinary cultures. To take only one example, confidentiality guidelines constrain public action—they limit what can be said where.

I am interested in formal descriptions of awardmaking in panel reviews, as well as in participants' representations and legitimating accounts. Here I focus in particular on the funding organizations' descriptions of the process. In the words of John Meyer and Brian Rowan, these can be viewed as "myths and ceremonies" that play a crucial role in legitimating the process—for instance, by making the criteria of selection available to the public on websites or by prefacing deliberations with an official introduction concerning the importance of the work of the panel and its rules.[2] Most of the unspoken and taken-for-granted aspects of interactions that shape panel deliberation are downplayed in this chapter, but they will take center stage later in the book.

An agreement not to focus on particular organizations was one of the conditions for gaining access to the funding agencies. Thus my analysis looks almost exclusively at similarities across competitions and panels and neglects many of the differences—for instance, that some competitions (such as the Society of Fellows) offer very big rewards to a few, while others offer smaller rewards to many.[3] I do highlight a few organizational contrasts that do not jeopardize the anonymity of the organizations—when discussing how applicants' seniority influences the weight put on letters of recommendation, for example.

If I had aimed to conduct a full analysis of organizational decision making, I would have proceeded differently. For instance, I would likely have drawn on the rich literature on the garbage-can model of organizational decision making, which considers how decisions that are made by many uncoordinated parties (as is the case with panels) suffer from uncertainty and may not be rational, although they may be presented as such.[4] Moreover, I would have examined the full stream of vetting applicants, the likelihood that different categories of applicants (from public and private universities, from more or less prestigious colleges) apply to competitions, and what (unevenly distributed) resources improve their chances of getting a fellowship.[5] Such an analysis would undoubtedly illuminate the elite character of resource distribution. Fortunately, although constraints on an organizational analysis require my downplaying some of the institutional mechanics of the evaluative process, the cultural aspects are fair game.

Program Objectives and Evaluation Criteria

The five programs I studied have as an objective the promotion of specific types of scholarship by providing income to researchers while they are on sabbatical leave or by providing grants to underwrite research expenses. The objective for each program is stated on the website of the sponsoring organization. The International Dissertation Field Research (IDFR) program sponsored by the Social Science Research Council (SSRC) is open to the social sciences and the humanities; so, too, is the Women's Studies Dissertation Grant program of the Woodrow Wilson National Fellowship Foundation (WWNFF).[6] The Humanities Fellowship program funded by the American Council of Learned Societies (ACLS) supports research in the humanities, and in humanities-related social sciences. The Society of Fellows funds work across a range of fields; and the anonymous foundation supports work only in the social sciences. These competitions also target scholars at different career stages: the SSRC and the WWNFF programs provide support to graduate students; the ACLS holds distinct competitions for assistant, associate, and full professors; the Society of Fellows provides fellowships to recent PhDs only; and the anonymous social science foundation supports researchers at all ranks. I take the funding organizations' stated objectives at face value in this chapter. Chapters 4, 5, and 6 explore the different meanings and levels of importance that panelists assign to the program objectives and target populations and see how these understandings affect the evaluation process.

Although many panelists emphasize in only a limited way the particular objectives of funding agencies, these goals influence panel deliberations. For instance, program officers will at times encourage panelists to "factor in" various kinds of diversity in distributing awards. Moreover, some competitions aim to promote distinctive types of scholarship and this objective contributes to the overall context of evaluation, because panelists may be asked how proposals measure up to such explicit goals. This is notably the case for the IDFR program, which was created in 1996 to replace older SSRC funding programs in area studies. In the 1990s, the SSRC leadership concluded that area studies needed to move in a more theoretical, interdisciplinary, and comparative direction.[7] They set up the IDRF program as a tool for agenda-setting, with the explicit goals of encouraging graduate students to

> use their knowledge of distinctive cultures, languages, economies, polities, and histories, in combination with their disciplinary training, to address issues that transcend their disciplines or area specializations . . . The current program operates on the premise that societies and cultures, from isolated villages to entire world regions, are caught up in the processes that link them to events, which—though geographically distant—are culturally, economi-

cally, strategically, or ecologically quite near. To learn more about values or social conditions in a particular area, then, means to learn more about how that area is situated in events and processes going on outside its borders, but not thereby outside its culture or economy or ecology.[8]

Similarly, the WWNFF's Women's Studies Dissertation Grant program was created to "encourage original and significant research about women that crosses disciplinary, regional, or cultural boundaries."[9] In the foundation's newsletter, WWNFF past president Robert Weisbuch justified support of research in women's studies by citing the interdisciplinary character of this field of scholarship, its questioning of hardened boundaries, its role as a catalyst for energetic debates, and its immediacy (women's studies is a field "not merely academic, divorced from our lives").[10] The WWNFF program has played a very important role in the promotion and development of the field of women's studies in the United States.

The five funding programs' formal criteria of evaluation are summarized in Table 2.1. These criteria are in line with those typically used at other funding agencies, such as the National Science Foundation. Making formal evaluative criteria public increases accountability and makes winning democratically available to all (since success depends on the display of technical proficiency), as opposed to a domain of the talented few. These technical criteria, which address the quality of the proposed research, are discussed in detail in Chapter 5. Beyond assessing quality, however, funding agencies also consider the interdisciplinarity of proposals, and the diversity (by institution, discipline, geographic location, race/ethnicity, and gender) of applicants. Chapter 6 takes a close look at the various meanings that panelists give to these criteria and how these are used in conjunction with the formal specifications.

Table 2.1 Criteria of evaluation used by funding agencies

Agency	Clarity	Originality	Intellectual and/or social significance	Methods	Quality	Feasibility	Others
Anonymous			Yes	Yes (appropriate methodology)	Yes (grasp of relevant literatures)	Yes (necessary skills and experience)	Fits with goals of foundation; interdisciplinary
ACLS			Yes		Yes	Yes (training; past experience; plan of work)	
IDRF	Yes (clear, intelligible prose; clearly formulated)			Yes (responsive to methodological concerns; provides rationale for field research)		Yes (knowledge of relevant concepts and theories; realistic in scope; appropriate level of training for fieldwork)	Multidisciplinarity; speaks to cross-regional panel
Society of Fellows			Yes	Yes	Yes ("scholarly excellence")		Teaching experience; contributes to an interdisciplinary community
WWNFF's Women's Studies Dissertation Grant	Yes	Yes	Yes (contribution to women's studies)	Yes ("scholarly validity")		Yes (preparation; readiness; reasonable timeline)	

Note: Criteria are from http://www.acls.org/fel-comp.htm; http://programs.ssrc.org/idrf/; and http://www.woodrow.org/womens-studies/index.php. Except as indicated by quotation marks, all the specific criteria noted are paraphrased.

"Yes" indicates the criterion is used in evaluating proposals.

Recruitment and the Role of the Program Officer

The evaluation process adopted by the ACLS resembles that of most of the other funding organizations I studied. As an internal ACLS document explains:

> ACLS has developed an intensive peer-review process to select its Fellows. The process combines screening by readers from the applicants' academic field with review by interdisciplinary panels. At the first stage of the outside peer review process, each of the applicants is prescreened by two scholars in the general field (seventeen prescreening fields include anthropology, art history, archaeology, classics, English, modern foreign languages, etc.) The screeners' scores and comments are used to eliminate about 50 percent of all the proposals overall. The remaining applications are divided into groups of approximately 60 and are sent to four panels of five or six distinguished scholars, all of whom read the applications. These panels then convene at ACLS to discuss each application and to select awardees.[11]

The most important actors in the evaluation process are the program officers, full-time employees of funding agencies who are responsible for running funding competitions. They typically hold a PhD in a discipline covered by the fellowship program. This expertise is necessary if they are to understand the substantive content of the proposals and help orient the deliberations. While some program officers have migrated to funding agencies from academic administration or research (in some cases, after being denied tenure), others are hired by the agency immediately after receiving their PhDs. Program officers' responsibilities include selecting screeners and panelists, communicating with and directing the two groups during the evaluation process, communicating with applicants, and supervising the organization and distribution of applications. They also preside over panel deliberations, or they appoint a panel chair who takes on this role (in close collaboration with the officer, who even if not officiating, remains present throughout the deliberations). Either way, they play a crucial role in setting the tone of panels. They facilitate interactions, promote collegiality, diffuse tensions (often through humor), ensure efficacy, and engage in "repair work" when customary rules of evaluation are broken.[12] They also help uphold the "sacredness" of the process, that is, the panelists' belief in the value of peer review (see Chapter 4). Although they instruct panelists about evaluation criteria and program priorities, program officers do not force panelists to respect these guidelines. As we will see, panelists are given full sovereignty over decision making.

Although program officers are not recognized as experts or "peers" (because they are not expert researchers), they have great discretionary powers that affect competition outcomes. First, they define the composition of individual panels, which many people believe is the single most important determinant of which proposals succeed. Program officers can also terminate panelists whose behavior or level of participation is disappointing, and they can promote good screeners to the role of panelists. These responsibilities give them some leverage over those academics who feel overly empowered by their position as judges or very eager to be asked back. For the most part, though, program officers' power is of the indirect, agenda-setting kind.[13] This is alluded to by a sociologist who compared his experiences serving on a panel for multiple years. He spoke appreciatively of a previous program officer, who privileged panelists who were "liberal arts people more interested in interdisciplinary work and in new lines of work." The current incumbent, who is much less to this sociologist's liking, seems to prefer panelists who are in "second-tier research institutions, who are very solid, reasonably productive, but by and large, precisely the inertial forces that maintain this merry core, if you will. No one who's about to push the envelope anywhere."

To understand fully the role and influence of program officers, we have to consider the selection of evaluators. Screeners and panelists can be chosen from various pools. Typically, they are academic experts who are very highly regarded in their field. In three of the five programs, they are chosen from among former award recipients; in another, the Society of Fellows, they are chosen from the faculty of a particular university. In the fifth competition, they are chosen among experts in the field.

Panelists are identified by the funding agency—that is, by the program officer—through consultation with other experts in the field. The process is similar across four funding organizations (the Society of Fellows is somewhat different). The description provided in an internal ACLS document is representative:

> All screeners and panelists are accomplished tenured faculty or independent scholars of comparable attainment. The ACLS board of directors approves screeners and select panelists. All screeners and panelists are drawn from a database built up through consultation with the Board, Delegates to the Council, Administrative Officers of the Learned Societies, and Learned Societies Presidents.[14]

Because there are some differences in the selection of panelists versus screeners, we will consider each separately.

The Selection of Panelists

The selection of high-quality panelists is crucial to the prestige of the fellowship program. As the ACLS's now-deceased president John D'Arms explained:

We try to make sure that our selection panels are composed of distinguished scholars, tough-minded but also broad-minded and prepared to learn from the work of others as well as to judge it. We believe that panelists' careful reading of applications, followed by a full day's discussion of proposals with their colleagues here at ACLS, enlarges panelists' own understanding of the scholarly Humanities, and widens their vision. And we believe that the consensus that panelists reach at the end of their discussion helps to establish national standards of quality. Our aim is to ensure that the ACLS Fellowship is regarded across the country as the result of a process that is at once rigorous, well-informed, venturesome, and fair.[15]

This description emphasizes the dispositions of the panelists ("tough-minded but also broad-minded") and the moral quality of the process ("venturesome and fair").[16] It plays up the role of funding panels in setting standards of quality nationwide. In all cases, the status of individuals who serve on panels is presented as an important (if not exclusive) guarantor of the legitimacy of the evaluation. The reputation of the funding organization also contributes to overall legitimacy, as does a tradition of funding significant work. Thus funding organizations often make the names of panelists public when announcing the outcome of a competition. It is the job of program officers to identify evaluators of sufficient caliber and commitment to ensure the ongoing legitimacy of the award programs. At the very least, these evaluators have to believe in the legitimacy of this system. That they have themselves often won fellowships and awards facilitates strong identification with a culture of excellence that is centered on the technology of peer review. After all, their awards are proof that they have submitted themselves repeatedly to this mode of evaluation.

Program officers, who typically cultivate relationships with a wide array of trusted academics and funding agency insiders, survey this network (sometimes through "gossip") to identify evaluators who present the desired intellectual and personal dispositions. The degree of autonomy that officers have in this selection process varies across organizations, but it tends to be considerable—at least, this is what program officers state.[17] They may consult with leading experts, panel chairs, members of the board of directors of the funding organization, heads of foundations, and other program officers in order to identify likely panelists. They draw on their networks, but within limits given their need to recruit a wide range of experts.[18] One political scientist highlights the role of networks in describing how her acquaintance with a program officer and a panel chair influenced her own selection as a panelist:

> I don't blame [the program officer and panel chair] for choosing people [whom the chair would] know, because [otherwise] you could really get yourself into a real mess. You could have a very inefficient and non-fair committee if you didn't have faith in the judgment of the people that you chose. And that comes from network[ing] . . . And I think I have a reputation for accepting a pretty broad range of work and not having a bias.

In putting together a panel, program officers consider the overall composition of the panel as it pertains to "balance in perspectives," complementary coverage of wide areas of scholarship and disciplines, and diversity. At a minimum, panels should include some women, individuals teaching in universities outside the Northeast, and individuals who teach in nonelite institutions. Ideally, they should also include some people of color—depending on the size of the panel (in this study, panels ranged from three to sixteen members). This diversity is essential given the character of the American higher education system, where legitimacy is grounded in expertise as well as in universalism and openness. An alternative model, where panelists are selected from among individuals affiliated with the most elite schools, would be unthinkable; in the American context, democracy, universalism, and rationality all must be present in the decision process.[19]

Panelists are expected to form an opinion on proposals covering a variety of topics and representing a range of disciplines. In the course of deliberations, they must be able to judge a large number of proposals while absorbing new information provided by other panelists. They are also expected to know how to offer convincing support for their determinations. These expectations are similar to those they must meet in their daily work lives as producers of research and assessors of evidence.[20] Not surprisingly, then, they generally are both more senior and more experienced than screeners. Panelists are also generally more broadly respected and have greater name recognition. Finally, while screeners do not interact with other evaluators, panelists are chosen for their good interpersonal skills, because they are expected to engage in face-to-face negotiation during panel deliberations. Thus beyond the bottom line—that the panelist "not be an asshole"—program officers look for academics who demonstrate such key qualities as "breadth, articulatedness, confidence, and friendliness," along with flexibility and the ability to work quickly. (Characteristics of a good panelist are explored in greater depth in Chapter 4). Panel members' ability to help maintain a pleasant tone throughout the deliberation is essential to the group's success, because it lowers the probability that individuals will dig in their heels and cause conflicts to erupt.

Once program officers have identified panelists who fit the bill, they need to convince them to serve. This can take some persuasion, given that high-level academics are often already shouldering many other professional obligations, and rigorous peer review can be "mentally exhausting," as a historian of South India puts it. The attractiveness of the invitation will vary with the potential panelist's career stage, whether she has served on other panels in the distant or recent past, and the level of her commitments in future months. Stated motivations range from a desire to define the agenda, provide a community service, be exposed to new ideas, measure oneself against other high-status experts, and test one's own status and self-concept.

The appeals of prestige and the opportunity to shape competition outcomes and affect the trajectory of other scholars ("power") are often attractive to prospective panelists. The same historian who describes panel deliberations as "exhausting" explains:

> [You have] a handful of people who for whatever reason have been chosen to kind of be the arbiters of future directions of doctoral work . . . This is one of the most prestigious scholarships for grad students in the United States. I can't think of any other that actually competes with it. [You're] kind of shaping the direction of the future in various fields by giving a certain message through the funding.

Another panelist, an anthropologist, similarly stresses that

> People who serve on important panels certainly are able to shape things, in terms of who gets accolades . . . It's defining who gets defined as excellent, and then gets to get ensconced in positions in universities to train students of the next generation, and on and on and on. Even who gets linked to the funders themselves to think about how they're going to redefine their criteria or reshape their grant giving . . . I'd like to see some really good studies of [these sorts] of political repercussions and dynamics. [They] aren't spoken [of], at least in my world. I mean we all know who the power players are to a certain extent and who's getting invited . . . to be readers for what.

Despite the attraction of the opportunity to exercise influence, many panelists deliberately do not publicize their role, in hopes of avoiding pressure from colleagues or questions about the details of deliberations. They prefer anonymity over awkwardness of this sort.

For some panelists, too, the prime motivation for service is not power but the highly pleasurable opportunity it provides for learning what is going on in a variety of fields. In the words of an African-American historian, "It's good to get just a sense of what's happening in the field and find out what is piquing the interests of the scholars writing their dissertations. When we come together as a group, it's fun to see what the other people are thinking about, what they find interesting and how our ideas kind of meld or don't meld together . . . I feel like I learn things, things that I didn't know, or get a better understanding." New information can of course influence the research agenda of panelists and improve their own grant proposals.

Others explain their willingness to serve in rather disinterested terms. One refers to a sense of "noblesse oblige. [This funding agency] had given me fellowships on two previous occasions and I felt a sense of obligation." A literary scholar says he agreed to serve because he "just took it as one of those burdens that I would one time or another have to bear. [Once] I was approached more than four times and I just saw it as, 'I can't escape it.' . . . I don't go out looking for extra work for myself. Plus, I don't know what is ultimately a gain for me." A third panelist, by contrast, cheerfully admits being lured by the combination of an honorarium (rarely offered) and the opportunity to travel to the attractive city where the deliberations were held.

Still others value the opportunity to interact with "other really smart people" and the associated pleasure that kind of interaction so often brings to academics. An English professor recounts:

I was very happy to find that I agreed with [a female panelist] on many evaluations where the two of us were different from the other panelists. I was very pleased by that because I admire her because of her field. What she does is maybe more akin to what I do, because some of her work is very strongly inflected with feminist influence . . . I remember enjoying her book immensely . . . We are interested in [similar topics], which created similarities in our evaluations.

Another panelist says, "I remember having a couple of moments of very pleasurable agreement with the medievalist. It had to do with reading major classics against the grain . . . There again, it just seemed a moment of connecting, but I couldn't really describe it in abstract term[s]." Such moments of connection are particularly important given the rather isolated character of academic work. They are also valued because relatively few people share the knowledge needed to appreciate scholarship in an informed fashion. A number of interviewees describe experiencing moments of individual or collective effervescence during deliberations. These feelings are prompted by a variety of factors, but some respondents note as especially powerful moments those times they felt they were in deep agreement with others on what defines good work, or times when they felt the group as a whole had forged a connection around specific research projects.[21]

If these academics have a personal interest in serving on panels, it appears to be as much about finding intrinsic rewards—the pleasure of reading good proposals—and in building relationships they find rewarding as it is about maximizing their position within intellectual fields. These elements of pleasure, which many respondents noted, are utterly absent from Bourdieu's description of the academic field.[22] For his part, Collins associates the effervescence of intellectuals with the emotional energy that comes from being at the center of attention.[23] But emotional energy can come from sharing important experiences. Considering the plurality of self-concepts among academics enriches our understanding of their motivations.[24]

In interviews, many evaluators expressed concern for their performance on the panel. Serving gave them an occasion to assess whether they measured up to the role they were asked to fill; they wanted to meet or exceed expectations. At a minimum, one must convince colleagues of the value of some of one's favorite proposals in order to come away from the deliberations with an intact sense of dignity. Thus deliberations are a context for presenting an ideal self or a perceived expected self, and perhaps even for measuring oneself against others. They are also a context where each panelist affirms the identity of others as valued experts. Although this aspect of peer review has not been discussed in standard accounts, it may be particularly valued because members of this group experience quite a bit of ambiguity about their relative status and worth, even as they spend much of their time judging the performance of others and are supposed to be strongly committed to quality.

Serving on panels also has the performative effect of sustaining faith in how the academic community identifies and produces quality. Service reasserts commitment to the process while also giving panelists a chance to improve it. This affirmation contributes to the feeling of effervescence, which can also result from the experience of distributing money to facilitate good work, from taking pride in participating in a process that is perceived as fair, or perhaps even from the collective exercise of "opportunity hoarding."[25]

The Role of Screeners

Screeners are generally highly regarded associate or (in a few cases) assistant professors whose mentors have recommended them to program officers. They are invited to serve because they are recognized as having high standards and good judgment, although, again, they are not expected to have the intellectual breadth and experience of panelists. Neither do they need the same interpersonal skills because they are not involved in face-to-face deliberations. As the description of the ACLS process presented earlier suggests, the screeners' job is to weed out unpromising proposals submitted by applicants working within the screeners' area of expertise. To borrow from Mitchell Stevens in his study of the admission process at an elite college, their task is that of coarse sorting, as opposed to making fine distinctions.[26] The rankings that screeners assign shape the list of proposals the panelists will evaluate and discuss.

In many ways, the role of screener has little to recommend it. These evaluators are not remunerated for what is often a very time-consuming task, their identity is often kept confidential, and they do not have the final say in which research receives support. But because being asked to serve is a badge of honor—a sure sign of the value that the academic community attaches to the individual's opinion—more junior and mid-career academics often are happy to serve in this capacity. Acting as a screener may add status and stability to their identity at what often is an unstable stage in their professional trajectory.

Screeners generally serve for one year and are invited to serve again if the program officer is satisfied with their work; they are rarely asked to serve for more than a few years, however. They are usually given several weeks to read and rate the proposals, but typically they receive very little guidance concerning what is expected of them. There is considerable variation in the care that screeners put into their tasks. For instance, some provide panelists with information regarding the proposals—they jot a few words or a few lines on each application—others provide nothing more than their ranking for each. Program officers exercise quality control. Their decision to "re-invite" screeners to serve is influenced by the care the screeners take in doing their tasks. For their part, panelists usually have the option of "checking" the work of screeners, but they rarely do so. In one of the competitions I studied, however, panelists became convinced, given the screener's written comments, that a particular type of project had been judged excessively harshly. Consequently, the panel elected to revisit all the eliminated proposals. Attributing such problems to a lack of experience among screeners, a historian explains:

> There were questions of both style and standard. Some people just are reluctant to give out high [ranks], and in a competition where a median figure might be enough to eliminate you, that could be a deadly . . . Others seem to have standards that we didn't agree with, where they reacted very strongly to a particular proposal. We looked at it and said, "Wait a minute. That's not a reason to eliminate this proposal." And one of those standards seemed . . . fairly arbitrary, [a] decision about the lack of a specific time schedule for the research. [This should not be] an absolute standard for making or breaking a proposal.

The Work of Panelists

Panelists are responsible for evaluating the applications of those in the pool of finalists. Typically, they assign a ranking to each, based on a scale of one to five (or A to E); build cases in favor of or against candidates; discuss these evaluations with other members of the panel; and make final recommendations concerning recipients. As suggested earlier, this job requires multiple types of expertise, the foremost of which are familiarity with several literatures and the ability to compare and assess a wide range of materials (the panelists I interviewed each had been asked to evaluate and rank anywhere from eighteen to eighty proposals). They usually have a month or so to study the applications and accompanying material and come up with rankings. In most cases, this reading and evaluating is "squeezed" into a schedule already overpacked with teaching; communicating formally and informally with colleagues; meeting with and advising graduate students; serving on departmental, university-wide, and professional committees; doing research; and writing books and papers.[27] Many panelists say they use time usually spent with their families to evaluate proposals, which often consumes weekends. For instance, a sociologist explains that he spent a whole weekend reading his eighteen proposals, allotting forty minutes to each.

Panel members recognize that they all do not put the same amount of time and care into their evaluations. A political scientist describes herself as much more careful than her fellow panelists: "I remembered the proposals [during deliberations]. I had much more detail about the proposals than some of the people. Some of them had read them a long time before the conference." An art historian, a first-time panelist, was frustrated and embarrassed to discover—during deliberations—that she had not put in as much time as others: "It comes at the worst time in the academic year. I had just gotten two piles of papers for grading for both classes at the time that these [proposals] arrived. And I did read them, but I obviously didn't read them the same way that [other panelists] did." Degree of preparedness affects how convincing panelists are to their peers.

In addition to relying on the rankings and comments provided by screeners, panelists normally base the judgments they make before their panel convenes on some or all of the following evidence: the applicant's biographical sketch, personal statement, curriculum vitae (specifically, past honors and awards, institutions attended, courses taken, employment, travel, and language competency), research project description, bibliography, project timetable, examples of past work, grade transcript, letters of recommendation, teaching experience and interests, statement of commitment to the goal of the funding program, and availability of other sources of funding. In one case—the Society of Fellows—the panel also conducts in-person interviews with finalists. As we will see in Chapter 5, panelists assign different weights to these pieces of evidence—particularly to the proposal, the project, and the applicant (including the letters describing her and her work). They may also mobilize additional resources. An American historian, for instance, describes going to his own bookshelf to consult a standard book on Middle Eastern history in order to better assess the claims of originality made by a particular proposal.[28]

Panelists typically serve for two or three years. A rotation system ensures continuity and helps new panel members learn the customary rules of deliberation. The benefit of this system is clear in the comments that panelists made contrasting their experiences from year to year (since they serve on panels for at least two years, seventeen of the panelists who participated in the study were interviewed twice). The art historian quoted earlier explains that the first year she served, she graded too liberally because she had "misunderstood" what was expected. "I suppose in many cases, my ones could have been two's and three's, and certainly my two's were three's and four's . . . That was very disconcerting because I did not come prepared to cite [from the proposals]." As a result, other panelists came to see her as having "low standards," which she found very upsetting. Another panelist explains that he learned from his experience the first year, when he had graded "easy,"

> a better sense of where to throw my ones and where to throw my lower scores, and when not to try and push it. Last year, for example, I gave a one to a proposal that was one-hundred-eighty degrees different than anything I think I myself would ever do . . . But it was so ambitious, and in a way so crazy, that I kind of liked it. Well, that was one of those discussions where essentially I made my case [and people] just looked at me and said, "That sounds more like you're arguing against this guy." . . . Everybody does a certain amount of role playing in these kinds of things.

Panelists note that the evaluation process is not straightforward because criteria change as one reads through the stack of applications. Most panelists take notes on each of the proposals and candidates while reading and then periodically revisit their rankings in an iterative process, with the result that, according to a political scientist, "One really does come to the session with a fairly clear recall of most of the applications." As they discover what the pool of applicants looks like, panelists often come to see that proposals shine under very different lights, that different standards apply to different proposals, and that proposals do not all win or lose for the same reason. As one panelist puts it:

> [One proposal] was very strong on originality, kind of ambitious, and weak on the actual presentation. It was overwritten. And the other proposal was actually uninteresting, but well presented. They had opposite pluses and minuses, so the argument was why should we fund this one and not do a similar kind of calculation for the other one, but in the opposite way.

Experience allows one to put incommensurable proposals like these on the same matrix and draw conclusions (more on this in Chapter 4).[29] Different characteristics—for instance, originality or significance—can push a proposal above the proverbial line. The evaluation process is not consistent or linear. As a historian says:

> If we could get fifty good, empirically grounded, significant proposals that had a reasonable comparative dimension to them, I would certainly go for those . . . [in practice] it's a matter of picking among twenty flawed proposals. [A proposal] that's sort of internally sophisticated and empirically important, but lacks that comparative or fashionable focus, is something that I would prob-

ably go for over something I thought was sloppy even if it was full of ideas.

Panelists perform much of their work in isolation and develop their own method of evaluation. One panelist, for example, first reads all the proposals in alphabetical order, and then by field, before giving any grade. Another describes her evaluation process thus:

> [The applications] are read about three times by the time I turn in my final grade, and some of them are read more than that. I read them once without grading them, then I go back and I grade them. Then I let them sit for a few days, then I go back and do the final grades. And in some instances, I might have read something several times . . . I knocked some scores up because I knew that they would get discussed if I gave them any kind of A, and I needed them discussed. Even though I do interdisciplinary work, I don't know everything coming out in history, and I needed help evaluating those.

This individualized approach is not surprising given that much like screeners, panelists do not receive formal training in the evaluation of proposals. Generally, the guidance provided by program officers to panelists is limited to information concerning the goals of the competition, the criteria to be considered, and perhaps a list of past awardees. Evaluators are not furnished with guidelines that dwell on what is being evaluated (the individual or the project), the specific meaning of the selection criteria to be used (for example, how to recognize originality and significance), or the weight to be given to each criterion (such as standards of excellence versus geographic distribution of awardees). Decisions in such areas are left to the discretion of the evaluators, who are expected to have learned how to conduct valid assessments over the course of their careers. And so most have—acquiring this skill in much the same way as they have learned many other tasks, that is, by themselves and by observing their more experienced colleagues and mentors.[30] An anthropologist explains how in the absence of "training," panelists nevertheless learn what is expected of them:

> I have been in a lot of grant review committees and I can't recall ever really [having] any training . . . It is a little bit difficult to think of training senior scholars. There are a lot of shared norms I think in academia, American academia, at least in research universities, from which most of these people are drawn . . . I think we, first of all, tend to judge people pretty heavily on their ability to contribute to major journals in the field . . . And we are impressed by people who are well-published, in that sense [of] publishing in major university presses and so on . . . The first time I was on a panel, I was probably thirty years old or something, I [wondered how we could do] it . . . Having now been on so many different kinds of panels, I would say I was curious to see whether there would be disagreement [among the experts] and so forth, but I [was not] struck by the difficulty of making evaluations. [It has become] natural.

Similarly, a political scientist believes that panelists do not need formal training in evaluation because

> It's the kind of stuff we do all our lives . . . Teaching, criticizing other people's work, reading articles for courses that you're going to teach. I mean, all we do is criticize and pick apart people's arguments, think about their variables, think about all the things that I talked about. No, I don't think we need any special training at all.

After a panel has completed its deliberations, the program officer often assesses the session and decides whether to ask the panel members to serve again. Among the panels I studied, there were a very few cases where an individual was not reinvited, either because he or she did not demonstrate the expected level of expertise (as evidenced by seeming wishy-washy or hesitant to express an opinion), or because of an apparent lack of essential interpersonal skills. Despite routinely making these "private assessments," program officers rarely provide panelists with information that would assist them in improving their own performance as judges—doing so could be awkward given the scholarly authority of the panelists. Nor do program officers provide information on the performance of past awardees, which could be useful for improving the selection process. When a formal evaluation of the panel is conducted—for instance, when a program is reviewed by an external committee—reports tend to remain in the hands of funding program personnel. Panelists are never confronted with the consequences of their deliberative choices, as they are when they select their future graduate students or when they approve tenure for colleagues. They are presumed to be responsible professionals who set high standards for themselves, and they are accorded full or nearly full sovereignty over the decision-making process. This autonomy adds weight to the selection process, and to the role that program officers play in it.

The Mechanics of Panel Deliberation

Panelists typically meet for a day or two, usually in the office of the funding agency, to discuss proposals. While some panels make funding decisions, others make funding recommendations, which are followed almost without exception. Commonly, once panel members have assembled, they are given a list of the proposals under consideration as well as the cumulative rating each has received from all the panelists.[31] The meeting generally begins with an explanation of the rules of deliberation, articulated by the panel chair and/or the program officer. These rules may specify, for instance, whether the panel operates by consensus or voting and whether all proposals (that is, even those with low ratings) will be discussed.

The panel chair and/or the program officer are responsible for orchestrating the deliberation, keeping the discussion moving, ensuring that all panelists have a chance to express an opinion on each proposal (if they wish), and seeing to it that applicants receive a fair hearing. They also in principle oversee the quality of the deliberation—by making sure that substantive arguments, rather than pure cost-benefit analyses, are made.

The chair and program officer must manage overbearing personalities (a sure sign of a poor panelist), prevent the formation of excessive alliances and allegiances, and forestall strong, potentially acrimonious disagreements. As we will see in Chapter 4, they also have to undertake emotional repair work when a panelist feels slighted (which may happen if his expertise is not given proper recognition, or if he believes that another panelist is not showing proper respect for a field or a topic).[32] Success in these endeavors requires that panelists respect both the chair and the program officer. Respect may be granted because of their skills and experience at running panels. Age, gender, race, known professional trajectory, and institutional affiliation (in the case of panel chairs) also have an effect.[33] One panelist explicitly attributed the success of her panel to the program officer: "I was amazed with how willing the panelists were and how accepting . . . It may have been because of the context, of the program officer . . . I don't know if it's the way she chose, I'm not even sure if she's the chooser, but the way she created the ethos was really exceptional [in setting the tone] and also moving us along, because we had a huge amount of work." A panel chair, by contrast, forfeited the respect of some members of his panel by alternating between the roles of an evaluator and a chair. This switching made it impossible for him to seem neutral when coordinating the deliberations; consequently, his credibility in both capacities was undermined. Another chair was strongly criticized for his patronizing and time-wasting managerial style. A panelist describes him as repeatedly saying, "'This is what we're doing,' when everyone knew what we were doing. It was time to move on. So there was a language that was employed that was exhausting and repetitious and maybe unnecessary. And I think it probably could have been cut off."

During deliberations, a panel typically works its way from the top of the list of applicants (those receiving the largest number of high marks) to the bottom. It is generally understood that applicants who received the highest total rating prior to the meeting will receive funding, so those cases may be noted at the start of deliberations, but they are not usually discussed. Likewise, applications that received low ratings often are not discussed. The bulk of the deliberations concern the applicants whose proposals have received mixed ratings, a group whose size depends on what proportion of the proposals will be funded. As an economist explained:

> The applications that were ranked six hundred and seven hundred, you could tell in ten seconds [that they were no good]. It just gets harder the closer you get to the cutoff and that's where we spent more time. So I think there's a time constraint in all our lives and we have to focus attention on some things. I don't think people got short shrift in terms of the amount of time. I think it was reasonable. You're not going to do any better than this.

The "middle of the pack" proposals, those that receive mixed ratings, are flawed, but their faults differ. The greatest challenge for panelists is often the comparison of incommensurate flaws. These middle-rank proposals consume the most time because individual panelists tend to weight differently the proposals' relative strengths and weaknesses. Hence debate about the relative importance of criteria and the meaning of specific criteria is a defining aspect of a panel's effort to constitute the "second half" of the list. When comparing proposals in this category, panel members also bring considerations of interdisciplinarity and diversity into the picture.

While on some panels someone is appointed to present each proposal, this was not the case in the panels I studied. The deliberations proceed at a fairly fast pace, with each panelist in turn being asked to provide an opinion. In order to refresh their memories, panelists often refer to notes they took when initially evaluating the applications and then offer arguments in favor or against proposals. Many have rehearsed arguments in advance, mentally comparing proposals as part of their effort to produce their own rankings in preparation for the meeting. After either only a few exchanges or more lengthy discussions, the program officer or chair gives his or her reading of the emerging consensus, and concludes with a recommendation. If there is no consensus, the proposal is generally set aside to be revisited later. A panelist describes the merits of this approach:

> Instead of anyone digging in their heels and saying, "If you don't fund this I'm going to . . ." which I have seen people do, we said, "Let's hold this and come back to it." Then by the time we've gone through the whole cycle of applications, things were clearer. I thought at the very end, where we were deciding for five [spots] among thirteen [applications], I thought that worked much more quickly than it might have . . . So I found it very congenial.

The discussion of the first proposals under consideration is lengthier than discussions held later because at the start of deliberation, panelists are also presenting their own expertise and background, defining their identity in relation to that of other panelists. As an economist puts it: "I suppose that's sort of what you learn during the first few hours of debate at one of these panels . . . you get a sense of each person, of well, they care about this, they don't care about that, maybe they're the only representative of this field here, but they come as the ambassador for that field." They also mark their territory, indicating the areas in which they believe they should be recognized as having greater authority.[34]

A political scientist points out that the first rounds of deliberation are also an occasion for individuals to "show off how smart [they] are"; that is, this is when panelists typically signal their particular fields and topic of expertise. As such, panel deliberations are also the occasion for "performing the self"—displaying one's verbal virtuosity and cultural capital among other academics.[35] As we will see in Chapter 4, such displays have a crucial effect on the interpersonal dynamics of the group.

As panelists get to know one another, and move from the "easiest" to the less consensual proposals, they develop a "group style."[36] Indeed, a historian explains, "When you sit on these committees, particularly from year to year, you increasingly get a sense of how other people see things, you can kind of predict [their arguments]." Many panelists also use the context of the panel to clarify their opinion about specific proposals and to gather additional information regarding currently available work on the topic. This aspect of deliberations is noted by a historian who, when asked if he was disappointed that some of the proposals were not funded, says:

> There were several cases in which I literally had question marks and I thought it looked like excellent and promising work, but I didn't think I understood it well enough. So I found myself asking questions more than making a case when I intervened in the dis-

cussion, and then was convinced that perhaps it was not my failure to understand something, but rather that the project wasn't completely thought through.

Conversely, this same historian explains that other panelists turned to him for his historical expertise:

> I knew that my colleagues would occasionally look to me to explain the situation [of the proposal] within the discipline—is this where the work is going, is this a valuable set of sources, what is this proposal missing, all sorts of things. So I tended to really focus a good deal on those, simply because I accepted it as my responsibility to be able to answer questions that others might have.

Undoubtedly, the multidisciplinary character of the panels I studied reinforces the interdependence of panelists when it comes to obtaining the knowledge needed to assess proposals. But across all types of panels, the evaluators also depend on one another for subtle nonverbal signals concerning the value of proposals (eye rolling, shoulder shrugging, nodding, smiling admiringly, and so on)—signals that help them "satisfice" or make the best choices possible given the limitations of their own knowledge and their current context.[37]

As suggested in Chapter 1, face-to-face conversations are seen as leading to better decisions. John Dewey, for one, believed that debating is important for the emergence of shared standards about fairness and for developing trust.[38] Accordingly, deliberating forces panelists to articulate their argument in the context of a dialogue—a process that may produce more transparent, less controllable decisions, and decisions that take into consideration contextual information. As a technology for decision making, deliberation helps neutralize conflicts and encourages interdisciplinary conversations, despite perceived inequalities of prestige and influence across disciplines.[39] It also makes room for improvisation and hunches, as panelists elaborate on their arguments in the heat of the moment.[40] This system is to be contrasted with mechanized forms of evaluation that attempt to remove all traces of the personal, the idiosyncratic, and the inconsistent.[41] Funding agencies use peer review because they can mobilize acknowledged experts, that is, an evaluative technology that puts connoisseurship and judgments at the center of the evaluation process.

Conclusion

As we will see, many applicants and panelists strongly support grant peer review because it is perceived as guaranteeing a relatively clean evaluation process. As such, it legitimizes the system of distribution of resources for evaluators and applicants, and beyond that, affirms the broader system of academic evaluation and promotion, including tenure. To some extent peer review is where agreement on quality is accomplished and where the principle of meritocracy is unquestioned. In contrast, to take only one example, in the French workplace studied by sociologist François Dubet, several forces are opposed to the meritocratic distribution of resources because it privileges the dominant and penalizes the subordinate groups.[42]

As a technology producing relative "cleanliness," peer review plays an especially crucial role in the American context, at least as compared to its role in "smaller" systems like those of Hungary, Finland, or Portugal. The sheer demographic size of American higher education, as well as the impersonal nature and level of social and geographic mobility that characterize it, generate uncertainty concerning shared norms and rules of behavior, and threaten to undermine organizational control.[43] Under these conditions, it is particularly important that individuals who have never met know immediately what is expected of them when they find themselves in the same room, and so they do, thanks to widely shared institutionalized norms that regulate the system of national competition.[44] Trust in the peer review system is crucial because, by definition, it rejects the vast majority of applicants, who could easily lose faith. Thus this system maintains representations of itself as open and driven by meritocracy, in strong contrast with a not-too-distant past when academia conspicuously favored more culturally homogeneous religious, ethnic, and class elites.[45]

As the next chapter will make clear, in the context of this clearly defined technology of peer review and the relative consensus that surrounds it, the evaluative cultures of academic disciplines vary greatly—so much so that it can seem like a minor miracle that consensus emerges from this sea of differences, and that the black box can actually produce awards.

3/On Disciplinary Cultures

The "gulf of mutual incomprehension" that Sir Charles Percy Snow famously posited as separating "scientists" from "literary intellectuals" also separates many social scientists from humanists, as well as many interpretative from more positivist researchers.[1] Long before they come to sit on funding panels, scholars absorb a variety of beliefs and perceptions about disciplinary cultures, especially each field's approach to producing and evaluating knowledge.[2] They become familiar with these differences through intellectual activity—graduate training, mentoring, reading within and outside their fields, and so on—as well as through the formal and informal activities of everyday life at colleges and universities. One panelist I interviewed, an analytical philosopher, playfully sums up some prevailing stereotypes this way:

Philosophers are known to be rigorous more than anything else, right? People in English seem to value a kind of ability to look at the underside of literary texts and see not so much what they are saying, but what they're not saying. In philosophy that is considered completely useless, whatever. In art history, some want to be on the cutting edge of every last French philosophical movement and be able to bring Lacan, Deleuze, Baudrillard, and Bourdieu into their discussion of the arts.

The differences in epistemological styles that this philosopher lampoons frequently fuel the divisive debates that occur across (and in some cases within) academic disciplines. By "epistemological styles" I mean preferences for particular ways of understanding how to build knowledge, as well as beliefs in the very possibility of proving those theories.[3]

In their quest for a monopoly on truth or science, social scientists and humanists often succumb to polarizing stances, arguing that there is only one correct approach to both theory and method.[4] In terms of theory, disciplinary preferences range from the view that authors should acknowledge how the formulation of their theoretical orientation is shaped by their own social location, identity, and political orientation, to the view that theories emerge from the observation of new evidence in light of existing explanations, without being affected by who the researcher is or how she apprehends her object.[5] The range with regard to methodological preferences is no less wide. Some disciplines emphasize hypothesis testing and privilege the role of formal models for proving theories; others vehemently reject such approaches in favor of a contextual or narrative method.[6]

This chapter identifies some widely accepted views that academics hold about the evaluative and epistemic culture of their own field and those of other fields. Such sets of conventions influence how disciplines define quality and recognize it. They include "inquiry beliefs" and "theoretical attachments" regarding, for instance, the proximity of fields to the natural sciences, the usefulness of reductionist approaches and strategies, and the roles of empirical data and theory.[7] Moreover, they include beliefs about whether academic excellence is "real" or located in the eye of the beholder, whether consensus can be reached, and what might ground it. They also encompass debates over standards, the role of theory, consensus in a field, the ability to judge, the importance of disciplinary boundaries, and the significance of subjectivity in the pursuit of knowledge.

Disciplinary differences are not only part of the funding panel experience, but also are at play in academic life more generally. As stereotypes, these differences often serve as grounds against which members of disciplines define themselves relationally, that is, in opposition to other disciplines. And like all stereotypes, disciplinary stereotypes are reinforced by lack of contact with the "other."[8] The frequency of interaction across disciplines typically is low, owing to the strong departmental structure of academia, the growing demands on faculty time, and the exigencies of keeping up in one's own field. Thus a consideration of disciplinary evaluative cultures is crucial for understanding the behavior of funding panels (as well as higher education more generally). The picture of disciplinary temperaments that emerges here is very different from that offered by Richard Whitley, who focuses on variations in dependency and task uncertainty across the disciplines.[9]

The discussion in this chapter draws on several sources. One is what individual panelists say—inchoate, unreflective responses as well as well-considered, theorized positions—about differences in disciplinary cultures and about how standards vary across disciplines. I focus on six of the eleven disciplines that the study's respondents hail from. These fields are roughly distributed on the humanities/social science and soft/hard axes, and include 75 percent of my respondents.[10] In order of presentation, the disciplines are philosophy, English, history, anthropology, political science, and economics. Because the social science competitions I studied are somewhat more humanistic than the social sciences as a whole (this is especially true of the SSRC and the WWNFF competitions), the anthropologists I interviewed are more likely representative of their discipline than are the political scientists and economists. This bias is unavoidable since I was unable to gain access to the more scientific social science panels, such as those of the National Science Foundation, where panel members from economics and political science probably are closer to their disciplines' "mean."[11] An important balancing factor here is that my description of each field, in addition to being informed by what their members say about it, reflects the perceptions of members of other disciplines, incorporates my own experience and exposure to these fields, and draws on broader analyses made by scholars who have studied academic life. I also benefited from discussion with and feedback from a range of experts from various fields.

Perceptions of disciplinary differences in panel deliberations. Representations concerning disciplinary differences are significant because they provide one of the frameworks through which members of multidisciplinary panels make sense of their roles and responsibilities. An anthropologist sketches the basic evaluative procedure this way:

> Before the meeting, you as a reader find something in a proposal that speaks to you or doesn't speak to you. And then you hopefully are able to convey some of that to the rest of the group . . . What you wind up doing is advocating or explaining to other people why something is a good project. And when other people are listening, as they were this time, then it's not so hard to come to an agreement.

Since by definition most of the participating scholars on an interdisciplinary panel come from different academic fields, members cannot count on others sharing their theoretical or methodological preferences. In order to be "able to convey" to colleagues "why something is a good project," a panelist needs to mount a case using arguments that others will be receptive to—that keep "other people . . . listening." Or, stated more broadly, what academics perceive as being the key cognitive conventions among all the various disciplines influences which characteristics of a proposal are accentuated (or downplayed) during deliberation. Which arguments are made, in turn, increases the likelihood that some proposals will be eliminated along the way, depending on the disciplinary make-up of a committee. A detailed content analysis of panel members' responses to interview questions shows that in making their proposal evaluations, they generally draw on one or more of the following epistemological styles, which my colleagues Grégoire Mallard, Joshua Guetzkow and I have dubbed constructivist, comprehensive, positivist, and utilitarian.[12]

The comprehensive style values *verstehen,* attention to details, and contextual specificity in proposals. As in Max Weber's comprehensive sociology, this style supports historically and culturally sensitive social science and humanistic research.[13] It is the most widely used style, mobilized by humanists (86 percent), historians (78 percent), and social scientists (71 percent).[14] (Historians are considered a separate group because of this discipline's hybrid status between the social sciences and humanities.) The constructivist style emphasizes proposals that "give voice" to various groups. It values reflexivity, that is, consideration of the impact of the researcher's identity and commitment on his analysis. It appeals to anti-positivists whose research is politically or socially engaged. It is most popular among humanists (28 percent) and historians (29 percent); it is favored by only 14 percent of the social scientists. The positivist style favors generalizability and hypothesis testing. It is used most often by social scientists (57 percent) and, to a lesser extent, by historians (23 percent); none of the humanists mobilize this style in their evaluation.

The utilitarian style resembles the positivist style, but it values only the production of instrumental knowledge. This is the least popular style. It is used by only 4 percent of the historians, 19 percent of the social scientists, and none of the humanists.

Disciplinary cultures and definitions of excellence. The definitions of excellence that panelists employ in evaluating proposals are influenced by their individual proclivities, and by various facets of their identity and of their intellectual and social trajectories. The epistemological criteria that panelists value most in judging proposals also often resonate with the definition of excellence that prevails in their specific discipline. As we will see in Chapter 4, multidisciplinary panels often loosen this association, giving preference to those criteria of evaluation valued in the discipline of the applicant rather than in their own discipline (a practice termed "cognitive contextualization"). Thus the interdisciplinary character of the competition affects disciplinary arguments and shapes how panelists go about convincing one another of a proposal's merits (or lack thereof).

But how is the goal of finding and rewarding excellence understood across disciplines? This chapter presents evidence of disciplinary variations in the extent to which panelists believe academic excellence exists (although serving on a funding panel signals a baseline commitment to the possibility of identifying some form of excellence); agree on what defines excellence; and believe that excellence is located in the object of evaluation (that is, the proposal), as opposed to the eye of the beholder (in the intersubjective agreement that emerges from negotiations among panelists). These variations can be explained in part by the epistemological culture of the field—the extent to which scholars understand criteria of evaluation as valid per se or as expressing and extending power dynamics ("whose standards are they, anyway?"). Fields such as English literature and anthropology, where post-structuralism has been influential and the "theory wars" have been fought, are more likely to take a relativistic stance toward evaluation, as well as to have a weaker consensus on what defines quality.

Disciplinary cultures of excellence are also likely to be influenced by demographic factors: these reveal patterns of growth and decline, which may reverberate on levels of consensus within a discipline. Over the past thirty years, students have fled the humanities, as well as the softer social sciences, for more practical majors such as business and computer science.[15] Figure 3.1 presents data on the number of PhDs awarded per field between 1975 and 2005. English, history, and political science experienced an important decline in degrees granted between 1975 and 1985. After 1995, these disciplines rebounded (to varying degrees) and stabilized or slightly increased until 2005. In the late 1970s, economics suffered from a less acute decline than the other fields (except for anthropology), and has shown continuous growth since, as have history and political science. Perhaps not coincidentally, economics and history are the two disciplines where scholars appear to have the most consensus concerning what defines quality. English, the only field to show a decline in PhDs granted between 1995 and 2005, is also the discipline where the very concept of academic excellence has come under the greatest attack. Of course, figures on the number of PhDs granted per discipline are not a conclusive indicator of the vitality or status of fields, and I do not present these data as evidence of a one-to-one correspondence between disciplinary status, market-strength, and consensus.[16] I do, however, see the association illustrated by Figure 3.1 as highlighting one of a constellation of conditions that sustain—or fragment—disciplinary consensus regarding the pursuit of knowledge and the associated question of how to define and evaluate excellence.[17]

In the context of peer review panels, one of the most vivid indicators of disciplinary differences is the place that evaluators accord to subjectivity in the pursuit of knowledge. Here the gulf of mutual in-

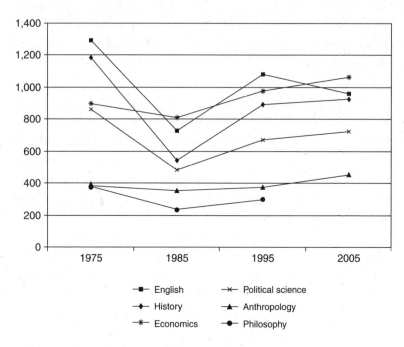

Figure 3.1 Number of PhD degrees given in selected disciplines, 1975–2005. Yearly data on the number of PhDs granted from 1975–2005 in the fields of English, history, economics, political science, and anthropology are taken from the *Survey of Earned Doctorates* (*SED*) conducted by National Opinion Research Center. See National Opinion Research Center (2006); Hoffer et al. (2006). Data on the number of PhDs granted from 1975–1995 in the field of philosophy are taken from two reports by the American Philosophical Association (APA): information for 1975 and 1985 is from "Degrees Awarded in Philosophy by U.S. Universities, 1949–1994" and information for 1995 is from "PhDs in Philosophy by Gender/Race/Ethnicity." The number of philosophy PhDs awarded in 1975 and 1985 was obtained by averaging the number of PhDs granted in 1974–1975 and 1975–1976, and the number of PhDs granted in 1984–1985 and 1985–1986. Since the *SED* data are obtained through a government research project and the APA data are taken from a survey conducted by a professional association, there may be some discrepancy in coding. Note that the APA has not yet compiled or released data on PhDs in philosophy after 1996.

comprehension finds most social scientists on one side and most humanists on the other.

Interpretative and Empirical Disciplines

Humanists often define interpretative skills as quintessential for the production of high-quality scholarship. Social scientists, especially those who champion empiricism, more often deride interpretation as a corrupting force in the production of truth. This basic distinction directly affects how humanists and social scientists evaluate proposals. Some humanists rank what promises to be "fascinating" above what may turn out to be "true." An English professor describes a proposal in the following terms: "I was just compelled by the sort of careful way in which she mapped this out, and my thing is, even if it doesn't work, I think it will provoke really fascinating conversations. So I was really not interested in whether it's true or not." Another panelist, a literary scholar who also supported this proposal, put originality above empirical soundness, explaining, "You can never prove anything." Such skepticism toward the concept of truth is more rarely voiced in the social sciences. Several panelists from political science, for instance, stressed traditional standards of positivism. One, noting that he thinks of himself as "a scientist, but in a very broad conception of that term," offers this description of the standards he uses to evaluate scholarship:

> Validity is one, and you might say parsimony is another, I think
> that's relatively important, but not nearly as important as validity.
> It's the notion that a good theory is one that maximizes the ratio
> between the information that is captured in the independent vari-
> able and the information that is captured in the prediction, in the
> dependent variable. [Also g]eneralizability across different histori-
> cal epochs, not across extraordinarily different societies . . . sys-
> tematic knowledge I think is important, too, so that you can be

shown to be wrong. In other words, to have discomfirmable knowledge.

For this panelist, the ability to replicate results is crucial. "Otherwise, what one is doing is a personal expression . . . what is interesting [about the work of scholars he admires] is not about their own view of the world, but about the world itself." Not all social scientists share this conception of subjectivity ("of the personal") as a corrupting influence on the production of knowledge, however. Much in line with standard practices in high energy physics and other scientific fields, there is a strong tendency in some quarters of the social sciences to acknowledge the role of interpretation and induction in research and to point out the researcher's back and forth movement between theory and empirical analysis (sometimes pejoratively termed "data massaging").[18]

Much like the gulf between the humanities and the social sciences, this split within the social sciences, between those fields where empiricism is more exclusively favored and those where interpretation is considered an essential ingredient, also influences panel deliberations. An anthropologist describes sociologists, political scientists, and economists as tending to emphasize "theoretical models" and "statistical framework[s]," whereas anthropologists and historians "put more emphasis on language proficiency, knowledge of the culture, spending time in the place you're researching." A sociologist elaborates on these distinctions:

> Sociology, political science, economics people share one set of criteria, and the people from anthropology and history share different criteria. Anthropology and history are much less positivistic, much more comfortable with single cases. Whereas the political science, sociology, [and] economics representatives want multiple cases and stronger research design. They are less comfortable with

a proposal that looks like it just wants to tell an interesting story . . . Anthropologists and historians are much more inductive in their approaches, much more sort of "empirical dirty hands," to a degree. Certainly much less inclined to [the] sort of typical deductive kind of process that you run into in introductory classes in sociology, for example . . . Political science is relatively narrower for what passes for acceptable science than sociology . . . on the dimension of do you need to be hypothesis-testing or theory-generating, as opposed to just engaging in interesting storytelling.

In addition to separating "generalizable theory" from "story-telling," academics frequently distinguish between the pursuit of pure versus applied knowledge. Some view the social sciences as having an applied dimension and the humanities as contributing to "the production of meaning," and to being "ultimately about the kinds of questions people ask of a range of kinds of texts." An anthropologist invokes this distinction to explain his preferences in scholarship:

I'm not the kind of person who tries to reduce a highly complicated social situation to a one-sentence synthesis . . . I'm much more interested in looking at the multiple layers and complexities of human social experience . . . I don't see myself as being somebody who's going to come up with a unified theory of all human life; I'm not particularly interested in doing that. So in a way, I guess my leaning is much more humanistic than is conventional in social science.

History, even more than anthropology, defies consistent categorization. Whether panelists consider the field as belonging to the humanities or to the social sciences depends largely on the place they accord narratives and theory in their own work. The social sciences have had a huge influence on history over the past forty years, and increasingly, historians follow William Sewell Jr. in arguing that history offers theory (about social change, for instance) to other fields.[19] Yet others, although also interested in theory (of the literary or cultural studies varieties), often identify themselves as humanists. The turn toward quantification in the 1970s also pushed history toward the social sciences.

By examining several disciplinary evaluative cultures individually, we can see that academics in each discipline consider that much is at stake in how their field is defined and understood, from within and from without.

The "Problem Case" of Philosophy

Four of the panels I studied included a philosopher and considered philosophy proposals. On two panels, philosophy emerged as a "problem field," seen as producing proposals around which conflicts erupt. Accordingly, some program officers warned panelists of the special difficulty of building consensus around such proposals and encouraged them to stay "open-minded" toward them. Such cautions and requests came as close to a plea for "affirmative action" toward a discipline as I witnessed during my study of funding panels.

Several panelists expressed at least one of the following views: (1) philosophers live in a world apart from other humanists, (2) nonphilosophers have problems evaluating philosophical work, and they are often perceived by philosophers as not qualified to do so, (3) philosophers do not explain the significance of their work, and (4) increasingly, what philosophers do is irrelevant, sterile, and self-indulgent. These views—especially the second—are problematic because the smooth functioning of multidisciplinary panels depends on all members' willingness to engage with other disciplines and to practice cognitive contextualization, thus assuring that each proposal is evaluated using the criteria most valued in the proposal writer's discipline.[20] Later, I suggest that views of philosophy as a "problem case" can be traced to aspects of the evaluative culture of the discipline.

Princeton philosopher Alexander Nehamas notes that American philosophers think of their field as a "second order discipline," superordinate to all other disciplines, because it investigates the claims made by other fields.[21] This in turn fosters a propensity among philosophers to see their field as uniquely demanding. This view can lead them to conclude that only philosophers are truly competent to evaluate philosophy proposals, an attitude that challenges the very possibility of multidisciplinary evaluation. A philosopher on one of the four panels expresses this view very clearly. He asserts that not all panelists are qualified to evaluate philosophy proposals because, like mathematics, philosophy presumes special skills that many panelists lack.[22]

Philosophy requires the ability to make analytic distinctions, the ability to clarify a position or an argument to a degree that hasn't been done before, a certain kind of rigor in working through the implications and details of a position and a mastery of the details but at the same time, a sense of the larger scale significance of detailed arguments and positions in the larger landscape of philosophical issues.

This understanding of the field as promoting a unique "rigor" and incisive clarity in arguments reflects the dominance of analytical philosophy as an intellectual style.[23] As a second philosopher explains, "Philosophy differs from other disciplines because there's much more of a sense of argumentation or debate . . . When you give a paper in philosophy, you give a paper and then you have an hour of people trying to find what's wrong with it. [The debates are] very clear, obvious, and not at all, so to speak, elegant." By contrast, "in

English or in comparative literature . . . the discussion is of a very different sort. I think it is, generally speaking, less ruthless." This ruthlessness—this toughness—may be a manifestation of philosophy's view of itself as one of the most exacting of disciplines. In trying to account for the fact that among all the projects selected for funding, "the philosophy proposals are the ones that need to be explained," another philosopher stresses, "Philosophy projects are by and large very, very difficult to understand." Along the same lines, the website of the American Philosophical Association states that "no other discipline is more attentive to the cultivation of intellectual conscience and of critical acumen."[24] Particularly in interdisciplinary settings, actions that reflect these field-specific characteristics may be interpreted by nonphilosophers as a form of misplaced intellectual superiority or as an inappropriate attempt to enhance disciplinary status.

Philosophy's "very autonomous" position in the humanities is another potential source of trouble on interdisciplinary panels. A historian observes that "it's very hard to find a philosopher . . . who has any common ground of discussion with the rest of the world." A geographer summarizes his panel's frustration with evaluating philosophy proposals with the remark that philosophers "produc[e] absolutely unintelligible research proposals, and so we just didn't know how to deal with them." Put differently, the philosophy proposals appear to have tested these panel members' ability to engage in cognitive contextualization. Some panelists interpret philosophy's "autonomy," "isolation," or "lack of common ground" with other disciplines as an indication of its loss of relevance. The geographer, for instance, dismisses the field as "sterile."

> I did a degree at Oxford and I did philosophy, politics, and economics [a typical Rhodes Scholar degree]. I decided it was pretty

sterile then, and I think it's become even more awful since . . . It's really still a playing out of the linguistic turn that took hold in Oxford in the 1940s . . . All these guys who taught me had been taught traditional history of philosophy, Kant and Hume, and so on, Descartes. But they dropped all of that because they heard there was this linguistic philosophy without any historical background, so you didn't get any sense of philosophy as an ongoing human preoccupation, what function did it play. Instead it had turned out into a way of solving puzzles . . . These guys had all been in British intelligence in the war, so they all love to sit around thinking up clever things to say, and that's a pretty goddamn sterile way of life.

This panelist did not hide his poor opinion of the field during panel deliberations. The philosopher recalls: "This [geographer] said right out at one point that he's had an encounter with philosophy in Oxford back in the fifties when he was there, that had left him with the impression that it was all just a parlor game . . . he seemed to be questioning the credentials of the whole field on the basis of some anecdotal encounters he's had with people who did it forty years ago, and I thought that was not professional and [not an] appropriate basis for an interdisciplinary panel."[25]

Other panelists were much more diplomatic in their view of philosophy, but they too saw it as a problematic discipline. An English scholar observes, for instance:

Although there was a huge range of views about many of the proposals, I just remember time and again there would be a very friendly, but pointed and not resolved, argument, either about a philosophy proposal that [the philosopher] really liked and that the rest of us couldn't stand, or about some other proposal that he didn't like and that other people did like . . . I really didn't appreciate a number of the proposals that the philosopher really admired. I also felt like I couldn't understand why he admired them, and I really appreciated his explaining. I thought [he] was a very articulate, patient explainer, but I just still didn't get it.

Some panel members opposed the philosophy proposals because they considered them boring, unfocused, or simply not as strong as proposals from other fields. One English professor was willing to defer to the philosopher in the evaluation of these proposals, a stance not supported by the other panelists. She explains her attitude this way:

Up to a certain point I was trying to defer to [the philosopher's] ranking. He had some kind of say over which of the philosopher candidates he liked most, which he liked least, why, who was doing what kind of philosophy, why it was important versus something else . . . in my balloting for alternates I tried to kind of go along with that, to sort of support him . . . because I felt that he was the expert and I was sort of out of my league. And I felt that they should have awards, especially if we had high-quality philosophers.

Disciplinary differences in definitions of excellence and, especially, how much weight should be given to "significance" (one of the two most frequently used criteria, as we will see in Chapter 5) also take their toll on philosophy proposals. According to a historian, these proposals are "in their own stratosphere." One philosopher, though, sees as the root problem that originality (the other most popular evaluative criterion) is manifested very differently in philosophy than it is in other fields. The predominant templates that interdisciplinary panels use to assess originality focus on the study of new objects. This handicaps philosophy applicants:

> We're grappling in much of conventional philosophy with very traditional problems that [have] defined the subject for, you know, thousands of years. It's not that entirely new problems come up that haven't been studied or investigated before . . . I think a certain kind of innovation and certainly originality is important in philosophy, but it's assessed very differently. That was one place where I consistently felt there was a difference between my conception of what the criteria for assessing good philosophy would be and the criteria that were sometimes used in our assessments: it would be held against people if they were doing comparatively traditional projects that might have been worked on in the past.

Finally, philosophy's reputation as a potential "problem case" is not helped by the fact that the discipline is defined by its own practitioners as contentious. Philosophers tend to approach each other's work with skepticism, criticism, and an eye for debate. Disagreement is not viewed as problematic; rather, it largely defines intelligence and is considered a signature characteristic of the culture of the discipline—with often disastrous results for funding. A similar contentiousness characterizes literary scholars.[26] But in the case of literary scholars, this rancorous debate occurs in the context of a great interdisciplinary openness, and so is not used to strengthen the disciplinary inward-looking impulse, as is the case in philosophy. The two disciplines have reacted in opposite ways to the decline of their disciplinary audiences—philosophy, with an increasing rigidity of standards, and English, as we shall see, with an approach to standards that is increasingly relativistic and diversified.[27]

The "Legitimation Crisis" of English Literature

Over the past thirty years, English has distinguished itself from the other disciplines considered here by broadening its mission—to the tasks of producing, teaching, and celebrating literary canons, the profession has added the job of reflecting on the canonization process itself.[28] It is perhaps the strong influence of post-structuralism, and of Jacques Derrida and Michel Foucault in particular, that has made literary scholars particularly aware of standards of excellence as power-laden and anything but platonic ideals. Much of Derrida and Foucault's writings concern the construction of arbitrary hierarchies of meaning.[29]

Given the commitment to deconstructive analysis that literary scholars evince in their classrooms and in their studies, it should not be surprising that many are ambivalent about the evaluative role of funding panels. The scholars whom I interviewed describe themselves as skeptical of whether "true quality" exists and, if it does, of their ability to recognize it. They tend to understand excellence as a construction resulting from the interaction of panelists, as opposed to an objective quality inherent to the proposal being evaluated. In responding to questions about whether they "believed in excellence" and whether the "cream naturally rises to the top," they emphasize intersubjective processes, such as how panelists collaborate to label specific proposals as being "high quality" based on agreed-on, but certainly "subjective," criteria. One English professor, when asked if she believes in academic excellence, says:

> My first impulse is to say no, I think I don't. Let me put it this way: Maybe I believe in academic excellence, but I don't think that's a natural category. I think that we have some kind of consensus around what we like for certain reasons, and then we call them excellence, and then that's what we hold for excellent.

Likewise, she asserts that she does not believe that the cream naturally rises to the top, "because it probably isn't natural." Then, elaborating, she adds:

> I could imagine that there is such a thing as a project that would seem to be absolutely excellent according to [some standard], but at the end of the day, that might not be the one that interests me more. Or I could also see something that strikes me as being bold and daring and might not quite have it right yet, but could be doing something that's so important that I would end up at the end of the day supporting that. And I don't think I'm the only person [who] would do that.

Another English professor, when asked whether she believes cream rises to the top, states, "I think if the cream is sort of the one percent, that's probably true. When you're deciding on [fellowships], you're [not] dealing with cream, you're really dealing with two percent [milk]. [*Laughs*.] [You have] a range of proposals and at any given moment that milk could become cream, but you're not exactly sure . . . It's always good to be a little more sort of self-conscious and self-aware and self-questioning when you come into these things. Our agreement about what constitutes cream, that percentage is very small." A third English scholar explains:

> One of the things that post-structuralist theory makes us do is say, "You can't just say something is good because it won this or NEH or ACLS," you have to be a little bit more hardheaded than that, you have to look at it for what it is . . . Excellence is constructed, that's true, but is it constructed so that anything I declare to be excellent and set a certain criteria is therefore excellence? Well, no. I'll go back to rigor. Someone who's just clocking time isn't [doing] enough either. [Someone who] has shown some

kind of principle of selection, has been willing to challenge their premises, has been willing to consider data even after you're well along in a study that completely challenges and overgrows the hypothesis you've been making. Those kinds of things I think . . . are things that every field can recognize as good . . . If somebody doesn't know the theoretical and critical literature on their subject, that tells you something right there. It tells you they haven't been doing their homework, [haven't] joined what I would call the intellectual conversations.

Even in the absence of such relativistic views of excellence, the question of how to evaluate literary studies scholarship would remain open. Until the recent past, mastery of close reading, defined as "making very careful observations about how the language works, about how meaning is produced by the interactions of individual words and their allusions to other literary texts," as one English professor explained, played an important role in determining the disciplinary pecking order.[30] Three simultaneous developments have rendered these skills less central to the practice of the literary craft, and thus have created a crisis in how literary studies scholarship is to be evaluated. First, the critique of the canonization process has gone hand-in-hand with a critique of privileging the written text, which has fed into a broadening of the disciplinary agenda toward cultural studies, defined as the critical analysis of visual, performative, and literary texts. This shift has transformed the meaning of close reading: deciphering popular culture requires less erudite, properly scholarly (that is, highly legitimate) knowledge than does studying canonized authors. Second, English scholars have widened their interests to include history and anthropology and have become more concerned than they were in the 1950s with locating literary texts within their social and historical contexts. In developing historical skills, English scholars may have indirectly lowered the value of purely literary analytical tools within their broader analytical toolkits. Third, social and literary theory has profoundly transformed their understanding of representations, as manifested in variants ranging from Marxist, feminist, psychoanalytical, and structuralist to post-structuralist theories. These changes have led scholars to value "smart" and "interesting" work over the "sound" and "rigorous" studies that were most praised in earlier decades.[31]

One result of these changes is that literature proposals are less competitive than they once were, particularly as compared to those submitted by historians (the latter garner and are perceived as garnering, the lion's share of humanities fellowships). The disciplinary broadening and diversification of criteria of evaluation may have led to a deprofessionalization that puts literary scholars in a vulnerable position when competing on theoretical or historical grounds with scholars whose disciplines "own" such terrains. Cognitive contextualization may be the link between "deprofessionalization" and decreasing awards. To judge a proposal on the basis of the criteria most appropriate to the applicant's discipline requires that panelists have a sense of what such criteria would be. In disciplines like English, where a laundry list of criteria might arguably be applied, panelists are much freer to choose their evaluative criteria as they see fit. So if a literary studies proposal makes much of its reliance on or expansion of work in history, this might prompt a panelist to apply criteria appropriate to the discipline of history rather than of English, and convince others to do so as well (a task made easier by the fact that there is little consensus within the discipline). An English professor recalls:

> At one point somebody said, "Gosh, we've giving all the awards to historians." And I remember thinking, "That's not surprising." There's an almost complete disappearance of literary proposals. English professors don't write literary proposals anymore. And when they do, they don't hold up very well . . . Why do people not write them? . . . [O]ne reason is that literary critics themselves

have turned more and more to doing historical work or social science work and so it's been a matter of a kind of internal self-critique, which is good; it's very healthy. I like it when I and other English professors turn their attention to non-literary materials because I think we're good readers of them . . . [But i]t may be that the historians know how to do this better than English professors do.

A second panelist, also from English, agrees that "the number of fellowships that go to people in language or literature [has] really gone down," and she draws similar connections between this and increasing deprofessionalization:

A lot of work coming out of the English department is less and less literary and more and more engaged in sort of cultural studies or what is called cultural material production. A lot of this material is familiar to people in history and anthropology and may just provoke them, in a sense that, "I know this material fairly well and none of this really computes." Or else "this seems to be over-arguing the importance of material which in fact doesn't really merit this kind of attention," or "the actual analysis being forwarded doesn't really correspond to my sense about what is going on in the particular film or this particular MTV video" . . . To go in that direction, you're moving into that sort of no-man's land or an open field where everybody can be kind of a media expert.

She muses that literary proposals may lose out to ones from history because

There's something about people doing history . . . there is a concrete body of information that you can assess. The interpretation refers to material that is subject to certain kinds of verification. Whereas with literary interpretation, part of it has to do with sort of subtlety, has to do with training, has to do with where you stand on the theory, how theoretical you want to be, or how formal your orientation is. We can't mount as convincing a case and it's harder to argue not only significance but originality because there's no real, no sort of set terms of agreement.

Regardless of "how theoretical" a literary scholar chooses to be, the discipline now considers mastery of "theory"—defined as a set of conceptual references, not as an activity leading to prediction—an essential skill because it can be used to bridge disciplinary and substantive boundaries. When combined with the lack of "set terms of agreement" regarding merit, emphasizing theory may, as the professor quoted above argues, only exacerbate the discipline's lack of coherence. But to the extent that theory makes it possible to communicate with nonspecialists about topics that cut across areas of expertise, it can positively affect the discipline by enlarging its audience. One English professor reflects on the centrality of theory and his relationship to it in the following terms:

> I wish I were a better theorist . . . I tend to love to do textual analysis, I love doing that, and I love doing it in film, and I think people love watching me do that, or reading me do that, but . . . I wish I could be more comfortable playing around with the ideas generated by the reading . . . Theory is something I seem to run away from . . . maybe because it requires me to think in ways that are not intuitive . . . [Theory] allows for a cross-disciplinary conversation. It allows us to put texts in wider conversations with each other, and I think that's important.

The effort to broaden the audience, to conduct "cross-disciplinary conversations," is a logical response to the demographic decline of the field of English literature.[32] To win acclaim, however, scholars must perform their theoretical acumen within limits. This in turn requires an additional skill—the ability to balance theorizing with readability. A different English professor points out, "Literary studies can just get too fancy, too complicated. I really enjoy writing very complicated new critical readings of things, but if people don't understand them, then there's not much point in publishing them." The emphasis on theory is also driven by a "star system" that may be the discipline's response to its loss of status.[33]

The panelists I interviewed identify and comment on many of the same aspects of their discipline's internal debates—over standards, the practical meaning and reality of excellence, the merits of theory, the importance of disciplinary boundaries—but they do not necessarily interpret the effects of this lack of consensus in the same way. One, for instance, sees English as nearly paralyzed by its internal divisions and laissez-faire attitude toward evaluative criteria:

> English is sort of separate as a discipline because it seems to be divided among itself, but also because I don't think it takes seriously how other [panelists] actually evaluate work in their own field and how important these other criteria are . . . English departments are also probably much more sensitive and responsive to some of the sort of ideological demands that are made upon teachers and on scholars to reflect on how literature does answer to certain kinds of social goals or sort of political ideals. How much should identity politics really enter into the way we teach about literature? Is there a point where that becomes self-insulated or self-segregating? Or is it a mode of empowerment? There often is a kind of reluctance to just have a plain conversation about these issues because it is just so ideologically fraught.

In the context of panelists' evaluation of English proposals, these disciplinary characteristics can be disadvantageous:

> There are still fields that have prestige, no matter what the apparent value of the project is. I suspect [that is true of] history, art

history, and certain forms of maybe philosophy. But when it comes to literature, there is absolutely no [a priori prestige] . . . [T]he sense in which projects [in English literature] are dismissed or rejected or questioned tend[s] to be more confident than the way other projects are evaluated . . . [O]ne of the real question marks is: Are these literary projects really calling upon information the way history does, or [on] a body of knowledge or a background that we can really trust to be scholarly in any even sort of commonsensical sense of that word?

Other panelists are more optimistic concerning the evaluation of excellence, disciplinary consensus, and the fate of the field. Pointing to the evaluation of student papers, rather than evaluation of journal submissions or book manuscripts, another English professor explains that English scholars frequently agree. By supplying examples of areas where judgments of quality are routinely made, he adds considerable nuance to how the question of excellence is conceptualized in the field:

I mean, people don't have the same views or the same preferences or the same tendencies or allegiances, but they usually have the same views about what constitutes excellence. So you could, say, grade a student paper with someone who is totally ideologically opposed to you, and you would recognize marshalling of evidence, strength of argument, persuasiveness, an element of flair, originality of argument. You could recognize those whether you happen to like that kind of thing or not. I don't know if this is true in other fields, but there is something slightly schizophrenic here that English professors like to claim they can't do, but they do it every day when they're grading papers.

He believes that "the left wing of literary studies" reproduces the notion that there is no agreement.

I could imagine a situation where I might want to say, "I don't believe in academic excellence." . . . What people usually [respond to] is that there is an absolute ranking: "I know for certain that Shakespeare is better than Updike." And then I think the rest of us are going to say, "Well, I don't believe that" . . . English professors also hate the form of question, "Is so and so a great writer? Is so and so greater than so and so?" I'm more drawn to a kind of worker's ethic, where it's impossible for me to imagine a writer who wouldn't like to write better than they do. I can't imagine a writer thinking, "It's all okay." . . . You might just limit it to a willingness to say some things work and some things don't work. But I can't imagine a world of literature without that.

Among academics who hail from other disciplines, there seems to be a widespread perception that literary scholars are divided, or perhaps even confused, about issues of quality. For instance, a historian draws on his experience sitting on grant panels within his university to describe the situation in English this way:

When you have people from Hispanic languages or English departments, basically they say, "I like this one." You try to find out why, and it's an extremely idiosyncratic thing. They like it because "I like football, and it's about football." People are given a very wide range of acceptable criteria and the criteria for arguing about excellence are much looser. There's not even a lot of experience in granting in departments. They may have experience in judging doctoral dissertations, but in granting they tend to not know how to do it at all . . . There's a range of fields, some fields are in continuous epistemological crisis, others have too much certainty, and the middle range would be the more fruitful. That is, people who are willing to have doubts, but at the same time are not paralyzed, are not arbitrary in their judgment.

A philosopher perceives English as more acutely affected by generational differences than other disciplines: "It seems to me that the differences in criteria don't cut so clearly among disciplines, but also across generations. I mean, what [an older scholar] thinks is good scholarship is not what [this other person] thinks is good or interesting scholarship. So you have at least two generations in addition to disciplines."

At the other end of the spectrum of perception concerning the evaluative skills of literary scholars, one English professor differentiates his standards from those of other disciplines by noting that "people from other disciplines did not read as closely as I did." He goes on to say:

I am coming from English, and in English today anything goes and most of our theories in English are . . . influential in diverse areas. So most of the time I feel like I know where they're coming from and they kind of know where I'm coming from. The discipline of English is extremely fluid, probably the most fluid. [For me the best proposal] is something that is very well written and does a lot of close reading of text and brings out very suggestive implications, conceptual and theoretical. The problem with us in English is that it is extremely difficult to define great writing, but when you see it, you don't miss it.

Historians also believe that "you recognize [excellence] when you see it," but this field is characterized by much greater consensus than is the case for English literature.

History, the Consensual Discipline

Historians are more likely than scholars in other fields to characterize their discipline as presenting a relatively high degree of agreement about what constitutes quality and how to recognize it. The contrast they draw with English literature could not be starker. According to one historian, in his field, "the disciplinary center holds." He explains:

> History hasn't been politicized in the way some fields have, in a kind of roughly post-modern sort of approach to history. In the wider field you get a range, but the range is reasonably narrow. There are not so many people who would be writing in the language that would seem empty jargon, [that would be dismissed as a] bunch of junk by people who consider themselves empirical historians. You don't have such a dominant group of people who are very engaged in cultural theory, who would just simply dismiss arbitrarily work that is narrowly empirical. The middle is pretty big, pretty calm, not overtly politicized, and the ends I think are relatively small. The idea that evidence does matter, that giving attention to theory at the same time is a good thing: I think both of those do probably hold.

This peaceful state of affairs is not based on a notion that the field is (or can be) unified around a common theory. Rather, in the opinion of a particularly distinguished historian of early America, what is shared is agreement on what constitutes good historical craftsmanship, a sense of "careful archival work." A European historian concurs:

> We are neither English, nor political science . . . We see ourselves as an interpretive, empirically grounded social science. There are a lot of clusters of reasons [for why this is, having to do with] how people are trained, the sense of community that they have while they're being trained. I think that grounding in [the] empirical is something strong that makes historians sort of have more of an

idea of "what's new here?" Research is oriented toward getting results. Theory is useful, but not paramount. Those disciplines that tend to have less agreement are based more on rhetoric, on personalism, that is, "I worked with da, da, da, or this is my theory," and they have no tangible way to judge excellence. I don't think that many of the so-called humanities have that, whereas the social sciences tend to have much more of a stronger sense of what's good and what's not.[34]

In his book *Historiography in the Twentieth Century,* Georg Iggers argues that if over the past decades history has "not only survived, but thrived," it is in part because it "demands adherence to a logic of scholarly inquiry shared by scholars generally by which the results of historical inquiry can be tested for their validity very much as they are in other disciplines." For Iggers, this empirical focus has prevented the threat posed by post-modernism from "com[ing] to fruition" in history. In place of a legitimation crisis, there has been an "expanded pluralism," accompanied by an expansion in the scope of historical studies.[35] Like English, history has benefited from a considerable broadening of its object over the past thirty years, fed by the turn toward microhistoria, women's and gender history, the history of other subaltern groups more generally, "history from below," and expanded coverage of geographic areas.[36] History also has had solid undergraduate enrollments for several decades, and unlike English, has suffered comparatively little from an internal split between its teaching and research functions—that is, between teaching history and producing historical studies. It has also had a fairly healthy job market for PhDs. While the number of PhD recipients exceeded the number of job openings throughout most of the 1970s, there was an excess of jobs in 2004–2005 (and earlier, in the 1990s, as well).[37] The hiring situation varies greatly across areas, however, with Europeanists facing a more difficult time than scholars working in traditionally less favored geographical areas. Were the discipline smaller, it might be characterized by more conflict. In several of the competitions I studied, historians were perceived as receiving the lion's share of awards, in part because they apply in such large numbers and are always represented on panels. The disciplinary fault lines might be deeper were I comparing tensions within subfields, such as American history or Chinese history.

The field's degree of consensus has fluctuated over the twentieth century. Along with rising disciplinary autonomy and professionalism, such consensus increased as the postwar college boom spurred a fivefold increase in the number of history professors (between 1940 and 1970).[38] During the 1960s, the discipline became polarized politically, with each side claiming objectivity. Influenced by cultural anthropology and hermeneutics, many historians grew increasingly critical of the idea of objectivity, but the discipline as a whole was able to find another basis of consensus in the practice of historical scholarship. Although anti-theoretical proclivities remained, epistemological issues came to be seen as "too hot to handle."[39] As a historian of China explains, "With other historians on the panel, as you know, we do tend to agree, but not too much . . . History is very subjective." As in English, divisions occur largely around the use of theory. This same Chinese historian describes tensions within the discipline that reflect the difficulty of accommodating some of the more recent theory-driven trends with the longstanding American tradition of thinking of "history as science," grounded in objectivity.[40]

> I would see the polarity as being less between evidence and storytelling than between being evidence driven and being theory driven—that is, where you're engaged in an enterprise which is driven by certain kinds of cultural theory that is outside history and you turn to history with those questions. [For one group] the

eye of the interpreter is given much more power, comparable to an art or literary critic who looks at a painting or feels the power to say, "I can tell you what this means. I can read this text." This is opposed to a much more old-fashioned sort of history that says, "My sources say 'x,' and that's what they say and I think it's clear what they say." These people are totally unaware that they are, in fact, still interpreting. In between, there is both a consciousness of what we're doing and a sense that, nevertheless, there are sources that can speak.

Also pointing out the polarizing role of theory, a young historian of France sees the discipline as currently in "transition":

There's increasingly a kind of fragmentation in the historical field in terms of what is good history, what is bad history, what's the direction that we should be moving in . . . It's over precisely the question of the extent to which theory should be used in the writing of history and to what extent one has lost touch with social and economic reality with the growing [dominance] in the last ten years . . . of cultural history. At the moment we're kind of in a period of transition.

A medieval historian summarizes what she sees as the main bases for division within the field this way:

One divide would be those people who do theory versus those who kind of don't do theory, just do straight archival work. Then there are those people who do a social kind of history versus those who have been informed by what is called a cultural stand and they discuss the construction of everything. Then there are people who seize old scholarship that's political versus that which is not. So those are the three kinds of divides, but those divides also often intersect with each other . . . I think that [the] sides carry a kind of stereotype of each other. I definitely see myself as somebody who is negotiating, though. I think I'm a strong disciplinarian in that sense. I think history as a discipline has a lot to offer and what it offers is a kind of careful archival work. But at the same time, I'm not naive enough to believe that empiricism is not a theory, so I also want to be more theoretically informed in my archival work.

The decline of social history and the hegemony of cultural history after 1980 have been detailed by intellectual historians, notably in analyses of the emergence of "new cultural historians" (exemplified by the work of the French historians Robert Darnton and Natalie Zemon Davis); the growing influence of Clifford Geertz, Norbert Elias, Pierre Bourdieu, and others; and the effects of post-structuralism.[41] Postmodern theory has been particularly polarizing, but as a South Asian specialist argues, consensus is again gaining strength:

Maybe certain kinds of consensus are evolving. There was a pitched kind of life-and-death battle for a while between people who felt that the post-moderns had taken over everything and were operating in some kind of gangster fashion, to only promote themselves and keep everybody else out, and wanted everybody to wear black, and all that. People's sense of desperation about that [has] passed, and I think people [have] kind of calmed down a bit . . . The people who really did the thinking about post-modernism were very important and they're always present in everything that I read or write or think about. But as for the jargonizing and the credentializing, that's a bit passé.

A very senior scholar sees generational tensions as overlapping substantive points of contention:

[You have] very painful debates, which run on a kind of rough generational fault line . . . : An older generation who did political, economic, intellectual history. A younger generation who works on identity, construction of the memory, who often uses race, class, gender, those group identity questions, as analytical criteria, but many of whom don't. It's most painful in American history, where there's a really sharp fault line. In European [history], my generation has somewhat at least a partial sympathy for those questions that were formed in part by some canonical authors of the new younger generation, so it's not as sharp a break as in American. But there certainly is a lot of generational tension.

Nevertheless, this scholar perceives strong consensus, at least when it comes to the evaluation of graduate students:

When I grade graduate application folders with an American historian with whom I have nothing in common generationally or in training, our grades will hardly vary . . . In history, certainly, we have very good consensus. In history, I think in effect we do have certain shared values about commitment to doing certain kinds of work, [the] ability to write in an effective and interesting way . . . I think English has much less consensus than we have, due to much more serious generational splits—due in the end to the lack of the method, since there are many methods competing. In history, for all the debates, there's a lot of consensus about how it ought to be done.

The intradisciplinary cleavages that these scholars acknowledge do not prevent them or any other of the panelists from history I interviewed from being strongly committed to excellence as a general principle. Some express reservations—for example, one would replace the metaphor of "cream rising to the top" with "a metaphor of cross, check, discussion, advocacy, persuasion, settling on a consensus, balancing." Still, the affirmative response of a very distinguished American historian to my query about whether he "believes in" excellence is representative of the panelists' position overall:

> It's something that it's important to strive towards, recognizing and practicing academic excellence. If we don't have some ideas of what is excellent, it's reduced to a total relative situation where everything is worth as much as anything else, and I don't think that would be a very successful path, either for training or turning out good research . . . There's always going to be some disagreement about academic excellence, but we need to work toward shaping it as best we can and to finding it, even though one knows that it's based on our own symbolic instructions.

Similarly, an African-American woman historian says:

> I don't think it's an objective standard that exists . . . but I'm always struck by how much of a consensus there seems to be about what excellence is. I don't know that it's necessarily objective, or consistent even, but I think that there is a sense of the kinds of standards that we can at least begin to agree upon. [*Such as?*] Integrity of the research. Is research based in some kind of rigorous testing, in terms of the way in which it's collected, the ideas behind [it], the methodologies that are used to follow up the conceptualization of a project. Clarity of thought, having very clear ways of articulating what it all means. Having some way of interpreting for others why [it is] important, and what it means, and what relevance it has to a particular field of knowledge or to a larger body of knowledge. Explaining what contributions it's going to make, and making some important contributions along the lines of originality, along the lines of . . . building on . . . the work

of others in very significant ways, perhaps branching out, expanding other important work.

Anthropology's Fragile Boundaries

Anthropology has four branches—archeology, physical anthropology, linguistic anthropology, and social/cultural anthropology—each producing its own type of scholarship. Since the character of the funding competitions I studied made them compatible mainly with social/cultural anthropology, the great majority of proposals (and panelists) were from this branch. Thus the observations here refer to these fields only.

The past thirty years have been characterized by a growing interest in things cultural across the social sciences and the humanities. This is reflected by internal changes not only in the fields of English and history, as we saw, but also in departments such as visual studies and communication, and in sociology.[42] The influence of cultural anthropology grew considerably during this period, as the work of Clifford Geertz, Mary Douglas, Victor Turner, and others began to feed development in fields outside anthropology. Some anthropologists viewed this proliferation as a threat to the discipline's monopoly over the concept of culture. This concern became more acute as the traditional object of social/cultural anthropology—so-called primitive societies—disappeared and/or was reconceptualized (as postcolonial societies). Worries over disciplinary focus also rose as the field sought new vitality by broadening its reach to include advanced industrial societies and by embracing topics that previously had been the privileged object of other disciplines (for example, immigration, political economy, and science). At the same time, the number of PhDs conferred remained relatively stagnant.[43] Accordingly, even recent writings often stress the field's state of crisis,[44] pointing out that disciplinary consensus has been replaced by permanent disagreement concerning "just about everything." According to Geertz, "One of the advantages of anthropology as a scholarly enterprise is that no one, including its practitioners, quite knows exactly what it is . . . [The result] is a permanent identity crisis."[45] This atmosphere of crisis seems to have led cultural anthropologists to perceive their discipline's boundaries as fragile and in need of defense against the encroachment of scholars from other fields. One aspect of this disciplinary boundary work has involved separating high-quality research on culture from work judged less sophisticated.[46] This in turn may have contributed to a tendency to seem inward-looking and self-referential. An anthropologist sees the effects of his field's insular leanings in the proposals he evaluated:

> This actually did come up in some of the proposals from anthropology [that we discussed]: they'll often not cite a single thing written by a non-anthropologist, just to give one manifestation of it . . . [A]long with that, there tends to be a certain sanctimoniousness, at least in a certain influential segment of cultural anthropology, that other disciplines, whether sociology or economics, political science, are following naive, positivistic epistemology and that maybe anthropologists are better than that. This also tends to be linked to certain kinds of political commitments as well. You know, we're doing things for the people and these other folks are working for evil governments. So you have graduate students working on a topic where there is a substantial literature in neighboring disciplines, but they'll know nothing about it and sometimes their advisers will never tell them to read it. Why bother—it's not anthropology, therefore it's not worthwhile. I have a grad student, the typical case, who wanted to do a project on illegitimacy among African Americans in Chicago. I mentioned a certain amount of sociological demographic literature on this and he was, first of all, totally surprised to hear it, and sec-

But this is also true of the other fields!

ondly, absolutely shocked that nobody else ever encouraged him to go read any of that stuff or talk with any of the people who were working on it. You see quite a lot of [this] in anthropology, unfortunately.

In this context of intense disciplinary boundary work, anthropologists are most clearly preoccupied with epistemological issues concerning the nature of the relationship that develops between the researcher and her object, and with how this relationship influences the researcher's ability to make sense of the object in a non-reductionist manner. Questions of representations, and of how one relates to one's subject, became particularly central and divisive after the 1986 publication of James Clifford and George Marcus's *Writing Culture,* which pushed scholars to acknowledge the literary quality of their writings and the epistemological and moral difficulty of speaking for others. One panelist recalls that "Geertz himself has been very critical of this position. As he puts it, [just] because we can never get the operation room one hundred percent antiseptic, does not mean that we may as well operate in the sewers . . . It's very apt here . . . If all we can really talk about is our own experiences, then that's not very interesting. I'd rather read a good novelist." While concerns with reflexivity are not shared uniformly by the respondents, the topic continues to be the focus of considerable attention within the field.[47]

As we will see in Chapter 4, when epistemological preoccupations lead panelists to adopt discipline-specific criteria of assessment, successful interdisciplinary evaluation is jeopardized. An anthropologist's criticism of a proposal to study changing public opinion in the former Soviet Union provides an example. He considers the applicant, a non-anthropologist who planned to travel to a British university to use survey data collected by other social scientists, alarmingly short on contextual knowledge. This leads the panelist to mobilize a set of evaluative criteria common in anthropology that may not be applicable to other disciplines:

> [These non-anthropologists] didn't speak or read a single language other than English, as far as I know never have been [to Eastern Europe], or if they have been, they probably stayed in some luxury hotel for a couple of days. They could just as easily have proposed to study Guatemala . . . That does get at this issue which tends to divide anthropologists from at least some of this stuff. Finding somewhere an anthropologist reviewing a proposal like this which he will like is never going to be easy . . . I think [the proposal is] more misleading than anything else; I wouldn't want to use funds to support it.

This panelist's comments suggest how readily preferences and evaluative criteria specific to one discipline can be seen as baseline standards for other fields. An anthropologist's summary of the situation also conveys how disciplinary boundary work contributes to the construction of the field's identity:

> There's certainly a number of anthropologists, including some very influential ones, [who] look askance at people who work with numbers, and tend to be dismissive . . . My own position on science would be seen as hopeless positivism in some parts of anthropology. For any kind of economist or 99 percent of demographers, I'd be seen as some terrible post-modernist . . . What I thought was most off-putting and most divisive was, at least some members [said that] . . . what they were doing was somehow politically enlightened and what other people were doing was serving the interests of colonialism, imperialism, racism, and everything else, and [they were] linking that to . . . epistemological issues as well as . . . even [linking] the utmost quantitative inter-

disciplinary work to the bad guys . . . What bothers me most is a certain kind of political sanctimoniousness, more even than a kind of anti-scientism.

Anthropology's efforts to protect its boundaries also are manifested in how panelists distinguish the object of anthropology from that of cultural studies. One anthropologist explains: "I heard several times anthropology being described as a discipline with really fuzzy methods, which is a very old misunderstanding of what anthropological methods are, but which I think adequately describes a cultural studies anthropology, which is kind of like journalism." This panelist deplores the blurring of the boundary between anthropology and cultural studies, and he is critical of Clifford and Marcus's argument, "which seems to me has led to a backing away from any belief that it's possible, through immersion or intensive study of a particular context, to get inside of another cultural form. Once you give that up, there's no reason to do intensive, long-term research." These views, which prompted "disagreements" with other panel members, reflect this anthropologist's understanding of his field's most essential boundaries. He says:

> Ultimately, I am kind of a traditionalist in that I believe that anthropology as a discipline has really only one feature that distinguishes it from what, say, journalists do or what anyone might do, and that is sort of the critical value of face-to-face field work or gaining people's trust; of getting at the social world through actual personal interaction. So whenever I see an anthropological project that involves more than two locales, or three maybe, it seems to me impossible that that person will be able to do that.

Several panelists involved in cultural studies rejected this "traditionalist" position as being at odds with the discipline's recent embrace of multi-sited research.[48] A sociologist portrays this anthropologist—who during deliberations had described work at multiple sites as "lite anthropology" and criticized "people who don't have twelve months to sit in one village or in one family"—as a person who "seemed to be a gatekeeper in this kind of very reactionary way, like he wanted to return anthropology to pre-1985. Not that I'm so into people just doing auto-ethnography . . . but I think that anthropology can go forward." These remarks allude to an ongoing debate over a larger and more fundamental issue for anthropology, that is, whether the technique of combining methods ("triangulating") is as desirable a methodological approach as traditional field work. This is a heavily loaded question, because extended ethnographic fieldwork is one of the most central ways in which anthropology distinguishes itself from qualitative sociology.

Debates within anthropology—over methodological issues or around questions of reflexivity—are pervasive and include the four departments that historically have been most centrally involved in graduate training (those at Columbia University, the University of Chicago, the University of California at Berkeley, and the University of Michigan), as well as other departments that some now see as being on the rise (those at Princeton and New York University in particular). Since these debates influence how anthropologists and anthropologists-in-training handle theory and frame their work, they also affect research proposals, and how academics from other disciplines react to those proposals. One historian notes:

A lot of Columbia anthropology, and we tend to get a lot [of proposals from them], it has a lot of jargon in it . . . In a lot of cases, the historical methodology side is pretty weak. I don't want to sort of be in a position of always giving low grades to Columbia anthropology, so I have given this [one] actually a higher grade than I would've [otherwise]. But in the course of the debate, other people said that the [proposal] didn't actually live up to what the person said he/she was going to do.

Anthropologists' relationship to theory may make their proposals particularly challenging for panelists. For instance, a political scientist comments:

I ended up getting a lot of the proposals in anthropology, but a lot of them I thought were pretty bad when it comes to sort of using clear language and being jargon laden. I mean I had to work harder . . . to try and figure out what the significance was. And sometimes, I must say, it worked to their advantage. I remember one proposal, it was on the measurement of waste, on refuse, okay? I think if you look at my score, I gave it a two. I remember reading this proposal and going, this is either a, no pun intended, but a bunch of shit, or it's just a waste, no pun intended again, or it's really brilliant. And it seemed to be very self-referential in terms of the language that he was using to craft the proposal. But I thought this may be one of these ones where I just don't get it. I'm worried I'm going to be overly prejudicial, so I'm going to give it a two . . . The other anthropologist gave it a five, and they looked at me and they went, "What did you see in this?" And I went, "I don't know!" I wanted to bend over backwards [to avoid prejudice]. They said, "Well, don't do that again."

This respondent's remarks point to the important methodological differences that exist between his field and anthropology. An anthropologist, acknowledging that he felt distant from the political scientists on his panel, confirms those differences: "In many ways, yes, it was one of the major divides in the room among panel members. It was the political scientists who had the nasty things to say about anthropological methods."

In anthropology, contested notions of excellence reflect the influence of post-structuralism, which emerges particularly in debates over whether excellence resides in the object being evaluated or is located in the eye of the beholder. A cultural anthropologist who teaches at a top university articulates the field's multilayered conception of excellence:

> There [are] places where everybody's in agreement, where this is excellence that's recognizable no matter what your field is. And then there are cases where excellence is something that's negotiated within the group of evaluators, who are subjective. But then there's something else, too, which is what you might want to think of as inter-subjectivity between the individual reviewer and the writer, so it's more of an author-reader relationship in that kind of collaborative recognition . . . I don't want to say that there are objective standards of quality, but there are certainly conventions of excellence that a good proposal pretty much, no matter what the field, can engage with.

Asked if she believes in academic excellence, she answers, "I suppose I'd have to say that philosophically and intellectually, probably not, but in some sort of visceral way, probably so . . . I was just reading political philosophy of post-structuralist sorts, and so I know that you can't really, that excellence is constructed. And yet, you know, constructed or not, it's still, it's the discipline that we're all kind of disciplined in. So it operates as if it were something real." Yet for other anthropologists, the consensus that emerges from the independent ranking that panelists produce prior to the group meeting confirms that quality is intrinsic to the proposal. As one interviewee says:

> A matrix was prepared which rated [proposals] by total score [i.e., the sum of the scores given by each panelist]. It was notable that

there was . . . considerable consistency, homogeneity of the scores. So in [the] meeting, in terms of the cream rising to the top, there was a general sense in which, you know, here are these that [have] practically perfect scores, so we don't really need to do much discussion of these.

As we will see, the more relativistic approach—the concept of excellence as constructed—is not central in political science or in economics. In these disciplines, very different evaluative cultures prevail.

Political Science: Divisive Rational Choice

If political science is in better health than anthropology from a demographic standpoint (see Figure 3.1), like anthropology, it has become divided over the past thirty years, largely as a consequence of the ascent of rational choice theory and the concomitant hegemony of formal theory and methodology.[49] In somewhat simplified terms, the rational choice paradigm posits utility maximization as the sole and universal motivation for human action and claims that all social structures and processes can be explained by aggregating individual choices. It is particularly concerned with group decision making and the handling of institutional constraints. Disciplinary commentators have discussed at length the divisive effects of the rise of the rational choice model, noting, for example, how it has amplified other divisions, such as that between researchers who use quantitative versus qualitative methods.[50] An important counterhegemonic response, dubbed the "Perestroika Movement," emerged publicly within the American Political Science Association (APSA) in 2001.[51] This pressure group (whose email list in 2003 included roughly 5 percent of the APSA membership) primarily sought three changes: a balance between quantitative and qualitative research in the *American Political Science Review*, the discipline's most prestigious journal; a more democratic process for selecting the APSA executive board (APSA leaders are not chosen through competitive elections); and more methodological pluralism, including greater disciplinary support for qualitative work, problem-driven (as opposed to method-driven) approaches, and area expertise in contrast to the production of generalizable theories.[52]

Ian Shapiro, Rogers Smith, and Tarek Masoud's analysis of the field identifies similar points of tension within political science: they single out the problem- versus method-driven research divide, the debate around rational choice, and methodological pluralism.[53] One panelist explains how the low degree of consensus affects the work of panels: "The lack of consensus relates to what questions are important. Some people will just look at the method and ask if it's been well done, and others of us will, I think, look at the *importance* of the questions and *then* the method and say [whether] this has been well done" (my emphasis). This panelist, who is a political scientist, notes that math and formalization have come to define "good methods": "If someone has a really good question—Adam Przeworski is an example of this—. . . and is using different methods and formalizing, it's fine with me if they're formalizing something that's important. But I think a lot of people don't react that way." Disparagingly, she concludes, "I think academics are a surly bunch. I think we're paid to argue. By surly I mean, you know, people are always yapping away about . . . questions of method, gossiping about who's good and who's bad."

The divisions within political science have worked to the advantage of proponents of rational choice theory. Many contemporary political scientists point to the epistemological homogeneity of economics as a model of "progress." By appealing to the argument that such intellectual consensus signals disciplinary evolution and status, backers of rational choice theory have been able to extend their paradigm's sway over the field.[54] Indeed, an economist, happily noting an increasing resemblance between his field and political science, asserts, "That's the field where the cancer of economics has spread most. So our field is kind of penetrating that field and perceptions in that field are to some extent shaped a little like economics in ways that [are] not true for literature, anthropology, sociology." Of the political scientists on his panel, he says, "I could see the cogs going around in their heads in ways that were similar to mine a lot of the time." During interviews, political scientists explicitly mentioned the influence of rational choice on their field and on the evaluations. In the respondents' view, the hegemony of the rational choice approach has translated into a redefinition of standards of excellence for everyone in political science, thus influencing how scholars define their goals and intellectual trajectory. For example, while one panelist states that now "it all comes down to how quantitatively sophisticated you are," a top comparativist explains that he would like to produce more quantitatively sophisticated work, and in particular, simulation, because this is where the action is now in his field. "I think that there are possibilities for tremendous creative breakthroughs. It's just a hunch that I have." Even political scientists who have not been fully converted by this revolution may still use its tools sporadically; and some take an eclectic approach, using rational choice models along with other paradigms and their accompanying methodologies. Others note that those who reject the rational choice paradigm are disadvantaged when applying for funds from some organizations. Many within the field believe that certain funding sources, such as the political science program at the National Science Foundation, are particularly welcoming toward rational choice proposals, while others, such as the SSRC's International Dissertation Field Research Competition that I studied, are more open to qualitative research. In short, different funders are perceived as using different standards and emphases for awarding grants.

The emphasis on rational choice theory in political science also raises problems for academics outside of political science. Among evaluators I interviewed, this was particularly the case for anthropologists. One offers this summary of a widely shared perspective: "Anthropologists think that [rational choice] is a totally misbegotten theory of human behavior, you know, actions are not produced by any kind of simple rational calculation. And even if they were, the variables involved, namely defining what the goals are in the model, [are] entirely beyond the model itself. So for all these reasons, I tend to take a very dim view of it."

Clearly, the ascent of the rational choice paradigm is important in its own right, but it is also tied to much broader questions within the discipline concerning the meaning of science. In their influential book *Designing Social Inquiry*, published in 1994, Gary King, Robert Keohane, and Sidney Verba invited qualitative researchers to produce the same kind of descriptive or causal inferences (or predictions about the nonobservable) as can be produced by quantitative research.[55] The book generated a strong response among qualitative researchers concerned with demonstrating their commitment to science through their methodological rigor.[56] *Designing Social Inquiry* has played an emblematic role for political science comparable to that which Clifford and Marcus's *Writing Culture* played for anthropology. As one political economist puts it: "People get kind of obsessed with writing in registers or genres that look more like science, even though these guys are really interpretivists. There's a lot of concern with things like case selection . . . to demonstrate that, in fact, qualitative research methods are really as rigorous as quantitative ones."[57] This panelist believes that the main debate in his field concerns whether a "person [is] contributing to a generalizable theory of politics, or nomothetic laws of politics, or universal theory, to the extent that someone is arguing this person has to be supported because he or she is making a theoretical contribution." Yet others believe that the conflict around rational choice theory is receding, or that it has been exaggerated.

Despite the divisiveness that characterizes the discipline, most political scientists I interviewed say they believe in scientific progress ("We stand on each other's shoulders. It is a collective enterprise"). They also tend to agree that quality resides in the proposals themselves, as opposed to resulting from the interpretation of the judges. One political scientist defines excellence in terms of successfully meeting disciplinary standards. He states: "I believe that there are scientific norms that are relatively well understood, that are pretty explicit. My view on this would be Lakatosian . . . There are certain norms that one can battle about. The battles are within, I think, pretty narrow parameters." This scholar believes that relativism applies to some kinds of knowledge and not others. For him, there are poles of relativism and certainty, and interpretations of the world are important when it comes to ethical matters. But, "I don't think it works well if we're looking, say, at thermodynamics or mathematics . . . the mathematics we have is not relative, you know, there are proofs there." Another political scientist dismisses as "silly" the view that claims to truth are just competing narratives. Of those who adopt such views, he says, "I think they believe in academic excellence, but defined differently. It's more defined in terms of intellectual virtuosity and the capacity to find hidden meanings in arguments rather than original contributions to knowledge. I think they have some very clear ideas of academic excellence, they're just different." When asked if she believes in academic excellence, another political scientist—a Europeanist teaching at a large Midwestern university—responds, "I mean, it's not like God or something, but I know when I'm reading something excellent and when I'm not. I don't know that there's consensus about it. I mean either someone has convinced me of something or they haven't. Either they have the evidence or they don't. If they have the evidence, then it's nicely done."

Economics: Unified by Mathematical Formalism

Economics is rivaled only by history in its level of disciplinary consensus. Unlike history, however, where the basis for unity is a shared sense of craftsmanship in research, economists' cohesion is grounded in a cognitive unification that was largely achieved by the 1960s, as mathematical economics triumphed over other approaches (institutionalist, Marxian, and anti-mathematical institutionalist, for instance).[58] This ascendance of mathematical economics has translated into a homogenization of the core courses in every major institution, which has further solidified its position. Of course, there is substantial diversity across fields. According to Harvard economist Elhanan Helpman, "The empirical methodology dominating labor economics is quite different from the empirical methodology dominant in industrial organization. Behavioral economics plays a much bigger role in finance than in international trade, and the degree of rigor varies across fields. These types of division are accepted, although with a grudge by some scholars."[59]

Disciplinary agreement is echoed at the international level, where the use of mathematical formalism has promoted an intellectual consolidation of the field around economics as practiced in the United States.[60] It is notable that the high degree of professional consensus among economists has been accompanied by a robust production of PhDs. Although there was a slight decline from 1975 to 1985, the number of PhDs conferred in economics has grown steadily and consistently over the past twenty years—to over one thousand such degrees in 2005. Relative to the number of doctorates awarded in all disciplines, degrees conferred in economics appear to have remained fairly constant. English, history, and political science, by contrast, all have seen their proportional representation decline by a percentage point or more over the past thirty or so years, largely due to the increased number of science and engineering PhDs.[61]

Perhaps owing to their discipline's epistemological cohesiveness, economists seem much less concerned with (or even aware of) the constructed nature of excellence. Panelists perceive economists as agreeing more readily on the quality of proposals than is typical of academics from the humanities and the more humanistic social sciences. They describe economists as behaving as if it were possible to draw a clear line between proposals. As a historian puts it, they all agree that "this is an A, this is an A−." Another, describing history as "subjective," differentiates it from economics, where "It's up or down." An economist endorses these views, observing, "I think in economics we're fortunate to have a fairly unified view of what is or is not good research." A program officer traces this approach to evaluation to the more homogeneous culture of the discipline: "I just find that the training is sort of set up by being a purely internalist discourse within the discipline. There's such a strong sort of epistemological hegemony within the discipline."

Economists' standards of evaluation, too, strike panelists as differing from those used in other disciplines. Historians acknowledge competing standards and often ask, as the feminist historian Joan Scott has, "whose standards determine the standards of the discipline."[62] Economists, in contrast, are seen as considering evaluation to be a fairly straightforward matter of separating winners from losers. Compared to most other panel members, they seem much less concerned with traditional markers of scholarship—contextual knowledge, linguistic competence, and so on. On one panel, for instance, the economist did not understand why an applicant who planned to study three countries, including Greece, would not be funded because she lacked familiarity with the Greek language. He viewed this objection as a red herring. For their part, noneconomists are often very critical of the assumptions that applicants from economics make in their proposals. An anthropologist comments, "They [applicants from economics] were viewed as living in their own world, defined by a theoretical worldview and both being unwilling to explain it and not interested in thinking about anything different." Similarly, a sociologist notes an economist's critical attitudes toward more interpretive proposals: "He was coming out of a sort of pretty positivist organization that most of the rest of the committee didn't care for. So he tended to be kind of critical of all the history proposals. But the rest of the folks, I thought, were quite open and were willing to change their minds."

In keeping with their discipline's positivist tradition, the economists I interviewed seem to believe that excellence resides in the objects being evaluated—in the proposal and the project themselves—as opposed to resulting from the negotiated interdisciplinary agreement reached by panelists. The sense economists have of a clear line that separates the best from the rest is associated, as well, with a more objectivist view of the value of knowledge. At the close of an interview, one economist reaffirms his belief in academic excellence by saying, "I certainly believe there are ideas that are valuable and discovering them is a mark of excellence in all kinds of ways . . . I certainly think there's something out there to look for, and people who are finding it. I guess that's the definition of excellence. I think we recognize now certain major ideas developed in the past that really changed our view of the world."

Conclusion

American higher education brings together disciplines that are remarkably different in their evaluative cultures, intellectual traditions, and professional languages. Disciplinary norms are stronger in some fields than in others, because American academia is also multidimensional, traversed by networks and literatures that are not always bounded by disciplines. The current state of American political science is a case in point. And although hiring and promotion decisions are made within disciplinary cultures, such is not the case for funding decisions made by multidisciplinary panels, which have to create shared evaluations across epistemological and other divides. This context primes academics to make explicit their shared, taken-for-granted perspectives as well as their differences—which may range, at the most general level, from the split between humanists and social scientists regarding the proper place of subjectivity in the production of knowledge, to divisions over theory, method, and standards of evaluation within and across individual disciplines. Panelists' understandings of the challenges facing their disciplines and their expectations regarding what is valued in other fields affect the type of arguments they make for or against proposals. That expectations for ethnographic research are higher for anthropologists than for political scientists illustrates this point.

It seems from my study that those panelists most able to form a consensus about definitions of excellence come from the fields of history and economics. In history, broad consensus is based on a shared definition of good craftsmanship in the practice of empirical research; in economics, consensus results from cognitive consolidation around mathematical tools. While economists are described as believing that they can clearly distinguish among high-quality proposals, and appear to downplay the role of intersubjectivity in the identification of excellence (perhaps because of the role of formalization), historians acknowledge the existence of gray areas and the importance of negotiation and debate in determining excellence. Having been influenced by post-structuralism, historians, like their colleagues in English literature, are more likely than economists to ask "whose criteria get universalized as disciplinary criteria." As is also true of English, history is cleaved around the role of theory and politics as criteria of evaluation. In contrast, economics is viewed as being influenced very little by politics. Thus although both disciplines are fairly consensual, history is more divided internally than economics. This can be explained in part by the fact that history is more defined by national spatial borders than is economics, which is more cognitively unified globally. Moreover, economists may be more self-satisfied with their consensual state than are historians—a clear indicator of disciplinary maturity according to some.[63] The alternative view, perhaps more in line with that of historians, would be to define the ability to tolerate ideological and methodological pluralism as a signal that the field has matured.

Of the six fields considered, English faces the most acute disciplinary crisis, both demographically and intellectually. Several panelists hailing from this discipline question the very concept of academic excellence. Panelists note the low consensus on what defines excellence (notably on what defines originality and significance), as well as the prevalence of disciplinary skepticism and relativism. There is a proliferation of criteria for assessing excellence, including through theories and authors that help bridge substantive topics. Panelists express concern over deprofessionalization and the decline of real disciplinary expertise at a time when close reading is losing its disciplinary centrality, when cultural studies is becoming more prominent, and when English scholars are increasingly borrowing their topics and methods from historians and culture experts. In this context, excellence is often viewed as residing in the eye of the beholder (or in interpretive communities, such as those described by Stanley Fish), rather than being an intrinsic property of the object being evaluated.[64] The increasingly interdisciplinary nature of English itself certainly may prepare literary scholars to accept the methods used in proposals emanating from a subset of cognate fields. The same holds for history.

Threatened by the popularity of cultural analysis in other fields, anthropology is becoming more inward-looking and engaged in disciplinary boundary work in an effort to distinguish what is worthy cultural analysis from what is not making the cut. In this context, epistemological positions, politics, and method are particularly important. As in English and history, theory can play a divisive role in limiting disciplinary consensus. Moreover, like English, anthropology is a self-reflexive discipline where there is a greater awareness of the constructed character of excellence.

Political science aspires to the level of consensus found in economics, but the new hegemony of rational choice theory has divided the discipline against itself, as have internal conflicts regarding the privileging of quantitative over qualitative research. In contrast, philosophy is unambiguously inward-looking. Many philosophers believe that only they are qualified to evaluate research emanating from their field, in part because significance and originality have to be measured using distinct, traditional discipline-specific matrices. The discipline is perceived by other panelists as too autonomous and increasingly insignificant and obsolete, in part because of its seemingly elitist stance. Thus some program officers and a number of panelists define philosophy as a problem discipline.

Given this diversity in disciplinary evaluative cultures and the associated potential for conflict, how do panelists succeed in reaching consensus and making awards? As we learned in Chapter 2, the technology of peer review panels brings scholars into the same room and creates a context that constrains and channels differences. The rules and exigencies of reviewing, and the constraints of making funding decisions within a delimited time frame, push panelists to reach agreement. So too does the promotion of a culture of pluralism by program officers. Although academics are contrarians, this culture helps counterbalance disciplinary differences by fostering a shared commitment to academic excellence. As I will show in Chapter 4, members of multidisciplinary peer review panels abide by a set of customary rules. Chief among these is the rule of cognitive contextualization, which requires that panelists use the criteria of evaluation most appropriate to the field or discipline of the proposal under review. In other words, they recognize that different standards should be applied to different disciplines. Panelists learn as well the importance of a willingness to listen and to defer to one another's expertise. As a geographer points out, despite the difficulties, the act of evaluating interdisciplinary work can bring its own pleasure and unique rewards:

> Even though it's a lot of work to read all these proposals, what was wonderful was to hear experts in fields acknowledge people for their scholarship . . . it was wonderful to hear the perspective from a person in the field on that topic and on that proposal. It was a process for me, it was like sitting in a lecture in a field that's not your own . . . [seeing] the imagination and the scope of that field revealed through a practitioner.

How evaluators move from a hypothesized (Bourdieuian) world where, to paraphrase Hobbes, academic men are wolves to each other, to one where deliberations are described by participants in a language of pleasure, consideration, and deference is the topic we turn to next. As we will see, the black box of grant peer review is characterized by colleagueship, but it is also a multidimensional space in which muscles are flexed and where networks compete in the forging of shared definitions of excellence.

4/Pragmatic Fairness: Customary Rules of Deliberation

It's just very pragmatic. You put twelve pretty smart people in a windowless room in [some city] for two days and you expect them to remain sane. They're pretty professional people, so they do their best. They have very different tastes so there's a lot of potential for conflict. They stay cool-headed and they have to make these heroic efforts to agree across big disciplinary differences on what constitutes a good proposal . . . We spend so much time on it and . . . there's so many people focusing at once on this proposal . . . This year particularly, there was a lot of movement: You had a lot of situations where something was ranked relatively high [prior to the meeting and] weaknesses were discussed and people in favor were convinced [not to fund]. And conversely, something [ranked] quite low, [but] the more you talked about it, the more it looked like you should give it a chance, that it had some promise . . . It would be sort of self-congratulatory to say that cream rises to the top and that we picked exactly the right set. I don't think that happened. But I think we chose on average the better proposals.

Economist

Academic excellence? I know it when I see it . . . If I didn't, I couldn't honestly do all of the selecting and advising I do. I would even go farther and say I'm extremely confident in my own judgment and contradiction does not affect me very much . . . Everything is relative in some ways, but I do believe there are real qualities, which I'm identifying, which are pretty related . . . What rises to the top is cream, but I am not convinced that all the cream makes it. I do worry about, for example, what happens to people who for one reason or another don't make it to the very best possible graduate program . . . My sense is that in every case you get a high degree of agreement . . . people will suppress a very strong outlying opinion, or perhaps briefly and mildly express it, in order to make the process work.

Historian

Almost without exception, the panelists I talked with consider their deliberations fair and their panel able to identify the top proposals.[1] Like the economist quoted earlier, the evaluators do not believe that their panel did a perfect job, but they do maintain that they identified the best proposals "on average." They agree that meritocracy guides the process of selection and that unfettered market mechanisms generally determine the outcome of the competition. Some qualify their views by referring to the "role of chance and passion" in the process, and some acknowledge that "mistakes are made." Overall, however, they are confident that panels succeed in identifying high-quality proposals, and that peer review "works" as a mechanism for quality control. As one art historian put it, "I think on the whole we do a pretty good job of identifying, not individually but collectively, . . . quality research that could be considered 'the cream.'" This belief resonates with their broader investment in a "culture of academic excellence" that precludes panelists from framing the outcome of the deliberations as an expression of cronyism. In fact, a tradition of not indulging in expressions of self-interest is one of the reasons that panelists say they enjoy serving on panels ("officiating as priest" as one of them puts it). "I'm really impressed," a historian says, referring to his experience on a panel, "when people can step outside of their own interests and out of their own interest groups and look at something from another perspective." A somewhat frequent outcome of group deliberation is a feeling of satisfaction that the group has shared an appreciation of good work and has come to a consensus regarding the evaluations.

Indeed, such heartfelt and personal aspects of academic life feature prominently in panelists' talk about their experience as evaluators. They enjoy deeply both seeing a brilliant mind at work and reading a perfectly crafted proposal. As suggested in Chapter 2, their commitment to the distinctive pleasures and virtues of academic life cannot be overestimated as a factor that shapes how they think about their responsibilities as panel members. The point here is that although panelists' beliefs in academic excellence and in the fairness of the funding process do not come "naturally," neither do they appear to be expressions of false consciousness or ritualized covers for self-interest.[2] Like all social actors, these academics rely on various, and sometimes inconsistent or contradictory, frames to give meaning to their actions.

In this chapter, I explore the social conditions that lead panelists to understand their choices as fair and legitimate. This is quite different from determining whether the process of peer review itself is fair. There is already a large literature on that question.[3] Typically, such studies have focused on those values and norms of the scientific institution that support fairness in evaluation by ensuring that no one is excluded from scientific debates due to purely subjective social factors.[4] In contrast, my concern is with the frameworks or meaning systems—the rules of the game—that panelists use to understand their actions and the environment in which they are operating.[5] Although the scholars I interviewed are almost unanimous in their belief that "the process works," they are not always sure how it works. A panel chair, for instance, stressing that "the consensus candidates were [agreed on] at a high level," concludes, "I think the process works very well," but then adds, "It's just hard to articulate what it is." This chapter aims to clarify the complicated dynamics of group evaluation.

Producing Legitimacy and Belief through Customary Rules

Max Weber and Emile Durkheim, two of the founding fathers of the field of sociology, each wrote about the production of belief. Weber identified various forms of legitimacy and suggested that the production of rational-legal legitimacy requires belief in the use of impersonal, abstract, and consistent rules.[6] This in turn requires the bracketing of individual interest. Durkheim, in his writings about the production of religious feelings and the mechanisms by which people come to invest in the sacred, maintained that the sacred is defined by its separation from the sphere of the profane through the use of rituals—rule-bound processes.[7] Weber's and Durkheim's insights are directly relevant to the actions of panel members. Funding organizations provide evaluators with formal rules. These institutional mandates constrain the kinds of arguments that panelists make by affecting the likelihood that specific criteria—whether a proposal is excessively or insufficiently humanistic, comparative, policy-oriented, and so on—will be invoked against or in favor of a proposal. Evaluators do sometimes refer to specific guidelines to bolster their arguments, or to resolve disagreements. But, as noted in Chapter 2, program officers give panelists full sovereignty and rarely enforce the mandates. A sociologist recalls that a proposal that did not have the focus specified by the competition, but which everyone judged to be excellent, was funded. Another sociologist, downplaying the influence of the formal guidelines, comments, "I doubt that most people read them all that carefully."

As I explain in more detail later in this chapter, the rules that panelists do pay careful attention to, the ones that lead them to assign great legitimacy to the outcome of their deliberations, are informal. I describe these rules as "customary" because they are not formally spelled out and are instead created and learned by panelists during their immersion in collective work.[8] Some of these rules are meant to standardize procedures, and they promote the bracketing of personal interest (for example, norms for abstaining from decisions involving one's students). Others, such as deferring to expertise, operate as ritual and are used to separate the "sacred" (excellence) from the "impure" (self-interest, idiosyncratic preferences, narrowness, disciplinary parochialism, and so on). As one panelist explains, replying to a question about how he thought about his experience, "I think it has to do with almost sacred value, with value that transcends institutions, individuals, networks, and things like that. What you're trying to achieve is something that goes beyond individual interest and perspective."

In a general sense, all the informal rules that guide deliberations are deeply familiar to panelists. In the process of doing their jobs as academics, panel members become accustomed to making judgments; they evaluate students' and colleagues' performance, manuscripts for publication, and tenure cases. What distinguishes the assessments that academics perform on grant and fellowship panels from those that occur in departmental evaluations is context. As we saw in Chapter 2, panelists are not engaged in a sustained relationship with one another; nor do they have to share the lives of awardees, as they do with newly hired colleagues or graduate students who have been admitted to their department. As a consequence of the limited personal stake in the outcome and of the lack of time, they are not likely to mobilize their networks to gather information on the personal qualities of the candidate, as they might do (in some instances) when serving on recruitment committees.[9] At the same time, since universalism is essential to the legitimacy of the process, panelists are expected to work hard to keep their personal connections and idiosyncratic preferences from affecting their funding decisions. But these rules are not always abided by and they remain ideals shaping the understanding of how panelists believe a successful panel should conduct itself. There are obvious tensions between, for instance, the ideal of methodological pluralism and the commitment that panelists have to their own disciplinary evaluative culture.

This chapter looks closely at how panelists struggle to identify and agree on criteria for academic excellence. The analysis reveals that making judgments about excellence is a deeply interactional and emotional undertaking, rather than a strictly cognitive one.

What Makes a Good Panelist

The legitimacy of panels rests mainly on impersonal rules (what Weber described as "rational-legal" grounds), but elements associated with traditional authority, where obedience is due to the person who occupies the position of authority, are present as well.[10] The authority of panelists is determined by their formal technical training (as PhD holders) and by their reputation, and is thus attached directly to their person. This means that although in principle all panelists have the same degree of legitimacy, their individual credibility and relative authority within panels are determined in important ways by their behavior. With this in mind, I asked panelists, program officers, and panel chairs to describe what in their view makes a panelist "good" or "bad." I also questioned them concerning the person who impressed them most and least on their respective panels, and how they perceived themselves to be similar to or different from other panelists.[11]

The interviewees often expressed enthusiasm when describing "good" colleagues, confirming that sheer pleasure and intellectual enjoyment motivate academics to add to their already considerable workload by serving on funding panels. The wonderment of discovering new domains of knowledge by interacting with smart colleagues is often palpable as respondents discuss their experiences on panels. At the same time, their answers frequently emphasize their colleagues' interpersonal skills and fundamental character traits. Program officers, in particular, uniformly stress the importance of "collegiality" when describing what they look for in a panelist and acknowledge that they take special care to select personable or like-minded participants. As the following list of traits or behaviors needed to qualify as a "good panelist" suggests, the quality of a panelist is defined not only in cognitive terms, but also in terms of "presentation of self," as well as moral and emotional characteristics.[12]

Show up fully prepared and ready to discuss the proposals. Demonstrating a strong sense of responsibility and work ethic is clearly key to being a good panelist. A political scientist describes the best evaluator on his panel as a historian "who always had very thoughtful commentary on the proposals. He had clearly engaged the proposals themselves; he did not get swept away by fluff or anything." A sociologist explicitly states that she assigns the most weight to the opinions of co-panelists who are the best prepared and best informed. Preparedness and command of details enhance credibility because they improve a panelist's ability to think on his feet when trying to convince other evaluators.

Demonstrate intellectual breadth and expertise. A good panelist demonstrates a command of large literatures within her field, has passive knowledge of several areas beyond her field, and is able to assess quickly the strengths and weaknesses of proposals in all these areas. One panelist recalls two notable colleagues: "I remember being really impressed by the amount that she [an architectural historian] knew.

When she was an expert about something, she was completely convincing about it. I remember being perhaps even more impressed with the American historian's range of knowledge . . . [He] kept talking about varying courses that he taught in which he had become expert on x, y, and z, and it seemed an enormously broad range. He's one of these people who read very widely and retained everything that he read and I was tremendously delighted by that; he was very helpful."

Be succinct. Panelists' work is conducted at a fast pace, because they generally have to accomplish a great deal in a very limited amount of time. It is crucial that members not waste everyone's time by talking too much or too slowly, making unnecessary remarks, or providing too much detailed information. A humanist remembers being put off by a panel member who "would kind of go off on tangents that were irrelevant and tell sort of anecdotes, and we had an agenda [a pile of proposals to go through]." A historian picks as the worst panelist an anthropologist who "talked way too much about proposals that he hadn't read, [and] had to make his views known about everything." A political scientist offers a similar indictment of this same panelist: "This guy was just so full of himself. For me, I sort of lost my tolerance when at the end [the chair] keeps saying 'let's move along,' and he keeps on name dropping on these proposals." Panelists who are not succinct lose credibility; "being smart" also means knowing how to use one's time effectively in a group.

Speak across disciplinary boundaries. Being able to articulate one's point of view to others outside one's field is essential. An English professor equates this with "smarts." She feels that her co-panelists all exhibited this trait. "Each of the people in the panel made remarks at different points that taught me something that was new and that was not just a person's opinion about a proposal. I felt like I was in a classroom learning something important about history or about music or whatever it might be." Of course, being accessible to nonexperts is a more valued asset for those serving on multidisciplinary, as opposed to unidisciplinary, panels.

Respect other people's expertise and sentiments. An appreciation of others' views translates into a willingness to listen and to be convinced by another person's assessment. A historian's explanation for why he felt closest to two women co-panelists sums up the importance of respect among panel members:

> I liked the way they interacted with other people on the panel, always respectful. Their interpersonal skills, I felt comfortable with them . . . I felt that I could say what I wanted to say and it would be heard respectfully. I thought that they had read the proposals very carefully. I guess I felt sometimes that the other guy's readings did not seem to be as detailed, although that may have not been the case. But in addition to that, the women I thought also commanded a kind of intellectual respect.

Conversely, the most negative comments made about other panelists often concern how they interact with others, handle differences of opinion, and contribute to shared goals. Although expressing differences of opinion is deemed acceptable, avoiding open confrontation is viewed as essential. Indeed, a humanist describes a co-panelist as follows: "[He] could be a little . . . bit contentious and confrontational in ways that seemed to be a little unnecessary. [He] made pronouncements, expressing his contempt for this or that." Another panelist, this same humanist recalls, "had a kind of flaky irreverence that I think grated on us a bit . . . He made any number of odd jokes of borderline sensitivity and appropriateness." Undoubtedly, the value assigned to interpersonal sensitivity is to some extent historically specific: it is more crucial in an environment characterized by uncertainty, where conflict avoidance, along with eschewing comments that might offend specific constituencies (defined in sexual, gender, racial, ethnic, religious, class, or national terms), may be the safest strategy. A more aggressive masculine style may have been more acceptable a generation ago, when higher education was more homogeneous or "clubby" than it is now.[13]

Preparedness, expertise, succinctness, intellectual depth and multidisciplinary breadth, respectfulness, and sensitivity to others: these traits and skills all go into the equation that defines a good panelist and establishes an individual's credibility. The ideal personality for a panelist is captured by a sociologist as he reviews the traits he feels made his panel's chair superlative: "[He has] a very good sense of [the field], [is] smooth, agreeable, charming, and very much blessed with a sense of reality, up on the literature, very well informed . . . he listened, [was] brisk, efficient, everything a chairman could be." Yet this description is very much at odds with that presented in most of the literature on peer review. Most studies emphasize exclusively cognitive factors and the exercise of power and downplay the role of emotion and interpersonal signaling (about one's morality, for instance).[14] The misalignment between the traits and behaviors that panelists single out and those that researchers have focused on hints at the importance of considering evaluation as an emotional process, as opposed to the more typical approach of focusing on cognition and final outcomes. These traits also suggest that the credibility of panelists seems to inhere both in their person and in their disciplines and institutions.

The Central Rules of Deliberation

Panel deliberations follow principles analogous to those that some theorists prescribe for deliberative democracy.[15] The standard of reciprocity applies, as does an overall orientation toward producing consensual decisions and realizing the common good. Moreover, panelists are expected to convince one another with the force of reason. The requirement that panels make specific, informed decisions necessitates that each participant be given full liberty to express her opinion without any reprisal, and that each be provided opportunity for full and equal voice. The meeting is deliberative to the extent that this full, equal, and free exchange of opinion is sustained. Although the panels are conducted in secrecy, evaluators are accountable to the funding organization, as well as morally accountable to the wider academic community.

There are limitations on these ideal conditions of equality, however. Panel members vary in age, race, and gender, and they represent institutions of uneven prestige (characteristics discussed in more detail later). More importantly, each of the panelists also claims expertise on a specific subset of topics covered by the proposals.[16] Thus their opinion is given more or less weight depending on the subject of discussion.

Deferring to expertise and observing disciplinary sovereignty.   For many proposals, alternative framings are possible. Is a proposal well-written or glib? Is it broad and daring or dilettantish? Is it current or trendy? Painstakingly focused or disappointingly obscure? Panelists formulate interpretive frames and attempt to convince one another that theirs is most apt. It is this context that gives rise to "deferring to expertise," a foundational rule for sustaining collective belief in the fairness of peer review. When panelists want to advocate a position regarding a proposal, they invest energy in staking their rightful claim to evaluate it based on their past research or teaching. That is, they mark their territory.[17] In other cases, they draw on previously established proofs of competence; in still others, they remain silent. A historian uses himself as an example as he explains how a panelist might openly claim authority. During a discussion of a proposal on modernity and the media in the United States, he mentioned to the group that he had done work on the period covered by the proposal, and that for this reason he was particularly well positioned to assess its contribution. "I think I had expert advice here, and I think that's why she got [the funding], because I had expert advice," he concludes.

Panelists defer to the expertise of others because the situation requires that they take positions on topics about which they know very little. An anthropologist says: "Philosophy, I didn't feel at all as if I were competent to evaluate those proposals. [I don't mention this] to say this is good or this is not good; I just did not know what was up with them. And in those cases, I always deferred to the people who did have some kind of expertise in that field."

Hearing the opinions of experts is also essential when panelists are comparing proposals that speak to a wide range of unfamiliar topics. An English professor who "tended to give high marks to some proposals [where] I had no education about the field" counts on the corrective influence of more knowledgeable panelists. While he found the proposed work simply "exciting," "some other panelist would be able to say very quickly, 'This is not original work, you know.' There'd be no way for me to know that in advance." Similarly, a historian notes that a proposal "looks good until somebody says there's a whole literature that you cannot reasonably be expected to know." Particularly when listening to someone who "comes in extremely expert and careful and [is] a person I respect a lot," this historian finds it prudent to defer. "[If this expert] says, '. . . this is really a fairly banal proposal,' then I just sort of say that must be true."

The most common form of deference involves what I call respecting disciplinary sovereignty. Panelists' opinions generally are given more weight according to how closely the proposal overlaps "their" field. Another historian spells out this culture of disciplinary deference:

For a couple of proposals, I had to "explicate" a research strategy that wasn't fully explained. [My historical expertise] on the whole had a lot of weight. Sometimes I almost felt uncomfortable about the deference that was given to my responses as a historian . . . There was a lot of credibility given to the way I responded to historical questions in particular. And I, of course, returned the deference to people in the other fields.

This willingness to recognize and defer to expertise can have drawbacks. An English professor's description of her tentative (and failed) attempt to save a proposal from being labeled "dilettantish" illustrates the way in which deference can limit rather than promote discussion:

I work in twentieth century, but I'm not an expert in post-war, post-modern literature [the applicant's field]. I think I know enough. I didn't find [the proposal] dilettantish. So I was interested that so many people did, and I was sort of willing to defer. I [should have] pushed it a little further, even just to sort of clarify: Why is it dilettantish in this area? How much of this really is disciplinary intimidation? Are you willing to go to bat for this person? I would, if I think I knew a little bit more about the field . . . I think they thought there was too much theory, that there was an element of sort of name dropping, where I wondered whether a lot of this was a kind of inexperienced way of indicating what the critical literature might be . . . I just didn't know enough to counter. If there was just another voice that was a little more enthusiastic, I would have, could have.

Maintaining collegiality.   In combination, the rules of deference to expertise and respect of disciplinary sovereignty lead to a third important customary rule: collegiality. Panelists are expected to adopt a consistently respectful tone toward one another, and not only as a nod to a long-gone era when academia was the private domain of honorable men of independent means. Collegiality has a concrete effect on panel discussions and their outcome; it is the oil that keeps the wheels of deliberation turning when panelists otherwise might not be willing to accommodate one another. Even if it at times limits the extent to which panelists engage in vigorous discussion as they compare proposals, collegiality is considered indicative of a "well-functioning" panel. A panel is described as "good" when panelists listen carefully to and are influenced by one another. This kind of respectful interaction diffuses the potential for frictions and tensions that could hinder decision making, and helps create an amicable environment. Indeed, many panelists mention being surprised at how friendly panels are, given the level of conflict that is customary in their respective departments. "I thought we were all listening to each other," a person who served on a women's studies panel says, adding, "[I] felt respected when I was speaking to something in my field."

Alliances, Strategic Voting, and Horse-Trading

Beneath the panelists' acceptance of the deliberation process as fair lies a second belief: that consistent and universalistic standards of evaluation are applied, which means that without regard to inessential differences, all proposals have an equal chance of being funded.[18] This belief constrains how panelists think about alliance formation, strategic voting, and horse-trading. Although these activities potentially skew deliberations, panelists frame them as compatible with universalism and the "natural" rising of the cream.

Alliances. Many interviewees report aligning themselves with different panelists at different times, and noticing that others seem to do the same. They did not witness strong alliances among their fellow panelists, perhaps because respondents' describe legitimate panel interactions as being among independent actors who act on a case-by-case basis. When probed further, however, most panelists reveal clear personal, intellectual, or theoretical affinities. For instance, a historian confesses feeling close to an English professor because

> she clearly had a good deal of critical and literary theory in her background. So that to some extent she and I over the years would have been reading similar work, and we happen to be sympathetic towards it. [She is] also concerned with social significance, concerned with the voices of the other, evaluating proposals on questions of originality . . . [This is important] because if you believe in liberal education and you believe that education has a role in the formation of the citizen, then it seems to me you have to pay some attention to the plurality of what constitutes citizenship.

These elective personal qua intellectual affinities are not conceptualized as corrupting or illegitimate.[19] From panelists' perspective, their task requires that they assess proposals using the more or less diverse intellectual tools they have at their disposal; these generally converge with those of at least some of their co-panelists. Thus particularism is to some extent unavoidable: the value assigned to proposals as cultural products depends largely on their embeddedness in the context of evaluation. That is, value is defined in reference to the other proposals under consideration, and by personal affinities and differences among reviewers.[20]

Strategic voting and horse-trading. Similarly, strategic voting and horse-trading are, if not unavoidable, at least very common during deliberations, despite the centrality that panelists accord to universalism in interpreting the group of proposals as a whole. Strategic voting refers to the practice of giving a lower rank that would otherwise be justified to some proposals ("low-balling") in order to increase the likelihood that other proposals will win. It may also mean boosting the ranking of a mediocre or controversial proposal to improve its chances for funding. Horse-trading means enabling the realization of other panelists' objectives in the hope that they will reciprocate. Some construe this as non-meritocratic, because the horses being traded are not necessarily equivalent, and one of them may "win" because of "politics" as opposed to intrinsic strength.

Many panelists, however, acknowledge strategic voting as normal, to the extent that they admit explicitly calibrating their own votes in anticipation of those of the other evaluators. An English professor, for instance, recalls ranking a feminist theorist's proposal highly

> partly because I knew that the other panelists would be put off by her style and I knew that I would want to argue very strongly in her favor . . . I've read her other work and I really admire it. She does something very close to what I aspire to do . . . Her style is very informal and very mannered, it's not standard academic prose by any means . . . I just thought her style would be so annoying that people wouldn't be able to see past it to the value of what she was doing. The other reason is, she takes psychoanalysis very seriously, and psychoanalysis is beloved only by a small remnant of literary critics. I figured that would probably turn some people away.

This professor describes her voting in strategic terms, but it is entirely legitimate for panelists to rank a proposal highly when they believe its quality justifies such a score. In every case, a vote aims to support a proposal or prevent its funding. It is strategic when it is guided primarily by a desire to facilitate or hinder the funding of another proposal, or to influence other panelists. The opposite of strategic voting is taking into consideration only the proposal itself, not the context of evaluation. While some panelists take pride in aiming for this goal, abstracting proposals from the context of evaluation is a social anomaly, and it is not easily or often achieved.

If strategically assigning a high rank to a proposal ("high-balling") is considered permissible, low-balling is not, because it unfairly penalizes better proposals. In fact, low-balling is the only form of strategic voting that panelists describe as illegitimate. A historian, who suspected a philosopher of deliberately assigning low ranks, explains the problem:

> I was a little bit concerned about [this guy's] rankings because he gave a lot of "threes." The problem with "threes" is they pretty much end a proposal. My sense in reading the instructions that we received is that all of the proposals had already gone through pre-screening and between fifty and sixty percent had already been eliminated, so that this was really the kind of *crème de la crème* . . . I can't impute intention, but the effect was three simply meant the end of a proposal. At a certain point I guess I began to feel . . . "Is this a sort of political [that is, strategic] evaluation?"

Strategic voting and horse-trading are particularly crucial at the end of panel deliberations, when panelists are parceling out the last available fellowships, choosing among proposals that each are flawed, but differently so, and thus are not easily made commensurate. This eleventh-hour context forces panelists to engage in calculation and quid pro quo to a degree that may have been unnecessary or unthinkable at an earlier point. (The influence of timing on proposal evaluation is discussed at greater length later in this chapter.) A historian explains that "one of the reasons I honestly don't mind making compromises is because [in the final stages, when] you're dancing through all these [deals], you realize your [own] judgment, to say the least, isn't perfect." An English professor reflects on her decision making in the final stages of deliberations this way:

> What I decided about two-thirds of the way through the meeting is that there was one file I was going to go to the mat for around these issues [of applied knowledge]. I decided it was going to require me to figure out what I'd have to lose in order to get this one . . . I think that the process of these committee meetings is about negotiations. And at the end of the day, it seems to me one may need to think about these files in terms of categories . . . you kind of [have] to figure out which of these files in these particular categories is going to be the one that I can win. People aren't going to want to concede everything; everybody has their thing they want to win. And so if I'm going to try to win on these two fronts, I'm going to have to put my weight behind the strongest one and kind of lose the others.

Horse-trading is described here as part of the ordinary order of things once the consensus proposals have been funded. A historian provides a very similar view, while also stressing the importance of negotiation. "There was one [proposal] that I didn't like and argued against a couple times earlier in the day. At one point I realized that the other four people liked that and so I said 'Look, I'm probably wrong. I still don't like it but I'm probably wrong, so let's put it on the list.' And I think to some degree, just politically, that gave me some credibility when I wanted something else . . . because I showed good will."

The dynamics of ranking are such that many judgments are relational and conjectural, and it is in this context that panelists come to think strategically about what they can realistically accomplish. This is evidenced in the comments of another historian, as he explains why he deliberately chose not to veto a project he opposed:

I said to myself, "You win some, you lose some." . . . One of the reasons I pulled back from vetoing is because we were quite sure that not all of the fellowships would be accepted, and that there would be an alternative source of funding. We were quite convinced that a person who I supported and ended up on the wait list would nevertheless be funded. And that trade-off ultimately made it seem acceptable.

In the end, panelists seem to support a pragmatic understanding of evaluation—one that is at odds with the ideals of using consistent standards and of ignoring proposals' contexts to consider only their intrinsic qualities. Panelists seem acutely aware that scholarly quality is relationally defined within the universe of the group of proposals being evaluated. Which one is used as point of reference shifts throughout the deliberation. Across all disciplines, contextual ranking is central to the art of evaluation.

Bracketing Self-Interest and Personal Ties

The influence of self-interest and personal ties on the outcome of deliberations is viewed as entirely illegitimate in a panel review. This is consistent with Weber's view on the production of rational legitimacy, which requires the application of impersonal and consistent rules. When I asked a panel chair how panelists would likely react to a member saying, "This is a student of a close colleague of mine and I'd love to see his work funded," she replied,

It's just not a consideration. It can't be a consideration. You probably noticed that the panel rejected quite roundly a student of [a panelist], who described him as the best student he'd had in twenty-five years . . . Nobody thought about that. There are other types of biases that other people bring to the meetings, but they tend to be well camouflaged . . . I hear criticisms from colleagues [such as] "Oh man, you're just funding Chicago anthropology, it's because you have all these Chicago anthropologists on your panel." . . . And what I can tell you is that in my experience it looks the opposite. The more specialists you have on the Middle East, the fewer Middle East proposals are going to get through. Because people tend to be really tough on their discipline, to the point where they're too tough and we have to think of ways to make them mellow to get them to say yes.

Taking perhaps an idiosyncratic stance, this panel chair also notes that the funding program tries to minimize the presence of panelists from Ivy League universities because of the large number of graduate students from such institutions who apply:

[We]'re looking for people who are not gatekeepers . . . I'm not sure how formal the policy is, but you did notice there was nobody from Harvard, Yale, Princeton, Chicago . . . And we definitely do not include people from those institutions [that produce] large numbers of area studies types of applications. No Michigan, no Berkeley. It's almost an unwritten rule that we're looking for people who . . . are not connected to the networks. We look for people who will decide applications on the basis of their intellectual merits, and not on who did it, where they're coming from.

Thus, following Durkheim, self-interest can be understood as the "impure" juxtaposed against the sacrality of academic excellence, which is defined through the rituals panels follow to insure that there is no corruption. The formal rules of funding agencies clearly delineate the obligation to abstain when the work of close colleagues, friends, and direct advisees is being discussed. Although there is no explicit requirement to do so, some panelists also volunteer information on indirect or informal ties ("this student's mentor is a close collaborator of mine" or "I know this applicant's adviser very well and trust her letter"). These disclosures are not offered systematically, perhaps because such ties are not uncommon. Given the degree of specialization in American academia, panelists are likely to know personally or by reputation most of the scholars whose areas closely overlap with their own, especially if they are very active in research circles, as are most evaluators.

Still, panelists' awareness of the importance of limiting the "corrupting impact" of personal relationships makes disclosing informal ties common enough to be a customary rule. A historian's reply to my asking him to describe his favorite proposal is illustrative: "That's a little bit difficult because to be completely honest about it, the one that I liked the most was by a student who quoted me at length. I recused myself. I didn't enter the discussion on that. She's not literally my student. She did some independent work with me." A sociologist, too, says she chose to remain silent when a former colleague's work, which she does not appreciate, was discussed.

Both these scholars were pleased when the decision the panels reached in each case endorsed their own viewpoints. In contrast, all of the panelists I interviewed who had written letters for applicants (and who therefore excused themselves from the deliberations) were upset when these proposals were not funded. Such decisions, they said, made them feel awkward, as if their fellow evaluators are giving them a vote of no confidence. They said they abstained from asking the other panelists for an account of the deliberations, and the other panelists did not volunteer such information. Interestingly, the "slighted" parties seemed to expect such a breach of confidentiality, despite their commitment to universalism, and were disappointed when details were not forthcoming.

Because scholarly expertise is superposed onto the social networks of those who produce the knowledge, it is impossible to eliminate the effect of interpersonal relationships, including clientelism, on the evaluation process. Nevertheless, discussions proceed as though panelists were free of these influences. Their individual preferences are usually construed in universalistic terms, despite the particularistic aspects introduced by real-world considerations. Evaluations of proposals are framed at least in part by what panelists believe are important topics, judgments that are tied to their personal view of the appropriate directions for a particular field. They are also shaped by letters of support that are more or less trusted, with the level of trust reflecting network connections.[21] Furthermore, as we will now see, some panelists view idiosyncratic preferences as an acceptable component of evaluations.

Beyond Idiosyncratic Taste and Self-Reproduction

Rational legitimacy, Weber reminds us, comes from applying impersonal and consistent rules. Thus by trying to bracket their idiosyncratic tastes, panel members help sustain a collective belief in the deliberations' fairness. An English professor advocates distinguishing between one's personal preferences and criteria of competence, and privileging the latter when the two are in conflict. Referring to "a completely chaotic proposal," he comments:

> The art historian and I both liked the kind of effervescence of the thing and thought it was probably worth thinking about, but I think others felt he was just too chaotic. What I found with these things, you need to use two sets of criteria. One is . . . your best professional judgment in as neutral a way as you can manage it, independent of your taste. And the other one is allowing for your tastes, if they don't get in the way of each other. I think one should always give up the personal one, if the arguments of other people seem sound, and not give up the other one.

In subordinating personal preferences to more neutral standards, this scholar protects the legitimacy of the process, but he also recognizes the role of individual subjectivities in evaluation. Similarly, a political scientist establishes a clear distinction between evaluating the choice of topic, which is not "objective," and the quality of the proposal, which is "amenable to the canons of academic excellence." A different panelist dismisses a colleague's assessments, noting, "He seemed to value some proposals for very odd reasons that were more like personal taste than any kind of other criteria."

Panelists' concern over the influence of idiosyncratic tastes is tied to a desire to aim for the most universalistic standard possible. A historian of China makes this point when she states that she works hard to be a good panelist because

> some would just say "Well, I don't like this kind of thing, I don't like that kind of thing." . . . Professions are only a set of codes and standards, so if everything is going to be completely spontaneous and just according to your own whims, there isn't going to be a profession. Plus, I just think the people out here submitting proposals to us should be able to understand what they're aiming for.

Likewise, an economist values attempts to bracket "subjectivity" and instead make "objective" evaluations as often as possible. He praises another panelist because "he had the whole game in mind. I mean he was viewing the whole set of proposals and trying to be consistent." An art historian is even more explicitly opposed to the use of idiosyncratic preferences in evaluation:

> Everyone brings their own baggage. Certain people would say, "Well, I think this should be funded in part because it's something that interests me, because it relates to my research, because it's something I would like to see published, because it deals with the period prior to the period I'm [working on] . . . and that says a

great deal. One has to remain open to a degree and not get quite so personal. So I was struck often about how personal people did get.

These panelists' concerns are somewhat exceptional, however. Most reviewers uphold the legitimacy of the process by seamlessly folding their idiosyncratic preferences and tastes into the formal criteria of evaluation. So, for example, they tend to define originality in ways that are in line with the type of originality that their own work exhibits.[22] As one interviewee acknowledges, evaluators tend to like what speaks to their own interests: "I see scholarly excellence and excitement in this one project on food, possibly because I see resonance with my own life, my own interests, who I am, and other people clearly don't. And that's always a bit of a problem, that excellence is in some ways . . . what looks most like you."

During interviews, multiple examples of how panelists' idiosyncratic interests shape their votes emerged. A panelist who loves modern dance confesses (without flinching), "The one on dance [I liked a lot]; I'm an avid dance person . . . in terms of studying dance, the history of dance and vernacular dance in particular. So I found that one really interesting, very good." Similarly, an anthropologist explains her support for a proposal on songbirds by noting that she had just come back from Tucson, where she had been charmed by songbirds. An English scholar supports a proposal on the body, tying her interest to the fact that she was an elite tennis player in high school. A historian doing cross-cultural, comparative work explicitly states that he favors proposals with a similar emphasis. Another historian doing research on non-Western societies gives extra points to proposals that look beyond the West. Yet another panelist ties her opposition to a proposal on Viagra to the fact that she is a lesbian: "I will be very candid here, this is one place where I said, 'OK, in the way that I live my life and my practices' . . . I'm so sick of hearing about Viagra . . . Just this focus on men, whereas women, you know, birth control is a big problem in our country. So I think that's what made me cranky."[23] Apparently, equating "what looks most like you" with "excellence" is so reflexive as to go unnoticed by some.

The tendency to frame preferences in terms of self-interest may occur in part because it is difficult if not impossible to think of a system of evaluation that would entirely bracket personal tastes. Panelists cannot spell out what defines an "interesting" proposal in the abstract, irrespective of the kinds of problems that captivate them personally. They behave as if they have no alternative but to use their own personal understanding of what constitutes a fascinating problem in order to do the work that is expected of them. After all, their connoisseurship and expertise, which cannot be separated from their ability to judge, is why they were invited to serve.[24] And indeed, there is a great deal of uncertainty and unpredictability involved in deliberation. This is why experts who are recognized for their good judgment are needed. Their expertise positions them to demonstrate creativity in situations of improvisation.[25]

Some disciplines and some scholars may be more open to accommodating personal idiosyncrasies, as we saw in Chapter 3.[26] Feminist standpoint theory, for instance, takes an anti-objectivist epistemological stance on the grounds that personal identity influences all aspects of scholarly work.[27] But regardless of intellectual position, many panelists are aware of the dangers of rewarding proposals because they aim to do "something very close to what I aspire to do." An anthropologist sums up this customary caution against succumbing to the pull of one's personal interests:

One of the lessons that we learn immediately as anthropologists is, there's a lot of different ways of being in the world. So if you can apply cultural relativism to proposal writing, then you're OK. But you never fully escape from your own interests, your own position, and so on, and so that is bound to have some impact. I don't know that that's necessarily a bad thing when you have a panel that's sufficiently balanced in all sorts of ways, including academic discipline, areas of expertise, the kind of schools that you come from, and then the obvious, race, ethnicity, and gender. So I do think it is important to bring all of those factors into play in creating the panel, because you aren't going to be able to get rid of those influences.

Promoting Methodological Pluralism

In defining the qualities of a good panelist, respondents, as we saw, put a premium on deferring to colleagues' expertise and sentiments. They also view disciplinary sovereignty as very important. These imperatives point to the value of broad-mindedness and tolerance of differences in evaluation. Panels are not a forum for challenging methodological or disciplinary traditions. The rules of the game require that methodological equality be recognized as a matter of principle. Thus panelists are strongly committed to evaluating proposals according to the epistemological and methodological standards that prevail in the discipline of the applicant—a principle called "cognitive contextualization."[28] This principle is summarized by an evaluator as he describes the dynamics of his panel:

> [There are] differences between people who work with large data sets and do quantitative research. And then the very polar opposite, I suppose, folks who are doing community-level studies in anthropology. There are such different methodologies that it's hard to say that there's a generalizable standard that applies to both of them. We were all, I think, willing and able to understand the projects in their own terms, fortunately, and not try to impose a more general standard, because it would have been extremely

difficult . . . I wouldn't hold a candidate in political science responsible for what seemed to me to be having overly instrumental or diagrammatic ways of understanding what they're going to do, because they have to have those. They have to have a certain scientism.

The premium put on "cognitive contextualization" acts as a counterweight to idiosyncratic tastes and pushes panelists to assess proposals through the lenses that are distinctive to the applicant's field. A political scientist makes this clear as he explains how other panel members misunderstood his evaluative criteria:

I was basically being accused of being a positivist. No one ever said that, because obviously that's like calling somebody communist. But there was a sense in which I was imposing my disciplinary bias inappropriately on another discipline. That's what I was picking up. And my response was "No, I actually am holding [the applicant] to her own standards and I'm not trying to be hegemonic on this."

"Cognitive contextualization" presumes a certain methodological pluralism, that is, the ability to understand that different methods serve different purposes. Panelists act on this understanding, even if it may not seem to be in their interest. For instance, a hermeneutically inclined historian says that he "even liked" the political scientist on his panel and argues that "committee[s] always need one fairly tough-minded, empiricist, scientistic, social scientist who can hold up that banner and articulate why his standards . . . are [what] they are." Methodological pluralism produces universalism, thus bolstering the legitimacy of collective evaluations.[29] But significantly, such methodological pluralism does not favor the use of consistent criteria across disciplines; instead, different proposals prime evaluators to use different standards. This complex, nonlinear method speaks to the pragmatic character of evaluation, which is driven by problem solving and satisficing (settling for the "best possible" outcome), as opposed to a more rigid cognitive coherence.

When evaluators describe the panelists who in their opinion were the least impressive, they often mention a lack of methodological pluralism. A geographer expresses her frustration with a political scientist who refused to use the most appropriate tools for evaluating a proposal that focused on meaning: "This [proposal] is not about how many people are actually sick in a population, but rather how many are saying they're sick in a population, which is about discourse. So it's not going to fit into nice little number crunching. It's about how people use issues to mobilize protests, and he was not willing to hear that or entertain that, and it made me mad." Similarly, a historian criticizes another historian for her lack of disciplinary flexibility: "She sort of has this one standard . . . I mean, she always had this one little test that she seems to be applying to everything. That just seemed to me to be not the most productive way." Others stress pluralism when describing the panelists they valued most. A historian who also appreciates creativity and "solid" work says, "When I'm trying to judge quality . . . I want to make decisions . . . [that allow] for the maximum diversified ecosystem, you know, the most [different] models of doing work possible." Another panelist, a political scientist, supports a proposal inspired by rational choice although he is very critical of the paradigm:

Because I am just a wonderfully secular individual, I evaluate [proposals] on their own terms . . . This guy was clearly so smart that if he wanted to do this, he should be allowed to do it. He knew what he was trying to do, he was likely to be influential with folks working in his wing of political science, and it should have been supported. It just seemed to me crazy, unethical virtually, not to support this proposal, even though you don't agree with it methodologically.

Finally, comparing two years of service on a panel, another historian lauds an "appreciative form of generosity towards what is good work in multiple traditions" among his colleagues the second year. That group embraced "more a kind of imaginative projection into work that is in a very different tradition than your own, you know, that is good work in its own terms. And it seemed to me everybody was to varying degrees committed to doing that." These quotes illustrate clearly how methodological pluralism is essential to the smooth functioning of funding panels.

Setting Aside Disciplinary Prejudices

The customary rules of methodological pluralism, disciplinary sovereignty, and respect for others' expertise and sentiments lead panelists to try to keep their disciplinary prejudices in check. A historian who chaired a panel describes the effort to manage disciplinary prejudices this way: "I think people try to be polite to other disciplines . . . You're not going to say things that other people might find offensive because you're not going to win any points by doing that. And most of the people who are on the committee are the type of intellectuals who realize that almost every tradition, almost every genre, has poor and excellent practitioners." A sociologist, summarizing the "give and take" that characterizes discussions, makes the point that feelings of proximity to or distance from other disciplines and types of scholarship are deliberately muted:

> Say it's an identity proposal, and I give it a low score because it doesn't stand up to the sort of criteria that I've laid out, but somebody else gives it a high score . . . The typical pattern in these

meetings is for the low score to listen very carefully to what the higher scores are saying, particularly if the higher scores are from areas where they have certain expertise . . . So there's a certain give and take and compromise, which is quite nice.

This same sociologist recounts how he manages his own disciplinary prejudices:

> As I was scoring these proposals, I started to be suspicious that I was giving lower scores to anthropology and history proposals than [those] from the other social sciences—in part because the criteria that I think are important are somewhat discipline-specific . . . It wasn't extreme, but it was there; you could see it in the confusion of scores [I assigned]. And so, when we met, I just 'fessed up. I said, "You know, I think I have a bias in terms of scoring lower for anthropology and history" . . . This particular panel, for whatever reason, could be just the luck of the draw, seems very open-minded and willing to accept the possibility that we each have our particular disciplinary process we use.

A historian tries to offset his biases by "giv[ing] disciplines very far from me the benefit of the doubt," and by being "a little bit harder on ones in my own discipline going in . . . a plus or minus easier or harder because I just don't want to just be bowing to people in American history one hundred percent of the time." This honorable attitude, which requires that scholars voluntarily hold themselves to the highest standards, is essential to the collective belief that the process is fair.[30]

The tendency to be "a little bit harder" on proposals from one's own discipline varies considerably, however. The historian quoted earlier also acknowledges that not "bowing to" his own field is "a luxury I can afford" because "history does very well" in funding competitions. Philosophers, classicists, and art historians, whose disciplines garner awards much less frequently—in part because these are small fields that generate far fewer applicants—may feel less magnanimous. Two philosophers were described by their fellow panelists as very eager to see their discipline represented on the lists of awardees. An inverse relationship between generosity toward other disciplines and scarcity may contribute to important differences in the degree to which members of different disciplines engage in disinterested behavior.[31]

Some panelists point out that favoring one's own discipline can be the unintentional result of knowing much more about that field and thus being better able to form an opinion. A musicologist, though, echoing the panel chair quoted earlier who noted that "people tend to be really tough on their [own] discipline," recalls that on her panel, "people cast a particularly critical eye on work from their own field, in part because they knew the field and could evaluate the claims more effectively than a non-specialist." Regardless of the motive for favoring one's discipline, doing so can have significant negative consequences. Panelists often lose credibility by pushing their own fields. A historian of France describes the panelist he liked least as someone who is "very interested in pushing her own field and is not as open to other fields. As she said herself, she's pushing time periods, you know, she'll sponsor anything in the Middle Ages, that kind of thing." Being able to sway colleagues' opinion and gain support for a proposal depends on the overall amount of credibility that one has accumulated. Respecting all the customary rules increases one's credibility with colleagues, in addition to promoting conditions for fair decision making.

The Limits of Legitimacy: Violating the Rules

The taken-for-granted character of customary rules is evidenced when these rules are perceived as being broken, or when they are moot.[32] Three of the twelve panels studied experienced disagreements important enough to require that program officers and some panelists repair relationships among evaluators.[33] Members of these panels recall them as "disappointing" and "nerve-racking," or as "a panel that turned into a two-day faculty meeting, which is not my idea of fun." Evaluators are particularly sensitive to the need to respect rules that pertain to collegiality, the use of consistent standards, and the exclusion of academic gossip from the deliberations.

Conflicts and collegiality. Across all panels, breaches of the rules of deference to expertise and respect of disciplinary sovereignty are the most frequent source of conflict and the most common threat to the maintenance of collegiality. Failure to defer can be deeply troubling to academics because so much of their self-identity is tied to their role as privileged expert. An anthropologist admits deliberately withholding deference in the case of a "controversial" co-panelist when that panelist "was, I thought, stepping outside of his field and into mine." Conflicts may also occur when a panelist is viewed as not upholding reasonable standards, despite having the relevant expertise. A historian explains how an art historian

> got noplace trying to sell [one of the proposals] to the rest of us. This proposal was just not put together very carefully, and she tried to argue that this is really a good person and that even if the proposal wasn't put together perfectly, [we should] think about it . . . you can throw your expertise out, but you do wind up having to convince at least two other people.

Other panelists say that they refuse to defer to narrow expertise ("I don't bow to the white lab coat"). When a specialist focuses too closely on detailed considerations that go beyond the general quality of the proposal, other panelists may withhold deference because the expert's opinions make it more, not less, difficult to differentiate what is important from what is obscure. The rule of deference is also voided when more than one person claims expertise.[34] As we will see in Chapter 6, this situation creates a challenge for the evaluation of truly interdisciplinary proposals, where multiple panelists can legitimately claim relevant expertise.

As noted earlier, respecting other panelists' opinions is an essential quality of a good panelist. Being respectful upholds the customary rule of collegiality. The comments of an anthropologist reveal the resentment that violations of this rule can generate. Describing a conflict over whether some proposals were eligible, he explains:

> I had a disagreement [with another panelist] near the start . . . I was a little taken aback because his response to me on that was very direct and kind of in your face. I found it . . . offensive is a little too strong, but I thought it was inappropriate, I guess. It came at a time very early in the panel where everybody's still sort of feeling one another out. It made me a bit uncomfortable.

Breaches of collegiality can go beyond creating discomfort. They can result in open conflict, as the following description of a panelist who was unable to convince others to fund a proposal in his own field shows:

> He ate by himself, as we broke after that [discussion] . . . He was extraordinarily upset. It took until pretty close to the end of the meeting for him to . . . get back into the swing of things . . . This was his top proposal that I recall, and so he had a huge stake in this. He couldn't get anywhere with any other members of the committee . . . He did not hear the criticisms that we were offering and they were quite substantive and detailed . . . There was a kind of an undertone that [he thought] we really weren't up to his speed on this.

Such conflicts have to be managed with great care, to ensure that collaboration remains possible until the collective task of the panel has been completed. To this end, program officers, panel chairs, and some panelists engage in "emotion work," helping their colleagues save face even after defeat and reintegrating them into the group.

When collegiality is low, the panel is considered "bad" or "polluted," because tension-ridden interactions among panelists undermine the group's ability to reach consensus regarding the worthiness of proposals. In describing why his panel did not function well, a historian explains:

> [Normally], if people have the outlying score, unless it is on a point of unbelievably crucial principle, they just sort of back off after making their case. [But in this case, m]ost of the people really dug in their heels . . . it was strange that people weren't quicker to get out of the way when they were the only person with a negative opinion . . . Some of it is precedent. If the first five or six that you discuss happen by accident to be ones where there really is a matter of principle at stake that the person objects to, then in a way it forms a model of how you talk about others. There were people enforcing a strong methodological vision, or a strong vision of what constituted quality . . . So they weren't backing off in a hurry on things.

In this context, a muted expression of enthusiasm can signal disapproval, and any more damning criticisms may be made allusively. Frowning, rolling one's eyes, sighing, blushing, and talking through clenched teeth are certainly actions that can be as powerful as words. And objections that are not fully articulated dampen debate because they are not amenable to contestation. Fortunately, such behaviors are much more easily controlled in the context of a two-day panel than they can be in, say, departmental deliberations, which occur regularly, have a history, and can be shaped by folk stories about past conflicts, interpersonal hatreds, and the like. Arguably, in comparison to other contexts of evaluation, it is on grant peer review panels that evaluators exhibit their best behavior and are most inclined to be generous, in part because the decisions made will have very little effect on their own working conditions and daily environment. Thus, panelists often report that they find colleagues from other universities more gregarious than their own immediate colleagues—a reaction common, as well, among academics who share a sabbatical year at a research institute.

Inconsistent criteria. Maintaining consistent criteria for judging qualitative and quantitative proposals is crucial to panel legitimacy, given that tensions between the two types of methods are found in several social science disciplines, and that explanation and interpretation, and positivism and hermeneutics, are fault lines separating the social sciences from the humanities. A political scientist who says he tries very hard "to judge the proposals on their own turf," also emphasizes,

> I try to be consistent in asking the same kinds of questions whether it was somebody who's going to build a formal model about corruption in Russia, or somebody who was going to access how changes in international legal standing . . . [modify] the perception [of corruption] . . . What I look for, first, is a research design that's fairly explicit about the nature of the kinds of calls and claims that are being made . . . I want to know the exact relationships they're trying to map out. I want to know something about the alternative explanations, which ones are being considered, which ones have already been rejected.

Consistency is complicated by the mechanics of deliberation. Panelists compare different subsets of proposals (defined by shared topics, comparable relative ranking, or proximity in the alphabet) at different times. The characteristics that are shared by any one batch of proposals vary and may make different criteria of evaluation more salient. As a historian of China points out:

> It does sometimes happen that we get some that are very close to each other, and I always go back again and look at the ones that I thought were really the best and really the worst and see if they're really all that much different. It's like working yourself through any batch of applications or papers or whatever: your standards kind of evolve as you go through it. I don't sort mechanically . . . Until I've read the whole batch, I don't even know exactly what the standards are going to be.

Maintaining consistency is also often at odds with the imperative of cognitive contextualism discussed earlier, which requires that the most appropriate disciplinary criteria be applied. A sociologist, reflecting on the challenge of consistency in criteria, observes:

> We were taking different disciplines and trying to make the rules up as we went along, really. We were saying, well, what counts as ethnography in sociology isn't what counts for ethnography in anthropology. It was quite hard, really . . . to remain consistent given that everybody had different consistencies, you know, we were all trying to be consistent in our own ways.

To respect "cognitive contextualization" means to adopt different criteria of evaluation for different proposals. But the resulting incommensurability is very much at odds with a social science epistemology that would suggest that the same standards (about falsification, for instance) should apply to all types of research.[35]

The application of consistent criteria generated one of the three serious conflicts that emerged on the panels I studied. A scholar de-

scribes a proposal that some thought was methodologically unsophisticated, yet that also seemed somehow grand and highly ambitious. The "fight," he explains, turned on whether the topic was
sufficiently enticing to overcome the proposal's many other flaws.

It was an absolutely wonderful idea and the people who liked it, at
least some of them, were swayed by the idea . . . But when you applied the criteria we often use for proposals to this one, it failed,
and it failed miserably. The fight was about do we overlook these
criteria or not because we like the topic so much. I couldn't help
but think there was, like, some sets of extrinsic things going on
too, like personalities, and there was a political, or ideological [di-
mension] . . . This applicant . . . was a kind of anti-globalization
lefty who was pretty naive about testing, assuming those assumptions are true and then running with them in the proposal as opposed to trying to defend any of them . . . His supporters would
go, "This is a cultural history, and that's really interesting, so . . ."
But the proposal actually says, "I'm going to do a social and economic history . . . and *test* whether or not it supported America's
hegemonic ambition." So [the economist] quite rightly said,
"Well, I don't think he has a clue about how to go about doing
that" . . . [Proposals often] fail on those grounds . . . a person
states he's going to do something and you take it on face value.
The supporters were going, "Well, no, he didn't really mean that,"
and [it] seemed to me, you can't really [do that].

Although the proposal was not funded, this panelist voices his
concern that standard rules were not applied during deliberation.
Later in the interview, he hints at a possible failure in the legitimacy
of the decision process when he wonders whether the panel chair
had some reason for wanting the project funded. Another panelist,
on a different panel, shares a similar concern over legitimacy. He

feels his panel was biased in favor of more humanistic social sciences, so that a proposal with a multi-causal model was penalized. Familiarity with languages also was favored, which meant that anthropologists were more likely to be funded than political scientists. Here again, the legitimacy of the deliberation process may depend on achieving a proper balance between "cognitive contextualization" and consistency, while also avoiding biases.

Two of the panelists most insistent about the use of consistent criteria are highly successful African-American scholars. Their own experience with biases and with being stereotyped and underestimated by professors and colleagues due to their race is likely to have made them particularly sensitive to the application of consistent criteria.[36] One, a senior scholar in his sixties, observes that considerations such as whether a proposed project seems to be already completed, or whether the candidate has already received several fellowships, were raised as objections for some cases, but not for other equally problematic cases. And indeed, my observation of panels suggests that all criteria do not remain equally salient from one proposal to the next; the saliency of criteria varies in part with what the proposal evokes in evaluators and how it primes (or prepares) them to frame their own further thinking about the issue.[37]

Gossip. For some respondents, disciplinary gossip and other extraneous factors have no place in deliberations. This position is illustrated by a younger, female African-American panelist who is adamant that panelists should consider only the evidence in the dossier. She recommends that all panel members be urged explicitly "to make their decision on the basis of the materials before them as opposed to going beyond that." She expresses her dismay over the fairly low ranking a proposal by a prolific and well-known scholar received prior to deliberations. She attributes this ranking to widely shared negative views about the applicant's reputation that she, the panelist, was not privy to. She finds it disturbing that other panelists were reluctant to take a further look at the proposal, and that they seemed to take for granted that it should not be funded. Reflecting on this episode, she describes how the norms of collegiality limit what can be said in the context of panel deliberations:

> The one thing that I could not do is what I wanted to do . . . [that] is, to just challenge [them] . . . But having just met all four of these people for the first time, I didn't want to question their integrity. So I [made what] I thought was a somewhat eloquent appeal based on the standard kinds of rationales . . . I admitted maybe I had been duped and all of you have seen through this hoax that he's trying to pull on us, but I saw this as a very interesting theme. And they admitted that, but they said, "It's a cliché."

In reference to an allusion made by a panelist that the applicant was able to secure large advances from publishers, she adds:

> That kind of innuendo I thought was unfair. They know about the proposal and what's going on sort of behind the scenes and so on, but they didn't even want to discuss [the proposal]. We never even discussed it, and I didn't push it. First of all, I didn't want to say, "Look, I'm the only [person in the applicant's field] here and although this is treading on everybody's turf, it seems like to me you should [have] at least, you know, talk[ed] about this for five minutes."

Nevertheless, this scholar is satisfied with the competition's overall outcome. She concludes, pragmatically, that "nothing is perfect," and that "human beings will find ways to bend rules, so the only thing that can really help is just to try to get people to have high-level integrity and a sense of fairness."

Extraneous Influences on Panel Outcomes

An array of other factors not directly related to the content of proposals can influence funding decisions. These extraneous factors may be categorized broadly as involving uneven personal influence and power dynamics among panel members (including the effects of racial identity, seniority, and gender); preexisting networks and reputation; and chance. All potentially affect the fairness and legitimacy of a panel's decisions, as well as the credibility that panelists vest in individual panel members.

The effects of uneven personal influence and power dynamics. Beyond the influence of race, seniority, and gender (discussed later), individual panelists' perceived levels of authority can influence outcomes. A pecking order emerges within the group during the process of deliberating. Although this hierarchy remains implicit, it manifests itself concretely. Panelists listen to some members more frequently than others and are swayed more by the opinions of certain members. Many of the conflicts that surround expectations about deference are triggered by perceived slights or challenges to positions in a pecking order. The questions a historian poses as a way to assess panel dynamics capture many of the ways in which personal influence can shape group evaluations: "Did anybody dominate the [deliberations]? Did everyone have a chance to express [themselves]? Was there any scholarly point of view that really didn't get a hearing? Were there times when people felt that their own academic field or standards or values were being challenged indirectly? Directly?" As these questions suggest, differences in degrees of influence across panel members and the power dynamics associated with these differences can affect whether a proposal receives a full hearing.

Panels provide academics with a context for measuring themselves against colleagues. Thus, an individual's panel performance—

as measured by, for example, how successfully she is able to champion a particular proposal—is important to each evaluator's self-identity.[38] Not surprisingly, then, when asked how they thought a meeting went, many panelists spontaneously discuss how much they believe they influenced others versus how much they were influenced by others. Similarly, when asked their opinion about other panelists, interviewees often compare degrees of influence. For instance, one woman, describing a co-panelist she thought made inconsistent judgments, said: "He often seemed to make arguments that no one else would pick up on, and that often seemed irrelevant."

One of the prime determinants of influence is institutional affiliation. Ivy Leaguers often are perceived as favoring criteria related to who studied with whom and where. And some Ivy League faculty members define themselves, and are defined by others, as undisputed authorities. A panel member from a southern college recalls the patronizing tone of a co-panelist from an Ivy League school when he, the southerner, presented his assessment of a proposal they both were competent to judge. The southerner remembers being surprised by this tone because he had more detailed empirical knowledge of the proposal's topic than did his co-panelist. Nevertheless, rather than challenging this panelist, he decided that the Ivy Leaguer simply was "used to being an authority."

A second factor affecting pecking order is personality. In one panel, an anthropologist was singled out as having a particularly strong effect on deliberation outcomes. A sociologist explains this panelist's influence by noting that "within anthropology anyway, there are so many different approaches" that "inevitably, these things often come down to strong characters who have very specific agendas." Of the same anthropologist, an art historian says, "In terms of the dynamics, he had a lot of power . . . If he decided he didn't like something, he would just simply say, 'Well, that work's all been done,' and he would list the literature and then everyone was silent. So he did have a very powerful influence." Aggressiveness, stubbornness, and determination can be a potent combination, quite apart from how knowledgeable or well-prepared a panelist may be. "In some cases [funding] really depends on an individual hold-out. If that person didn't hold out, [a proposal could] get funded," a sociologist attests.

Some evaluators downplay power dynamics, framing the role of all panel members as consultative. An economist comments: "I didn't feel like it was gladiatorial combat. I wasn't there to fight to the death for my proposal . . . I was there to try to give input on stuff that was closest to what I'm knowledgeable on." He adds, "It's not like Capitol Hill [where you have to] bring home the bacon for your constituents." For others, though, posturing is a useful way to make the pecking order visible. Panelists who extensively trash proposals that they know others like sometimes do so in order to flex their muscles and openly assert their position in the pecking order of the panel. While some view this behavior as wholly inappropriate, a political scientist recognizes that other panelists often "get interested in the games that are played around these things," as though they were watching power matches and following who makes points.

Of course, characteristics such as racial identity, seniority, and gender strongly facilitate or hinder the accumulation of influence, independent of personality and motivation. Social psychologists have shown that people have clear expectations about the kinds of performance and contributions that members of different gender and racial identities will offer to a group. Low expectations for blacks and women are typical.[39] This certainly may affect how academics approach the experience of serving on panels.

I did not find any specific instances where the racial identity of panelists directly affected their influence on deliberations. The absence of data on the topic is hardly surprising given the very few people of color who were involved in the panels I studied. Moreover, those panelists may have been reluctant to mention experiences of stereotyping on panels to a white interviewer, especially since, as was true of most respondents, they did not know of my academic interests in comparative anti-racism. The same can be said about the marginalization that panelists may have experienced due to their lack of seniority. Nevertheless, the social psychology literature gives us good reason to anticipate that both race and seniority affect how much influence panelists exercise and the extent to which they are the object of low expectations.[40]

In contrast, a few interviewees did mention the effect of gender on panelists' level of influence. One woman scholar, an inexperienced panelist, relates the advice she received from another, more experienced panel member:

She said to me afterwards that the gender dynamic often in these meetings can be difficult. She said, "You have to learn how to use language in a way that is almost like a form of warfare, rather than get at the issues. There is a drama to attack that has nothing to do with talking specifically about the projects, but it's how you launch yourself." She said I was just too nice . . . Ultimately my take on it is . . . really this whole committee meeting was a kind of performance. You have to learn to perform in a more bombastic manner to get your points across, and this has nothing to do with really what you say, but how you say it . . . [Another woman] said the same. She said, "You have to do things with a flourish and a dramatic sort of [style]" . . . She said, "You're altogether too nice and diplomatic about it."

Other respondents also referred to gendered patterns of interaction and self-presentation among panelists. For instance, a woman says about another panelist, "He's very bright and was in a performance mode, like a lot of males get into, you know, they're like bred for it, I swear, in academia . . . They need more women next year, to tone the testosterone down. Seriously, the year before this was not . . . [like that]." Of the other women panelists, she notes, "We tend to defer a little and maybe not be as assertive as perhaps we'd like to be. When I get . . . in a situation with a hard-hitting male, I just want to not say anything. It's like, 'I'm not playing this game.' I don't want to perform, I just want to do my thing and try to do as good a job as I can."

A final determinant of personal influence is whether a panelist is perceived by others as having similar standards. This is suggested by a history professor who explains how her appreciation of a co-panelist was rooted in shared theoretical frameworks:

There were just a couple of cases where she and I agreed and we together disagreed with others, and I remember feeling pleased about that, although I really felt quite at peace and attuned to the whole panel. I felt that we understood each other quite well . . . She and I share a post-structuralist intellectual background and perhaps for that reason we share a liking for those projects that took problems that had previously been considered in a binary framework and did something creative with that . . . She has a way of framing problems [using] very broad terms that are not just drawn from her field. I mean, she really reaches out to the humanities for philosophy and all kinds of frameworks that were familiar to me. So I had a good appreciation of her knowledge base and her approach to things. In some respects, that made the conversation much better because I knew where she was coming from . . . When I saw that she had given a proposal a high mark, it encouraged me to spend some time explaining why I thought it was really good.

This panelist's admission that her co-panelist's high opinion of a particular proposal "encouraged me to spend some time explaining why I thought it was really good" might be interpreted by outsiders as an example of personal influence violating the norms of fairness. But evaluators can legitimately use intellectual similarity as a criterion for determining the quality of mind and the level of influence that they are willing to accord fellow panelists.

The effects of preexisting networks and reputation. It seems intuitive that panel deliberations would be affected by personal connections among panelists and by the amount of information they have about one another prior to the deliberations. Indeed, as the comments of the panelist just quoted show, extraneous connections may influence how much weight panelists give to their peers' opinions.

In most of the cases I studied, however, panelists had no common personal ties and in fact had very little or no information about each other prior to the meetings. (Panelists of the Society of Fellows are an exception, since they all are drawn from a single institution; and in some other cases, evaluators knew one another from having served together on panels in previous years.) That all but a few had no preexisting connections is not surprising, given the size of the American academic community and that program officers for multidisciplinary competitions explicitly aim for diversity, constructing panels that include scholars from various disciplines, regions, and types of universities.

Some evaluators were familiar with the reputation or writings of colleagues in their own or a closely related field before meeting them; some others were connected indirectly, through mutual friends or colleagues. Indirect relationships were more frequent among those living in large metropolitan areas that include many colleges and universities, and among individuals teaching in elite institutions that often sustain dense cross-institutional networks. In one case, two panelists were former colleagues and knew each other very well. In another case, two panelists were involved in overlapping professional circles. As one panelist, a historian, explains, such familiarity can be welcome:

> The person that I felt closest to was the person I knew in advance, someone whom I didn't have to become acquainted with. I can't at all claim that we [are] close friends, but we've had an occasional dinner and we've been at a couple of conferences together, and I knew coming in that it would be relatively easy for us to discuss these issues.

Few evaluators took time to gather information on others prior to the meeting, even though the Internet makes data-gathering easy. For instance, a historian says: "In most cases, I knew the name by reputation. I had never met the anthropologist before last year, but I knew his work. And I think both years I didn't know the economist, and I didn't research. Interestingly, both of them were locals." This paucity of information about academic achievements or personal reputation makes it more likely that candidates will rely on preconceived notions about disciplinary differences as they prepare arguments for and against proposals in response to anticipated objections. The English professor quoted earlier, for example, shaped her defense of a psychoanalysis-inflected proposal based on what she assumed would be her co-panelists' negative reactions to the applicant's "mannered," nonacademic, and potentially "annoying" prose style, based solely on their academic disciplines. The dearth of information on others may also push panelists to be conservative in criticizing what they consider the foibles of other disciplines. Under conditions of uncertainty, it may be safer to err on the side of prudence and excessive collegiality, in order to avoid antagonizing the allies one might need later to label a proposal as a contender (or noncontender).

Chance. Although panelists view their deliberations as legitimate and fair, they also acknowledge an element of randomness in the outcomes. For instance, an English professor says, "Every panel kind of gets its own rhythm going and there is a kind of randomness having to do with who got picked to be on the panel, and the results could be very different on another day . . . I guess I hoped that all of these people are applying to lots of different fellowships and the cards will fall a different way for different people." She does not describe the process as unfair, but neither does she see it as fully controlled by the participants. This same panelist also notes that judging academic excellence can be a frustratingly inexact undertaking:

> I don't put a huge amount of faith in my or anybody else's ability to measure it [excellence] exactly. [Just because of] all the subjectivity involved, [there are] field-by-field and even day-by-day or minute-by-minute variations in what might count as excellence for any given person or group of people. Certainly, so much is involved in writing a proposal that has to do with cleverness, and that could be totally different from the excellence of the end result. Things like that, I guess, . . . make me uncomfortable.

Other panelists also readily admit the limitations of panels. An art historian explains that because one cannot predict the composition of the committee, "It is a tremendous game of chance that you can manage to get something funded. That was my sense, that it's a real crap shoot of who will get the funding and who won't." A historian maintains that the best projects do get rewarded, but "with mistakes" because there is "bad judgment, dominating personalities and the review [is done by] people who don't see the true beauty of some project over another. Mistakes are made. You're reading a lot of these things in between doing everything else."

For an English professor, these elements of chance work against the more innovative proposals:

> The alternates, sometimes to me they're the ones you really like to see sort of get in because they're just quirky enough, they're just odd enough, and they're just daring enough that they really might come to something so unexpected and unusual and provocative. But those are the ones that really are subject to these other variables, such as: What are the interactions among the members of the committee? Where are the proposals alphabetically? Or in terms of [the order in which they] are being decided? So it's by no means an objective process.

For a historian, luck is especially important in discussions of the more creative proposals, for which usual standards do not apply and which require collective risk-taking: "We have to make decisions that are based on these intangibles about creativity and pushing the envelope, and those are harder, more intuitive, as you probably noticed. You can't say this person's grades are higher or their letters are better; you can't use those criteria."

The sequence and time at which proposals are discussed are also crucial. At the end of the day, people are more pressed, eager to go home, and more disposed, of necessity, to negotiate and reach quicker judgments on each proposal under consideration. In addition, the more contentious proposals often are discussed at the end, after all the easier cases have been dealt with. A political scientist describes the context that emerges at this final stage:

> This is one of the last proposals we talked about, one of the very last. At that point we knew we had many grants to give away, and we also knew that we were at number twenty-four or twenty-five,

and we had like three or four proposals to go. [Some] were sort of on the fence, [and] there were a few people who were pushing hard. At this point there was no displacement effect because you knew that if you funded this person, it wasn't going to displace somebody else who might have more [merit]. And so I think they might have just simply said, "Look, you know, it's four-thirty on Saturday. We're at the end of the day. I'm tired. You feel passionate. I don't really care." I don't think [the last award] was [made] on the merit.

Timing and sequence are crucial because each award is made without knowing for sure that there aren't other, more deserving, applications farther down in the pile. Reconsideration at the end is always a possibility, but it is somewhat unlikely given that it requires the energy-consuming challenge of refocusing the panelists' attention on the specifics of a particular proposal. As one anthropologist explained: "I feel that if the meeting had gone another day, and if we had been allowed to pull people out of the 'yes' list and change our minds, there might have been six or seven or eight switches."

Panelists' intellectual exhaustion after two days of intense work also affects how they carry out their task, especially near the end. In particular, during the two days they spend together, panelists often develop a common sense of humor, a group culture of sorts, which may disrupt the seriousness of the deliberations. An art historian observes, "I think as people get more and more tired, certain topics that emerged, people made fun of and became sort of the butt of the joke right through to the very end."[41] Interestingly, because of time pressures (panelists had flights to catch), one of the panels I studied did not distribute all the fellowships it had at its disposal. This is a strong reminder that despite its many otherworldly aspects, judging academic excellence is a process shaped by real-world constraints.

Conclusion

Scholars engaged in grant peer review claim to pursue and honor excellence, and indeed excellence is what holds the academic enterprise together, if not consistently then at least some of the time. The sense of fairness in the pursuit of this objective is maintained by the technology of peer review and by the customary rules described here. Following the rules, which are sometimes revealed most fully when breached, discourages corruption and thus helps ensure that the best proposals are identified.

This chapter has focused on the conventional (that is, widely agreed on) supra-individual rules. Following these rules influences the likely success of arguments—how they will be heard—at least as much as their content (the focus of Chapter 5). The world I described is not one where elites from different evaluative regimes mutually bless one another, nor is it one where narrow social networks coordinate their efforts to engage in opportunity hoarding.[42] I do not deny that such logics of action are present in academia, but my analysis has revealed that it is not all there is—and it may not be the main thing there is. Breaching some of these rules (the rule about bracketing self-interest, for instance) offends panelists' sense of how things are and should be. Other rules have more to do with the emotional management of panels and are oriented toward ensuring that the process works and that the self-concept of panelists is not violated (the rule about respecting disciplinary sovereignty is one example). These mandates influence the overall feeling that emanates from panels and help generate an emotional energy that makes the enterprise of peer grant review more "sacred" and legitimate.[43]

The picture that emerges from this review of the customary rules is that of an imperfect but satisfactory system. Strategic voting, horse-trading, self-interest, and idiosyncratic and inconsistent criteria all are unavoidable parts of the equation. Equally important, panelists' comments and observations show that the act of evaluating is an eminently interactional and emotional undertaking, rather than a cognitive process corrupted by extra-cognitive factors. More specifically:

- The context of evaluation is crucial.[44] Proposals are evaluated relationally, in comparison with other proposals. The universe of comparison is not stable, nor are the criteria.
- Panelists support a pragmatic understanding of fairness that is at odds with the ideal of considering only the intrinsic qualities of proposals. Because many of the judgments are relational and conjectural, panelists have to think strategically about what they can realistically accomplish.
- The influence of interpersonal relationships, including clientelism, cannot be totally eliminated from the evaluation process, because scholarly expertise is superimposed onto the social networks of those who produce knowledge, including, in this case, both applicants and evaluators.
- Idiosyncratic evaluations are almost unavoidable, yet they are usually presented in universalistic terms and seamlessly folded into formal criteria of evaluation.
- Respecting the customary rules of deliberations is crucial for accumulating credibility with co-panelists (a necessary condition for making one's label "stick" to a proposal) and for facilitating deliberations.

It should be remembered that belief in the fairness of the process is not shared throughout academia. It is likely that scholars invited to serve on panels have strongly internalized the view that peer review "works." Moreover, it is reasonable to surmise that the more successful the scholar, the more likely he or she is to accept and endorse the sacred values of the group—and further, that panelists are generally very successful, given that program officers consider prestige when recruiting members. Those who never apply for or receive grants and fellowships may be more likely to believe that the allocation system is particularistic and based on cronyism. Nevertheless, the belief in its legitimacy is strong enough to animate the general process of grant peer review, in the United States at least.

The processes of evaluation documented in this chapter apply to multidisciplinary panels. Unidisciplinary panels follow different rules.[45] The rule of disciplinary sovereignty, for instance, may not apply, and there may be more competition to appropriate the right to speak on a topic when members all are from the same discipline and know one another, at least by reputation. Moreover, the fact that panelists must convince one another of the value of a proposal certainly contributes to their belief in the legitimacy of the process. In contrast, evaluations of journal submissions are conducted in the privacy of a reviewer's office or home and are not defended publicly. This may leave more room for greater personal arbitrariness.

The analysis in this chapter downplayed the effects of panelists' disciplines and institutional affiliations on how they are heard on panels, that is, how much weight is given to their opinion, who gets the benefit of the doubt, and who defers to whom. It also underemphasized the degree to which the same rules apply whether the knowledge being evaluated is more or less technical. Addressing these issues would require having detailed observational data on pecking orders, and paying attention to differences across panels rather than similarities. Nevertheless, I have provided clear evidence of the importance of both collegiality and respect for customary rules. Future research should detail which rules are most faithfully respected by panelists from various disciplines, and which rules are most respected across all panels, including those for competitions not considered here.

5/Recognizing Various Kinds of Excellence

I
n *The University in Ruins,* the literary scholar Bill Readings remarks that "the idea of excellence" is ubiquitously evoked in academic contexts, yet little consensus exists concerning its meaning.
As a term, it "has the singular advantage of being entirely meaningless, or to put it more precisely, non-referential."[1] As panelists are
very much aware, excellence is a quintessential polymorphic term. A
sociologist notes, "There are different standards of excellence, different kinds of excellence," yet is nevertheless "pretty confident that I'd
know it when I see it." This chapter spells out what this "it" is that
panelists easily recognize but cannot always clearly articulate. As we
will see, understanding the various meanings that reviewers attach to
the evaluative criteria they use is at least as important as identifying
the criteria themselves. In addition, the weight given to criteria—favoring intellectual significance over social significance, for instance—
imponderably affects the outcome of deliberations and may have to
do with differences in "intellectual habitus" across disciplinary clusters.[2]

In their classic work *The Academic Revolution,* Christopher Jencks and David Riesman observed that in the modern university, "claims of localism, sectarianism, ethnic prejudice and preference, class background, age, sex, and even occupational plans are largely ignored."[3] This remains the official credo of American higher education. The only sectarianism that is deemed acceptable is that of "high quality scholarship"—and it is in this context that particularistic considerations gain a footing. This is why it is crucial to look closely at how excellence is coded, signaled, and recognized.

In this chapter, I draw on the concept of "scripts" to analyze the meanings and relative importance panelists assign to the criteria they use to evaluate excellence." Borrowing from the sociologist Erving Goffman's concept of script, we can posit that individuals do not invent their standards of excellence anew. They draw on their environment and use shared conventions to make sense of their world.[4] To show how panel members go about making sense of their role in the world of evaluation, I begin by discussing the evidence on which they base their judgments: the proposal, the applicant, and the letters of recommendation. As we will see, these types of evidence receive different weight; the proposal, for example, counts much more than the letters. Next, I turn to how panelists interpret the formal categories that funding agencies ask them to consider. Again, the literature on peer review has focused on the weighting of evaluative criteria, leaving unexplored the meanings that evaluators assign to the criteria they use to assess excellence.[5] Here, I analyze responses provided by panelists during post-deliberation interviews to gain a better understanding of such meanings. I start by discussing clarity and "quality," the latter being shorthand for craftsmanship, depth, and thoroughness. I then turn to the more substantive criteria of originality, significance (scholarly and social/political), "methods" (which includes the articulation between theory, method, and data, and the proper use of theory), and feasibility (the applicant's readiness and track record, and the plan of work). Finally, I address the more evanescent qualities that are valued by panelists, most of which pertain more to the applicant than to the project. These evanescent qualities include which proposals and applicants generate "excitement" and which are "elegant" and "intelligent." Informal standards also include the proper display of "cultural capital" and perceptions of the moral quality of the applicant, particularly in relation to the authenticity of her intellectual commitment.

For seasoned evaluators, the ground covered in this chapter will be familiar; for more junior scholars and others still attempting to find the magic formula for winning fellowships, the discussion will provide a (sometimes surprising) picture of what defines a good proposal. We will see not only how frequently panelists mention the formal and informal criteria just noted, and which criteria they weight most heavily, but also the breadth of meanings attached to specific criteria. In the case of originality, for instance, the range of meanings used by panelists is much wider than has been posited by the positivist tradition. And with respect to evanescent qualities, we will see that more than half of the panelists accord these criteria sizable significance. I argue that moral considerations and class signals (namely, "elegance" and "cultural capital"), although they are somewhat antithetical to a merit-based award system, are intrinsic to the process of evaluation in academia.

Elements of the Proposal

As we saw in Chapter 2, the evidence on which screeners and panelists base their judgments normally includes information concerning the research project (project description, including bibliography and timetable), information about the applicant (biographical sketch, personal statement, curriculum vitae, publications/portfolio, grade transcript, teaching experience and interest, and statement of commitment to the goals of the program), supporting material (letters of recommendation), and, for the panelists, comments and a ranking assigned by the screeners.

Panelists understand proposals as part of a genre—as having certain recognizable characteristics and following certain known conventions, all of which give evaluators a basis for comparison and a common language for discussion. An anthropologist alludes to an element of this established genre when he remarks, "The first paragraph [should] make it clear what's going on . . . [we're] reading a twenty-page grant proposal in five minutes." And an English professor underscores the convention of discussing the "significance of [the] project, to convey a certain importance or excitement about the project [even if it is] a study of Greek coins from the second century BC. Why this is something that's worth doing, whether it's because it'll change the way we think about money or because it will tell us something about Greek society at this particular time, or simply because it'll tell you something about these objects that's new and interesting." Proposals that do not adhere to such conventions are doomed, despite any intrinsic interest they might have.

Yet some conventions also generate skepticism, because "anyone who's ever written [a proposal] knows that you [have to] sound convincing even about things you're not sure about." Thus panelists understand that proposal writing requires a certain amount of "impression management" or "bullshit."[6] A convincing proposal does not guarantee that the applicant really knows what he or she will be doing. But such limitations are construed as unavoidable in an imperfect and sometimes opaque system in which all parties have limited control. As we will see, many panelists believe that the authenticity of an applicant's intellectual engagement shines through in a proposal—and in fact they may impose what they call a "bullshit penalty" on proposals that seem shallow and formulaic. This is why proposals describing projects that are well advanced often are selected for funding, even when such decisions are at odds with a funding program's explicit objectives (such as to support fieldwork).

Advanced projects strike reviewers as almost "always better" because they are more specific, complete, and "elegant." Here the "bullshit penalty" does not necessarily apply because, in the words of one evaluator, "What difference does it make at what point the person gets the money? It's a reward for doing the work." Thus panelists, as well as applicants, appear to understand the rules of the game as being somewhat fluid and fuzzy.

Competition guidelines (described in Chapter 2) often emphasize that evaluators should focus on the strengths of the proposal, as opposed to the past record of the applicant. This is in line with funding agencies' commitment to a merit-based ethos. An economist feels that "it's unfair to those that spent a lot of time on those [proposals] to give . . . preference to someone's record." An English professor also makes the case for focusing on the proposal because "it is not always the case that [people who have the best track record] have put together the best proposals." Whether the competition supports graduate students or senior professors influences how much weight is put on track record or, alternatively, on likely future trajectory (measured in terms of promise and/or projected mobility). In either case, funding agencies do require consideration of the applicant in the assessment of merit. A standard question posed to panelists is, "Is this person well equipped to complete the project that is proposed?" Letters of support written by advisers and other supporters answer this question, but they address issues well beyond technical competence and preparation. Letters signal cultural capital, elegance, and other class-based evanescent qualities. The influence of letters is limited, however: a surprisingly large number of panelists (twenty-five of seventy-one) say that they pay little or no attention to letters, mainly because they are so often formulaic, hyperbolic, or uninformative.[7] As a historian puts it, "We had so many superlatives that, sometimes, it's hard to know how to interpret them."

Against this skepticism, panelists develop distinctive schemas to assess the value of letters, taking more seriously those that "conveyed a sense of excitement about the project," which can be produced only if the letter writer has immersed herself in the work. "All of the others, 'This is the best person in his or her field,' and of course, 'this is crucial and should be funded,' blah, blah, blah . . . They are assembly-line letters," an anthropologist says dismissively. "You know, everybody was 'the best in the field,' everybody was doing something that was 'the most important research.'" Similarly, a philosopher counterintuitively declares, "The more terms of praise I see in a letter, the less attention I gave to it. The more description I see, the more attention. If you just say 'it's great,' you're just passing the buck, in a way. We can't tell if it's great without knowing it, and knowing it is itself a sign of admiration . . . I see it myself, people I admire, I write about their projects. When I need to throw something off, I write 'Great! Brilliant!'" For an economist, "It's the specificity that matters . . . about what a student has done and how specific skills will influence a research topic." But if the applicant is unable to make a convincing case, no letter will tip the balance. It is the combination of strong letters and a great proposal that creates the conditions for building a consensus on quality, or even on "hotness" in fields that are more subject to bandwagon effects.[8]

The letters that count most are of two types. Those that explain a project's importance in specific terms and locate it in the literature can be, as one historian explains, "very, very helpful if they help someone like me who might not be particularly well read in a field to understand precisely why we should be interested." Similarly, those written by individuals whom panelists know personally or through their work can be very persuasive (see Chapter 3). An English scholar's explanation of why he particularly values a colleague's opinion illustrates how such a letter can influence one's judgment:

Diane Middlebrook is somebody I know, not real well, but we
have a lot of mutual friends. I've read her work, I've read other

letters of hers. I trust [them] and her intellect. She's not going to pump a candidate up, and she's also not going to deflate a candidate because they have some kind of [conflict] . . . She's somebody who has intellectual integrity.[9]

Similarly, a philosopher says that he assigned significant weight to a letter by the Nobel Prize–winning economist Amartya Sen because "He knows how to judge brilliance. He's had a lot of very brilliant people around him in his life." The same is said about another Nobel laureate, the Berkeley economist George Akerloff. To the extent that applicants located in more prestigious universities have greater access to well-known and well-connected letter writers, these applicants will likely be advantaged by those evaluators who put considerable weight on letters.[10]

Some panelists believe that letters are important in their "signaling" role, independent of their specific content.[11] Indeed, letters convey prestige, or a measure of quality, by association—the famous halo effect.[12] As one political scientist says, "I make judgments based on my knowledge of how distinguished the writer is, but I pay very little attention to what the writer actually says, because it's very hard to discriminate among the letters." The signaling effect of letters can be so strong as to override other factors. A philosopher provided this cautionary tale about a graduate student in his department: "We had to write his dissertation for him, but the description I had given on it was so good, he had twelve interviews. No one looked at him again after the interview. Since then, I've tried to be careful [to better align the letter with the accomplishments]." One political scientist says that because she "wants a clean sense of things," she makes up her mind solely on the basis of the proposal. She uses letters to revise her evaluation or as supporting evidence. Another panelist avoids reading the names of the letter writers until he has read the entire dossier, so as to equalize the playing field.

Six Criteria for Recognizing Excellence

Chapter 2 described the formal criteria that funding agencies ask panelists to consider in making awards (see especially Table 2.1). Chapter 3 provided a general analysis of disciplinary peculiarities with respect to what constitutes excellence. Here, I identify trends in panelists' understanding and use of evaluative criteria by regrouping these disciplines into the standard categories of humanities and social sciences, but I continue to treat history as its own category, standing between the humanities and social sciences. Table 5.1 shows the relative salience of formal criteria (defined as the number of times that respondents mention using each) across these disciplinary clusters.

The six criteria do not each receive the same weight. Originality, for example, is more heavily weighted than is feasibility (see Table 5.1.) Conflicts emerge over how much weight should be given to each criterion—to rigor versus innovation, for instance. One historian describes how he supported a proposal on what seemed to be a "cool idea": "My attraction to it was that I just could see the book, you know, and I was thinking this would be a really excellent, readable, teachable book, around a compelling idea . . . [It would] produce a kind of quality different than the usual more kind of massaged and theoretically sophisticated and careerist [project]. You know, I mean, it was something outside." An economist, who puts much more emphasis on methods and rigor, strongly opposed this proposal, despite its innovative character. Thus different standards are applied to the same proposals. Moreover, proposals do not win or lose for the same reasons. The social sciences and the humanities make up a multifaceted academic world; there is no single, integrated disciplinary hierarchy. Different pieces of scholarship shine under different lights. Many cross-cutting scholarly approaches partly reinforce one another, but also sometimes cancel one another

Table 5.1 Number of panelists mentioning each criterion, by disciplinary cluster

Criterion	Humanities (N = 22)	History (N = 20)	Social sciences (N = 29)	Total (N = 71)
Clarity	15 (68%)	16 (80%)	12 (41%)	43 (61%)
"Quality"	9 (41%)	8 (40%)	15 (52%)	32 (45%)
Originality	18 (82%)	19 (95%)	26 (90%)	63 (89%)
Significance	19 (86%)	19 (95%)	27 (93%)	65 (92%)
Methods	9 (41%)	11 (55%)	21 (72%)	41 (58%)
Feasibility	10 (45%)	11 (55%)	15 (52%)	36 (51%)

Note: A "mention" occurs when a criterion is used during the interview.

out. One anthropologist directly connects the valuing of a wide range of topics and types of scholarship with different standards of excellence. She traces this connection to the emergence of feminism in academia, and to the awareness of how power relationships shape criteria. "[There is] more than one model of excellence," she asserts. This view will be confirmed throughout this chapter, as we examine the main criteria of evaluation, starting with clarity and "quality."

Clarity and "Quality"

Only the ACLS, WWNFF, and SSRC specify clarity as a formal criterion of evaluation, but it is often the first characteristic that panelists mention when describing how they separate the wheat from the chaff. Although clarity is of greater importance to historians and humanists than to social scientists, in the aggregate, 61 percent of panelists who were asked to name their most important criteria for measuring excellence mentioned clarity, defining it in terms as varied as luminescence, transparency, precision, analytical articulation, crispness, and tightness (see Table 5.1.) That it is not explicitly mentioned by more reviewers indicates how taken-for-granted it is as a sine qua non for excellence. Particularly with respect to the proposal, form is as important as substance: it is a prerequisite for running the race. This is in part because of the time constraints typically faced by panelists as they make their way through a pile of applications. Panelists "are paid very little," a musicologist notes. "They're given a mountain of material, which they have to plow through and assess . . . What they principally do is deselect . . . as opposed to looking for ones that they really want to fund. So if you write poorly or you simply write in such a way that bores people, you're not likely . . . to surface." Similarly, a political scientist says, "The best proposals are the ones I didn't have to work at."

For many panelists, a clear writing style is a manifestation of a clear and orderly intellect. "The quality of writing says something about the clarity of the mind," an English professor remarks, adding, "To me, it is more important than whether the proposal is completely precise." Another English professor sees "a prose style that can handle complex ideas in a clear fashion" as indicating a sharp intelligence. Clarity is also taken to reveal competence ("It was written with a kind of clarity that made me feel that a person knows what they're talking about") and how much care applicants put into their proposals. This is because luminescence, transparency, precision, analytical articulation, and "crisp, tight, taut sentences" can be achieved only through the repeated polishing of successive drafts. Thus, a clear proposal, according to one English professor, "makes me feel confident that they will write a good book . . . if it's not carefully written, it makes me worry about thoughtfulness . . . the depth of thinking."

"Quality," like "excellence," is a catch-all referent that panelists persistently mobilize. Mentioned by 45 percent of the respondents, quality manifests itself through "craftsmanship," "depth," "attention to details," and "soundness." These in turn are associated with "rigor" and "solidity," with all of the terms used interchangeably to designate applicants who invest extra effort in creating their proposals.

Craftsmanship is admired by a sociologist who, when asked if he believes in academic excellence, answers, "If what we mean by excellence is honest work, well-crafted work, pretty much scholarship as craft, I believe in it." Elaborating, he stresses "work that's true to the data." He associates excellence "with [producing] work that is based upon good quality scholarship . . . *It is ethics, plus the craft* [my emphasis]." Similarly, a political scientist who "cares very much about the finished product" cautions that "to be a craftsman without insight or creativity, you know, that wouldn't work to create good objects. You have to be creative as well." Depth, another aspect of quality, is the dimension that humanists tend to stress most. A historian of China's description of a high-quality proposal reflects this concern: "There was a lot of historical work going into this one . . . but also depth. The statement had nuance in it. It was authoritatively written. You felt that this guy was full of respect and engagement and at the same time, had a certain kind of distance that would allow him to do really high-quality studies." Prevailing definitions of quality also frequently include praise for attention to detail. Thus a sociologist emphasizes thoroughness and describes his own work as being particularly strong on "rigorous historical analysis, which means not just sticking to the secondary sources, but also going to the primary sources." A historian emphasizes the applicant's thorough deliberation of research choices.

Finally, in defining quality, many respondents emphasize scholarly and empirical soundness. For the humanists, scholarly soundness is measured by the details and accuracy of the proposal. Thus, proposals that include factual errors are eliminated promptly. A historian recalled a losing proposal that was "riddled with historical anachronisms, historical assumptions that were just wrong, and yet [the applicant] used buzz words that were sort of trendy and would attract interest. It was kind of disingenuous." Empirical soundness is defined in opposition to the use of anecdotes and to what a music scholar describes as "spouting opinion." It is also frequently contrasted with the haphazard collection of evidence and with superficial "trendiness." A sociologist compares losers and winners this way:

> This one proposal on eighteenth-century Romanian national history was highly scholarly, absolutely in [the] forefront of debates on nationalism. It was empirically sound in particular research lights. And it seemed very detailed and he got the money because the Good Lord lives in details . . . Some of the trendy ones [that were not funded] were so much concerned with concepts . . . They were more about how we address certain things rather than actually the things themselves.

A political scientist concurs, describing scholarship she likes as work that "brings a lot of evidence to their arguments . . . I like Adam Przeworski's work, although it, like mine, takes a different form. I like projects where the author has really gone to a lot of trouble to legitimate what they said. And they can do that with case studies or through large and quantitative studies." In teaching her graduate students how to produce high-quality research, she directs them "to look at their variables very critically," "to look carefully at feasibility," to marshal "lots of evidence," and to bring many "different kinds of lenses" to their research problem.

Originality, Significance, Methods, and Feasibility

In discussing what defines the substantive quality of a project, respondents from all three disciplinary clusters seem to draw on shared "scripts" of excellence—sets of definitions and decision pathways in which originality and significance play a central role, with methods and feasibility also in crucial, but less widely agreed-on, positions. No clear patterns differentiate humanists, social scientists, and historians in how much importance they attach to any of these four criteria. As shown in Table 5.1, originality is mentioned at least once by 89 percent of the panelists, significance by 92 percent, methods (meaning theory, data, method, and the articulation of the three) by 58 percent, and feasibility by 51 percent.

Many forms of originality.   The canonical sociological literature on the place of originality in scientific evaluation has defined originality, following Robert K. Merton, as the making of a new discovery that adds to scientific knowledge. Merton asserted that "it is through originality, in greater or smaller increments, that knowledge advances."[13] Thomas Kuhn expanded this understanding of originality by pointing out distinctions in how novel theories are received. Characterizing scientific communities as generally resistant to paradigmatic shifts, Kuhn argued that new discoveries confirming the theories of "normal science" are the mainstay of the scientific endeavor, while anomalous discoveries and consensus-challenging theories are seldom welcomed, and usually ignored.

Numerous scholars have built on this literature, and others have examined various aspects of the peer review process. No one, however, has yet questioned the specific assumption that originality consists of making new discoveries or producing new theories. For instance, although Bruno Latour and others have criticized the literature's emphasis on priority disputes, how academics define and go about assessing originality remains unexamined.[14] And although the canonical definition of originality arose from studies of the natural sciences and was not—at least not explicitly—intended to apply more broadly, it often is applied to the social sciences. The extent to which this definition characterizes the understanding of originality in the social sciences or humanities is still an open question.

Elsewhere, my colleagues Joshua Guetzkow, Grégoire Mallard, and I analyzed the way the panelists describe originality and found that their descriptions point toward a much broader definition than that posited in the literature.[15] We constructed a typology to classify the panelists' definitions. These categories of originality, shown in Table 5.2, include using a new approach, theory, method, or data (for example, original research is seen as "bringing a fresh perspective" or "drawing on new sources of information"); and studying a new topic, doing research in an understudied area, or producing new findings (such as when the researcher ventures "outside canonized authors"). We found differences by disciplinary cluster. Humanists and historians tend to define originality differently than do social scientists: they clearly privilege originality in approach, with humanists also emphasizing originality in the data used—with the uncovering of new texts and authors given special prominence (see Table 5.3). Social scientists most often mention originality in method, but they also seem to appreciate a more diverse range of types of originality, stressing the use of an original approach or theory, or the study of an original topic. Overall, this diversity strongly confirms the need for a more multidimensional definition of originality, at least as far as the humanities and social sciences are concerned.

Scholarly and political or social significance. Four of the five funding agencies I studied specified significance as a formal criterion of selection. Yet most funding institutions allow some ambiguity in how the term is defined. Here, following the lead of the panel members, I distinguish between scholarly (intellectual or theoretical) significance and social or political significance. Scholarly significance is determined on the basis of whether a project is likely to produce generalizable results and/or speak to broad theoretical questions or processes, as opposed to addressing narrowly defined or highly abstract topics. A project with social or political significance is believed to give voice to subordinate groups or produce socially useful knowledge. Further distinctions include those between the significance of a

Table 5.2 Frequencies of mentions of generic and specific types of originality

			Generic types (N = 217)											
Original approach	Freq. (%)	Understudied area	Freq. (%)	Original topic	Freq. (%)	Original theory	Freq. (%)	Original method	Freq. (%)	Original data	Freq. (%)	Original results	Freq. (%)
New approach	5 (7)	Understudied region	7 (54)	New topic	9 (28)	New theory	5 (13)	Innovative method or research design	5 (19)	New data	15 (52)	New insights	5 (56)
New question	21 (31)	Understudied period	6 (46)	Non-canonical topic	20 (63)	Connecting/mapping ideas	12 (30)	Synthesis of methods	10 (37)	Multiple sources	10 (34)	New findings	4 (44)
New perspective	11 (16)			Topic choice is unconventional	3 (9)	Synthesis of literatures	12 (30)	New use of old data	7 (26)	Non-canonical data	4 (14)		
New approach to tired/trendy topic	10 (15)					New application of existing theory	5 (13)	Resolve old question or debate	3 (11)				
New connections	8 (12)					Reconceptualizing	4 (10)	Innovative for discipline	2 (7)				
New argument	6 (9)					Unconventional use of theory	2 (5)						
Innovative for the discipline	6 (9)												
Total	67 (100)		13 (100)		32 (100)		40 (100)		27 (100)		29 (100)		9 (100)
Total as % of all types	31		6		15		18		12		13		4

Specific types

Source: Guetzkow, Lamont, and Mallard (2004).

Table 5.3 Frequency of mentions of generic definitions of originality, by disciplinary cluster

Originality type	Humanities		History		Social sciences		Total	
	N	%	N	%	N	%	N	%
Approach	29	33	26	43	12	18	67	31
Data	19	21	6	10	4	6	29	13
Theory	16	18	11	18	13	19	40	18
Topic	13	15	6	10	13	19	32	15
Method	4	4	5	8	18	27	27	12
Outcome	3	3	4	7	2	3	9	4
Understudied area	5	6	3	5	5	7	13	6
All generic types	89	100	61	100	67	100	217	100

Source: Guetzkow, Lamont, and Mallard (2004).
Note: A "mention" occurs when a criterion is used during the interview. Some columns do not sum to 100% due to rounding.

research topic and the significance of the likely impact of research findings—on academia as a whole, on one's discipline, on knowledge—as well as the social and/or political impact of the research. Table 5.4 shows the distribution of panelists' references to these categories as they discussed the proposals during post-deliberation interviews. Significance of impact is mentioned slightly more often than significance of topic. Overall, panelists are more concerned with the project's likely influence on knowledge and on academia than with the social or political impact of the research. But there are differences among the panelists by discipline. Predictably, humanists are most concerned with the intellectual significance of the topic, while historians and social scientists are slightly more concerned with the topic's political and social significance.

As mentioned in Chapter 3, and explained in detail elsewhere, panelists use one or more of four different epistemological styles as they evaluate and discuss proposals.[16] These styles—"constructivist," "comprehensive," "positivist," and "utilitarian"—vary in terms of the

Table 5.4 Number of panelists mentioning significance criteria, by disciplinary cluster

	Humanities		History		Social sciences		Total	
	N	%	N	%	N	%	N	%
Significance of topic	16	73	16	80	17	85	49	69
Intellectual	15	68*	10	50	9	31	34	48
Political and social	10	45	13	65	17	59	40	56
Significance of impact	16	73	18	90	24	83	58	82
On academia	8	36	9	45	14	48	31	44
On field	8	36	8	40	6	21	22	31
On knowledge	7	32	12	60	14	48	33	46
Political	5	23	2	10	9	31	16	23
Social	5	23	5	25	13	45	23	32
Total	19	86**	19	95	27	93	65	91

Note: A "mention" occurs when a criterion is used during the interview.

*Percentage of all humanists who use "intellectual significance" as a criterion of evaluation.

** Some panelists referred to more than one type of significance.

methodological approach they privilege (in a nutshell: reductivism versus *verstehen*), and whether they are grounded in "knowledge for knowledge's sake" (privileged in the comprehensive and positivist styles) or "knowledge for the sake of social change" (privileged in the constructivist and utilitarian styles). In Table 5.5, the main styles that panelists referred to during our interviews are delineated and contrasted according to the elements valued and prioritized by each style. As Table 5.6 shows, three-quarters of the panelists favor the comprehensive style, which privileges knowledge for knowledge's sake, in describing how they evaluated proposals. This style predominates in all the competitions but one. Overall, it is used by 86 percent of the humanists, 78 percent of the historians, and 71 percent of the social scientists. Use of the other three styles is as we would expect—far more social scientists favor the positivist style than do either historians or humanists; and considerably more humanists and historians use the constructivist style than do social scientists. What is of most

Table 5.5 Most important epistemological styles, as indicated by panelists' interview responses

Epistemological style	Positive evaluation	
	Theoretical style	*Methodological style*
Constructivist	When the proposal presents personal, political, and social elements as relevant to research	When the proposal shows attention to details and to the complexity of the empirical object
Comprehensive	When the proposal emphasizes a substantially informed rationale for research and a theoretically informed agenda	When the proposal shows attention to details and to the complexity of the empirical object
Positivist	When the proposal aims to generalize empirical findings, disprove theories, and solve a theoretical puzzle	When the proposal seeks to test alternative hypotheses using a formal model enclosing the world in a defined set of variables
Utilitarian	When the proposal seeks to generalize findings, disprove theories, and solve puzzles related to "real world" problems	When the proposal seeks to test alternative hypotheses using a formal model with a defined set of variables

interest here is not the detail of these distributions but the variety and range of panel members' understandings of what constitutes significance. How do these various understandings shape the way in which these panelists make distinctions regarding scholarly versus social significance?

In *Of the Standard of Taste*, the philosopher David Hume suggests that the appreciation of beauty is "best construed as an idealized, counterfactual ruling, or as the combined opinion of near-ideal critics," that is, "true judges" and experts.[17] Similarly, judgments about scholarly significance can be made only by those who have great

Table 5.6 Number of panelists using each epistemological style, by disciplinary cluster

Epistemological style	Humanities		History		Social sciences			
	N	%	N	%	N	%	N	%
Constructivist	4	28	4	29	3	14	11	22
Comprehensive	12	86	11	78	15	71	38	78
Positivist	0	0	3	23	11	57	14	29
Utilitarian	0	0	1	4	4	19	5	10
Total	14		14		21		49	

Note: Since each interviewee may use more than one style, columns do not sum to 100 percent.

expertise regarding the current state of knowledge in a particular field and about what remains to be done. As one such expert explains, "I'm much more surefooted in my own field, where . . . I can make silver judgments, or more confident judgments, where . . . I'm intimately familiar with the research topic." Of course, there are often disagreements about how much work is needed on a topic. A political scientist addresses this question: "[A panelist] was saying, 'There's too much work on the welfare state.' Frankly, I think he's wrong that there's a bunch of stuff on the welfare state on the particular country she's looking at. Even if you threw that part away, [the proposal] is at the intersection of the "transitions to democracy" [literature] as well . . . It spoke to two huge, maybe the two biggest literatures, in political science today." Thus, determining scholarly significance can depend on personal taste as well as on expertise. An English scholar confirms this fact as he contrasts his own intellectual inclinations with those of a friend who is a literary critic: "[My friend] thinks cultural currents, trends, intellectual history, that's where the action is. The kind of stuff I do in my last book, where I show how much is going on in simple words or paragraphs, he thinks that's just a kind of self-indulgence, like playing around."

Determining significance is also a question of perspective, of the lenses that one privileges. This too is influenced by personal taste. For many social scientists, "to go beyond the anecdotal," to "generalize," are elements of a shared script of excellence. To wit, an economist estimates significance by "theoretical contribution," defined in terms of generalization. "Fundamental theory should apply [everywhere]," he says. When evaluating the significance of a project, he inquires, "Is [the project asking] a detailed question or is it a question that really covers multiple countries and multiple constituencies in multiple countries? If it's an issue that looks at specific aspects relevant for other countries, I would define it as having a broader relevance." A political scientist, though, is skeptical of generalization and law-like statements, "because you can't do it. And, in fact, most people now understand that they can't do it, but there are things about the discipline that reward it anyway." The alternative to generalization is to demonstrate scholarly significance by discussing the theoretical implications of particular studies (in line with the comprehensive epistemological style). This is the approach valued by a panelist who describes himself as a "micro-level social historian." He explains that "it is possible to do detailed studies and place them in a broader comparative framework that brings out its significance for broader things" (such as identity, globalization, inequality, aesthetics, meaning, race, or gender). This approach contrasts with that of a "narrow proposal" that will not be of interest to other scholars. A political scientist justifies the rejection of a "superb proposal for research on a very narrow period" in French history because there was no "knowledge of potential interest outside the specialization of that particular scholar." In all these examples, panelists express taste preferences that are informed by expertise.

Socially and/or politically significant research usually is equated with producing instrumental knowledge and "giving voice" to underrepresented groups. These approaches correspond to the utilitarian and constructivist epistemological styles. The concern with instrumental knowledge is illustrated by a panelist who, in citing John Maynard Keynes as one of his intellectual heroes, says of Keynes: "He was another one of these people who combined very advanced theoretical and abstract thinking about economics, but would never be drifting off the focus on the real world, from a concern with [what to do] to solve problems of the day." For her part, a political scientist takes policy implications very seriously because "it's the only way that we can justify what we do . . . my bias is towards things that are going to make people's lives better . . . Because I think intellectuals are leeches if they don't do that." She favors research "that has some real meaning in the way that power is distributed, or in terms of the solution of social problems."[18]

Illustrating the concern with "giving voice," a cultural studies scholar explains that significance means "potential social significance, as opposed to more narcissistic or solipsistic activity, or . . . simply a sort of gentleperson's activity . . . Scholarship ought to have more impact than simply personal pleasure of a hobby . . . It's important to consider the work of diasporic peoples, of women as opposed to simply men, of popular and folk idioms in addition to elite music." In the 1960s and 1970s, the "invasion" of French theory and the growing influence of Marxism, feminism, and post-structuralism put the "power-culture link" at the center of the intellectual agenda for many humanistic disciplines.[19] This perspective permeates the evaluative scripts used by many panelists, as illustrated by an English professor who remarks, "I don't think a cultural study even comes close to completion if it doesn't offer some reflection on how this cultural phenomenon intersects with power relations . . . I would think that something's missing if gender wasn't included, if race and/or national identity, or some other factor of that kind, is left out." A historian assesses a project's significance in terms of its urgency and timeliness for our understanding of society. So of studying racism, he says, "If we can understand the dynamics of how this arises and how it is preserved . . . that could be valuable." One Marxist historian of post-colonialism admits that political considerations influence his evaluation of proposals. Inspired by the British Marxist historian E. P. Thompson, this panelist is unsympathetic to "certain types of transnational post-modern bit of stuff that follow a particular line that I don't have much of an instinctive sympathy towards."

Unlike assigning weight to scholarly significance, for some panelists, factoring in social relevance raises many concerns. A South Asian historian says, "I would hate to think that academics and academic excellence [are] purely instrumental," in part because the effects of knowledge are rarely immediate. Similarly, an English scholar advocates knowledge for knowledge's sake and beauty for beauty's sake: "I think that the arts and humanities don't need to be justified on the grounds of social usefulness. It is a capitulation to try to talk about that." Others are critical of an instrumental conception of knowledge because they view it as leading to "subjectivism." Indeed, 45 percent of the respondents mention concern with bias when discussing the evaluation of proposals. Yet others echo Bourdieu's analysis of the functioning of scientific fields when they refuse to subordinate research to what they perceive as neoliberal instrumentalism. They defend the autonomy of academia against logics of action driven by political or economic pursuits.[20]

These tensions surrounding social significance are illustrated by differences in opinion between a geographer and an anthropologist. The geographer explains that he is inspired by issues of inequality: "I love . . . thinking about issues of the subaltern, the disadvantaged, and sort of trying to be a medium of communication in their situation and plight, and to also work with concepts of indigenous knowledge . . . I'm very much politically committed to diversity of lived experience on this planet." But an anthropologist criticizes this panelist as too easily swayed by political considerations: "There were proposals on environmental issues he would read and argue for, even though they were terrible proposals and everybody thought they were terrible proposals. He said, 'Well, this is an important environmental problem.' . . . It could be an important problem, but if you don't know how to study it, you're not going to really help to solve it." Reaffirming the positivist credo, an economist believes good scholarship is incompatible with advocacy: "The definition of an academic is someone who doesn't believe anything until [proven]. That begs the question of what are your hypotheses, what is your default position, which could be subject to all kinds of intrinsic, political, ideological, or just national bias." But a political scientist criticizes what he calls this economist's "pseudo-neutral" position of objectivity. "His politics were different from mine and he was very clear about, you know, 'I don't have a viewpoint. Either the person is biased or unbiased.' But he would pull the [neutrality] card when he was reading proposals by lefties." This political scientist questions whether social significance is an appropriate criterion of evaluation. He says: "I've never seen proposals that are socially useful . . . I don't think it's more significant that someone wants to work on refugee camps in Rwanda . . . [or on] French Maoism, because we really are social scientists who are defining [ourselves] in a particular career path, which is going to be about theory and teaching in universities."

Methods and the proper use of theory. Four of the five funding programs I studied, as well as others, often mention methods as a criterion of interest. Here again, there is a great deal of variation and ambiguity regarding the aspects of methods that are emphasized. For instance, the SSRC program mentions "responsiveness to methodological concerns" and "rationale for field work" as aspects of method that proposals should address. The anonymous social science foundation asks that proposals adopt a methodology appropriate for the goal for the research. Given this variation, I focus here on a specific aspect of methods that is correlated with quality: the articulation of theory and data. This is a topic of concern for roughly half of all respondents, but nearly three-quarters of the social scientists rank it as important (as compared to less than half of the humanists). It also figures prominently in graduate training in the social sciences. A historian of China provides a good description of the importance of the alignment between theory and data when she explains that combining several types of evidence helps produce a solid proposal. Drawing an analogy with crafting a table, she says, "The size of the table and the sturdiness of the table depend on how many legs [it has] and where they're placed . . . The table with one leg that is a broad generalization with one little foundation doesn't work. Four solid foundations, well, that's solid." A political scientist's account of the strongest proposal focuses on the articulation between theory and method: "[The applicant] had a clear sense of how to use a case to address theory. He took us through some of the main theories [of genocide] and showed how the Rwanda case . . . didn't confirm them in any straightforward way. And used that as a basis for establishing both, one, [that this was a] clear puzzle, [a] clear question . . . [and two,] what it was . . . obviously a case of. He inserted a comparative dimension into it in a way that was pretty ingenious, I thought, looking at regional variations."

Panelists wax poetic—evoking a language of beauty and appreciation—in describing proposals that reach perfect articulation between the research question, the theory informing the research, the method proposed, and the evidence mobilized to answer the question. This is where one can see craft at its best. Thus an economist provides this appreciative description of his favorite proposal, written by a political philosopher: "It's very rare that you find someone that can go from the very abstract political philosophy kind of literature and also design a good feasible empirical social science proposal to actually study how [international philanthropic organizations] work." In assessing how applicants achieve this ideal alignment, some panelists are most concerned with the theoretical dimension, echoing the assessment of intellectual significance. But here the issue is typically the presence or absence of a theoretical rationale for case selection. For instance, a political scientist criticizes a proposal on the grounds that "it was very unclear why she picked one place versus another place. The logic didn't seem to have been worked out. Reading her proposal you could see she was trying not very convincingly to respond to those very criticisms that other political scientists would formulate: . . . 'Why should it be a case study if you're pretending to make more generalizable claims?'"

Some more inductively inclined evaluators do not require a tight fit between theory and data because they expect the theoretical contribution to emerge in the process of gathering data. "Some people want a hypothesis before you go in," a sociologist observes, "[and] some people are quite prepared to accept that those hypotheses come out of the work. I thought if [this applicant] went in without it, he would actually probably get something more interesting."[21] An economist expresses the opposite view: "A general argument that people will make in this debate is, 'Well, this is an interesting idea and it's a bit of a fishing trip and this person will sort things out once they get there.' . . . For me, personally, this one was so far wrongheaded at the start that I didn't have faith that the person would straighten it out . . . If you haven't got the tools, you're going to write about something that's cool and interesting, but you're not going to do it in a scholarly way. That's a waste of money."

Panelists' discussions of the proper articulation of theory and data reveal differing perceptions concerning how theory should be handled and how much is too much or too little. This is in part a matter of taste and a response to varying disciplinary sensibilities—to varying intellectual habitus—as illustrated by a historian who describes the appropriate use of theory as follows: "There is a kind of high theory that is [in] and of itself beautiful and elegant when it's done right

. . . I want a sense when I read a proposal that there is a mind select-ing theory and working theory and an aesthetic to which a candidate is sort of responding deliberately."

As sociologists Charles Camic and Neil Gross note, theory is an-other polymorphic term.[22] The meanings given to theory vary widely across the social sciences and the humanities, and within each cluster of disciplines. Among our interviewees, a third of the mentions of theory refer most often to the articulation among theory, data, and method, followed by references to schools and to anti-reductionism, including reflexivity (roughly a fifth of the mentions), and to con-cepts (one in ten)—the remaining 15 percent are spread across vari-ous subtypes. The only noticeable differences in emphasis across disciplinary clusters are that humanists are more concerned with ref-erences to schools than are historians and social scientists; and social scientists and historians are more concerned with the articulation between theory and data than are humanists.

The diffusion of theory in the humanities that began in the 1970s (see Chapter 3) significantly affects how panelists from these disci-plines factor theory into evaluation. A music scholar, agreeing that in the past decades there has been "an importation as well as an adapta-tion of theoretical models that in particular came out of literary dis-ciplines . . . a whole panoply of post-structuralist scholars from Foucault to Baudrillard to Bourdieu to God knows who," also pro-nounces the role of theory in the humanities "extraordinarily impor-tant." A historian who mobilizes the term "theory" to refer to self-positioning is less enthusiastic. He describes those who adhere to "traditions of interpretive work as opposed to empirical work" as potentially "more vulnerable" to a "sort of posture or positioning that isn't about theory as tool, but about theory as statement of fidelities to all of the proper figures . . . It's merely a way of . . . saying, 'I'm on this guy's side' and 'I'm this guy's guy.'"

Humanists are particularly concerned with reflexivity, which is opposed to a naivety associated with earlier forms of humanistic scholarship. According to one panelist, reflexivity involves being "self-conscious about the very nature of historical narratives, about one's own practice when one inserts oneself into the telling of history . . . Because these kinds of academic practices are cultural practices, you know, they're not natural, they have their own culture . . . What's involved in being theoretically astute is that this is a form of ongoing self-criticism." To this, he opposes an unsophisticated proposal that he defines as one devoid of theory, that is "just kind of seat-of-the-pants descriptive scholarship . . . it is really unclear what is the guiding principle organizing the study. It's sort of popular chitchat . . . it struck me as scholarship lite." Thus, for some evaluators, the proper use of theory may play a crucial role in pushing a proposal above the proverbial line of funded projects. What may be seen by humanists as essential positioning and self-reflexivity will be viewed as narcissistic self-indulgence by more positivist social scientists. Unavoidable differences affect outcomes, but as we saw in Chapter 4, the influence of individual tastes is counterbalanced by cognitive contextualization and rules about consistency.

If theory is deemed essential by many, panelists, especially historians, also heavily criticize the abuse of theory. In fact, panelists appear to be more aggravated by this failing than by most others. An English scholar condemns this practice in strong moral terms:

Clarity trumps elegance, even in the English proposals, because what are we all doing if we're trying to build knowledge and [if] we can't communicate . . . [?] If I feel someone's using the jargon just to throw it around and say "I read Gayatri Spivak," forget it, that dog's not going to hunt with me . . . Now do I want to use a word as strong as dishonesty? It's a kind of trying to parade a supposed sophistication . . . It's also a kind of superficiality or laziness, not wanting to really think through either a theoretical proposition or the application of it . . . I'm not anti-theory at all

. . . [what] I don't like to see is theory using people . . . scholars should be using the theory.

An anthropologist sees the abuse of theory in the use of convoluted sentences and an overly abstract language that, to her, signals preciousness. About one proposal she particularly disliked, she says, "I also found the writing style just insufferable." In this instance, however, the panel "overlooked the style and went for the content."

Many of the historians interviewed reject the use of theory as a tool for generalization. One evaluator states that she "only likes middle-level generalizations, because that's where you have the possibility of saying something that's actually useful . . . I'm not interested in the connections at the level that will explain three societies at once across all time." For historians, theory is particularly irritating if it is not adequately integrated with the empirical material. A French historian explains that she is not opposed "to theory itself," but she was put off by a particular proposal because it "seemed to kind of tack on theory about the public sphere, and it isn't well integrated . . . I found that it was kind of intellectually pretentious." A similar commitment to a restrained use of theory is clear in the comments of a historian associated with cultural studies. He is irritated by the aura of "hipness" that is associated with theorists, the "kind of originality that consists of somebody trying to ride the sort of leading edge with a lot of buzz words and jargons that's kind of compulsive . . . Somebody like [a certain well-known anthropologist] annoys the hell out of me a lot of the time . . . He would be a good case of somebody who went from useful experiment to compulsive originality, where . . . everything you write has to look fundamentally unlike the last thing that you wrote." Considered together, these quotes suggest that theory, a polymorphic term, can be the source of different types of tensions.

Feasibility. The final formal criterion of evaluation provided to panelists by funding programs is that of feasibility, which refers to both the scope of the project (including its timeline, plan of work, and budget) and the preparedness of the applicant (including language skills, past experience, and advisers). Half the panelists mention factoring in feasibility when making an evaluation, and it is of roughly equal concern for historians, humanists, and social scientists. As a political scientist explains, evaluators typically ask, "[Is it] the right proposal being done by the right person? Oftentimes you see really great proposals and you think it should be being done by somebody else." Another panelist observes, "We're wasting our money and they're wasting our time if they can't do what they think they're doing." She assesses feasibility based on whether "they have a concept that can be examined, given the human limitations of the student, the people that they're looking at, or the evidence that they're looking at." Summarizing the importance of the plan of work, a political scientist says, "People can't know all the answers, but at least [they should] have a sense of where they're going to go when they get in the car. They should have [a] road map. Obviously they can make mistakes, but they should at least be in the right country." The track-record aspect of feasibility is important because all academics recognize how difficult it is to remain productive, given the many demands that accrue with seniority (many panelists themselves describe being less productive than they would like to be). Nevertheless, as noted earlier, factoring in an applicant's track record can cause problems because panel members may disagree about its proper weight. Some see past level of activity as correlated with excellence, and indeed, some empirical research supports this claim; others feel it can be misleading.[23]

Informal, "Evanescent" Criteria of Evaluation

In addition to applying the formal criteria prescribed by the funding agency, panelists use other, unofficially acknowledged criteria as part of the evaluation process. They are not necessarily always aware that they are doing so, however. As an English professor notes, "intuition and flair" play important roles in judging excellence, as does "just having a sort of eye for it." In many cases, these more evanescent criteria—the presence of "elegance," the ability to generate "excitement," a display of cultural capital—all combine to create a sense that an applicant is (or has) the "it" that everyone is looking for. Such considerations influence the signaling process as well as collective definitions of what is "hot." A historian, chair of a panel, recognizes the influence of such evanescent qualities. Rather than viewing their use as idiosyncratic or capricious, and thus as incompatible with making fair decisions, he sees panelists' application of evanescent criteria as an essential part of identifying true excellence:

> There are these intuitive aspects to it, and at the same time, I believe we're doing social science. These aspects have aesthetic sides to them, like "This is a very elegant or striking proposal." This is an important part of the individual and group processes. That doesn't mean that . . . we don't have standards. I think that those two things can go together quite well, especially if you're looking for things that are just a little bit outside the norm. You're actually looking for some of those qualities in the spark, the godlike qualities in the proposal.

These informal criteria appear to be used equally by panelists across the three disciplinary clusters. Even scholars from disciplines that view subjectivity as corrupting and as a source of bias (such as economists) show no special reluctance to judge who has "it" and who does not. Similarly, humanists are not less likely to factor in moral considerations. Instead, all panelists reference these informal criteria throughout their accounts of the deliberations. And recourse to these criteria does not appear to be limited only to times when reliance on formal standards has resulted in deadlocks. Panel members seem to appeal to evanescent criteria as the inspiration strikes. This is probably because such considerations permeate academic life, motivating scholars as they go about doing research and interacting with colleagues. Who is smart and less smart, who has a sense of analytical elegance and flair, who is boring or pedestrian, who is a mensch and who is not to be trusted—such preoccupations are routine for academics. Thus it is hardly surprising that panelists factor in these concerns when they find themselves locked in a room for a few hours, or a few days, and asked to make judgments on their peers. Far from corrupting the process of identifying and rewarding excellence, I see these considerations as intrinsic to it. In any case, they are unavoidable.

Divining signs of intelligence. As Table 5.7 shows, three-quarters of the respondents mention at least one dimension of "signs of intelligence" in discussing their assessment of proposals. An applicant's intelligence, according to an English professor, can be seen in the "subtlety and complexity with which the project is framed." For this panelist, intelligence is an "ability to understand and present complex ideas in an orderly fashion, to balance potentially conflicting positions or information and present that kind of complication clearly." The importance that evaluators attach to signs of intelligence is further indicated by the descriptions they provide of their intellectual heroes, who tend to be scholars who excel at making sense of complex phenomena. For example, a political scientist who singled out the political sociologist Seymour Martin Lipset emphasizes the complexity of Lipset's thought: "He's a primitive genius. He's able to pick up an enormously complex literature and he's able to take an angle on it that somehow captures some essential elements of those questions in the literature . . . He can kind of figure out what is going on. He can smell it." Similarly, a historian describes Robert Palmer's book *The Age of the Democratic Revolution* as impressive for "its abil-

Table 5.7 Number of panelists mentioning informal criteria, by disciplinary cluster

Criterion	Humanities N	Humanities %	History N	History %	Social sciences N	Social sciences %	Total N	Total %
Signs of intelligence (all)	18	82	15	75	20	69	53	75
Articulate	7	32	8	40	5	17	20	28
Competent	12	54	10	50	16	55	38	53
Intelligent	13	59	6	30	11	38	30	42
Talented	4	18	0	0	7	24	11	15
Elegance and cultural capital	16	73	14	70	16	55	46	65
Cultural ease	13	59	9	45	10	34	32	45
Cultural breath	8	36	8	40	10	34	26	36
Personal qualities								
Interesting	17	77	9	45	22	76	48	67
Exciting	7	32	4	20	7	24	18	25
Boring	3	13	3	15	7	24	13	18
Moral qualities (all)	8	40	9	46	11	37	29	41
Determination	8	41	4	20	9	31	22	31
Humility	7	32	4	20	4	14	15	21
Authenticity	6	27	2	10	6	21	14	19

Note: A "mention" occurs when a criterion is used during the interview.

ity to treat the distinctiveness of particular cases, yet discern a larger transformation that transcended those particular areas, [seeing] a larger story within all of those smaller stories."

Conversations with members of the Society of Fellows, the most elite of the five funding organizations, and the only one to conduct interviews with finalists, offer a look at what counts as intelligence in a highly rarefied stratum of the academic world (in this competition, applicants' odds of being awarded a fellowship are less than one in two hundred). These respondents tend to see intellectual refinement as a mixture of various traits held in delicate balance. An English professor, for example, describes the top candidate thus: "This person is extremely impressive and articulate, but in a way that actually establishes a circuit of exchange rather than everybody says one smart thing to sort of [lead] the discussion . . . So I take this as a sign that he is really listening. He [is] extremely successful in the way he describes [his work] and extremely interesting. But it has to do with a kind of nimbleness of his own mind and his questions and answers." The classification system used to assess intelligence in this setting appears to allow for finer gradations and nuances. As we will see, moral factors combine with intellectual factors to define who is considered a truly meritorious intellectual.

Elegance and cultural capital.   Who better epitomized the virtues of scholarly elegance than the anthropologist Clifford Geertz? His classic essay on the Balinese cockfight is often singled out as a particularly felicitous illustration of elegance in the interpretative social sciences.[24] For several respondents, it also illustrates a particular script for evaluating excellence. An anthropologist, after explaining that all the proposals she ranked highly were well written, refers to the cockfight article as "a model of what it is that we do best when we're doing what we should do." She defines her own understanding of academic excellence as oriented toward a "kind of perfectionism, trying to get the language right." Elegance also is often associated with the display of cultural capital—that is, it is linked to the ability to demonstrate familiarity with such high-status signals as cultural literacy.[25] For instance, a French historian says that she appreciates good writing, which she defines as the ability to express oneself with "some literacy." Nearly two-thirds of all respondents mention elegance and display of cultural capital when describing the evaluation of proposals and applicants (see Table 5.7). There are differences across disciplinary clusters. Humanists and historians particularly value elegance and cultural capital, and social scientists give it less emphasis.[26] About elegance a philosopher says, "I think it's wonderful. Elegance means clear, not rococo prose, though rococo prose can be elegant. It means not trying to sound like a social scientist," which would be "an effort to submerge the individual style altogether. I want to have a strong personal voice."[27] With respect to cultural capital, panel members are particularly concerned with cultural breadth and cultural ease.

It is often difficult to disentangle elegance from the display of a cultural capital that is very unevenly distributed across disciplines, as well as across types of academic institutions and across the class structure. In *Homo Academicus*, Bourdieu describes not only the humanities as carrying considerable cultural capital, but also traditional elite universities and the culture of the "dominant class" (the upper middle class).[28] Valuing elegance and the display of cultural capital may mean conflating excellence with elite or upper-middle-class membership.[29] When this occurs, Bourdieu would suggest, panelists penalize applicants from working-class backgrounds, who routinely suffer from class-based discrimination.[30] In a Bourdieuian logic, the applicants who are construed as most brilliant are also those who have the greatest familiarity and ease with the academic world (for instance, those who are offspring of academics). Students of working-class origins operating in elite academic environments often feel stigmatized, experience ambivalence toward their past, and learn to conceal their backgrounds. This is likely to influence their degree of ease—which in turn is likely to be associated with their degree of demonstrated elegance and poise, and thus also with the likelihood of being defined as doing "exciting" and "interesting" work (on this topic see also Chapter 6).[31]

Valuing what is "exciting" and "interesting."   Positive perceptions of work as "exciting" and "interesting" cannot be bracketed out of the evaluation process. But what exactly do these terms mean? In his article "That's Interesting: Toward a Phenomenology of Sociology and a Sociology of Phenomenology," Murray Davis examines a large number of sociological contributions deemed "interesting" and concludes that "interesting theories deny certain assumptions of their audience, while non-interesting theories affirm certain assumptions."[32] An anthropologist's description of a good proposal as one "that seems intrinsically interesting to me" states: "I want the writer to be able to convey that this is a project they're interested in . . . It's a sense that it's something important, because if it's not important enough to excite them, then why should they get funding?" "Boring," the opposite of "exciting," is equated with repetition (a historian observes, "if a person has had some success at a certain kind of analysis, [she should not] keep doing more of it"). But boringness can also have a more damning connotation. One of the most antagonistic exchanges reported during the post-deliberation interviews with panelists involved a historian who told a political scientist that proposals from that field were "not so much difficult to evaluate, but just extremely, well, boring, and sort of filled with jargon. [They were] just sort of artificially constructed . . . around these kind of criteria that were intrinsically uninteresting." Panel members' preferences for "exciting" work may indirectly advantage applicants (and their recommenders) from elite universities, to the extent that these individuals are better positioned to tap widely shared understandings of what is "cutting-edge," "exciting," or "boring" at any point in time. This possibility suggests one way in which informal criteria may work against meritocratic evaluation.

In Chapter 4, we saw that panelists often use idiosyncratic standards of evaluation (an ex-tennis star was drawn to a proposal on the body, a fan of modern dance to a study of dance, a bird enthusiast to work on songbirds), but there are also important variations in how panelists believe subjectivity—their own view of what is exciting versus boring—affects the evaluation. As Table 5.7 shows, humanists cite work as "interesting" or "exciting" slightly more often than do historians and social scientists. Humanists and more interpretative social scientists (anthropologists and cultural historians) may be more at ease with the role played by their subjectivity in evaluation.[33] After all, their interpretative power is their main analytical tool. In addition, their expertise, being more purely interpretative in character, does not employ technical black-boxing tools of the types that Bruno Latour describes in *Science in Action* and *The Pasteurization of France*.[34] The production of social science knowledge, in contrast, relies on specific data-collection techniques (surveys, interviews, observation) and tools for data analysis (qualitative content-analysis software or statistical analysis packages) to settle controversies.[35] Competition between opposite views of what "excites" and "interests" thus are perhaps more intense in the humanistic fields.

Panelists in noninterpretative disciplines, however, sometimes are extremely critical of using "what is interesting" or "cool" as a criterion of evaluation. Suspicious of idiosyncratic tastes, these panelists try to balance an appreciation of the researcher's ability with the project's intrinsic interest. A historian, for example, wants to couple appreciation of interest with an evaluation of competence: "Heavily quantitative proposals with a lot of arcane equations and things like that in it would have a hard time sparking my interest. I try to overcome that and make sure it's not just a matter of taste and try to understand what it is really that's being tested and what the chance of a significant result will be here, even if it's not my taste." A sociologist explicitly subordinates interest to competence. Referring to my own area of expertise, cultural sociology, he says: "If there [are] some really fine projects that come along looking for funding you would just get extremely excited about it at the level of intrinsic interests. But I might just say, 'Well you know, here's another culture project,' whatever. But why should I stand in the way of a really excellent project because it doesn't get my blood boiling?"

Moral Qualities of the Applicant

The vernacular of excellence that panelists use is laced with references to the moral character of applicants. As my colleagues and I have argued elsewhere, these references to moral character—particularly to "courageous risk-takers" and to "lazy conformists"—contradict the literature on peer review, which frames extra-intellectual consideration as corrupting the evaluation process.[36] Again, this literature ignores the extent to which self-concept shapes the way panelists appreciate and evaluate the work of others. Among the panelists, an English professor notes this influence, remarking that "the older I get, I've realized more and more how my own intellectual preoccupations really do spring from concerns that I just meet in my everyday life, and the kind of everyday major decisions I've had to make in the course of my own personal life and in my career." As we have seen in previous chapters (especially Chapter 4), scholarship is far from being an abstract and disconnected pursuit; instead, it is intimately tied to the image that academics hold of themselves (including their relative status), and to how they think they should lead their lives.

Table 5.7 shows that 41 percent of panelists refer to applicants' moral qualities when assessing proposals—enough to support the conclusion that doing so is not exceptional, but part of the normal order of things. Panelists privilege determination and hard work, humility, authenticity, and audacity. They express how the management of the self—the display of a proper scholarly and moral habitus—is crucial to definitions of excellence across fields. These qualities suggest that at least some panelists select not only scholars, but also human beings whom they deem worthy of admiration for moral reasons. Thus a political scientist says he recognizes excellence "first of all, by the willingness of someone to stick their neck out seriously to propose to produce disconfirmable knowledge"; and a historian praises "the person who is in control of their own intellectual work, who sort of has made their own choices, who has reasons for doing everything they're doing. That to me always stands out and it always distinguishes the very best people." Some of the specific moral qualities most frequently mentioned by panelists are discussed below (and shown in Table 5.7).

Determination is associated with one's ability to overcome hardship, and with a strong work ethic. Of his best student, a distinguished philosopher says, "The trajectory and the sheer will . . . and good will with which she did all this, I really admire that immensely . . . the fact that she overcame what I felt were actual weaknesses [which] were strengths that neither she nor I, nor anyone else had seen at the time, and that she ended up finding that there was a lot of talent and ability there."

Humility or unpretentiousness is viewed as an added measure of excellence, especially when coupled with superlative expertise. This is expressed by a panelist who describes a winner of the ultra-selective Society of Fellows competition: "Without seeming like an old pedant, he seemed to have the control of his area that only somebody who's worked for thirty years has. And without being either overbearing or patronizing or boring, he just communicated an immense amount of information, all of it articulate and structured at the same time." An anthropologist who served as a panelist for a different competition recalls an applicant who received funding despite an overbearing self-presentation. The panelist had disliked the "relentlessly self-promoting, arrogant tone of the proposal," which he equated with the applicant's personal characteristics:

> What troubled me was the performance aspect of it. He was going to prove that everyone was wrong about their interpretation of this [historical event], and he was going to make this, his idea of truth, into the general[ly] accepted one . . . But I could take the point, and it was certainly a brilliant piece of work, aside from his own recognition of his own brilliance . . . As much as I hate to give anything to this guy, he deserves it, and that's fine.

A geographer also stresses morality when he describes his intellectual hero: "Peter Wood . . . [is] a model person, very modest. I think there's too much arrogance in academia . . . I always find restraint and modesty marvelous qualities in a first-rate scholar."

Authenticity, which often goes hand in hand with audacity, is also singled out as a valued trait. Panelists appreciate applicants who are true to themselves, even if that means pursuing less popular paths. For instance, a sociologist says of his favorite applicant, "I appreciated her willingness to take on a very risky project, but [one] that potentially had a huge payoff in terms of reshaping or fundamentally challenging the received view on Japanese politics, and hence on comparative politics about advanced industrial societies." He compares her to those who succumb to the pressures to reproduce the work of their advisers and are slaves to "what is hot." A well-known and highly regarded historian speaks regretfully of the "very clear vision of career" that he sees as animating "the current generation." Similarly, referring to the "sterility of professionalization," an English professor explains:

> Students very much begin to pick up early in their career how they have to signal to different interest groups that they are of their persuasion . . . The students that I've been most excited about and whose work I learn the most from are those who really are passionately attached to an author, to a subject, to a problem. And it shows, it shows in their writing, it shows in how ultimately fearless they are in pursuing a track . . . So when I'm on panels, those are [some] of the things I immediately [look for] . . . sort of originality and a distinct sense of engagement. [Others] make me feel that I'm kind of in an echo chamber, that there's no original sound that I feel that I've experienced.

Authenticity is especially central in the accounts of the Society of Fellows panelists. One philosopher, pointing to the sincerity of a winner's intellectual engagement, notes that this applicant had "a kind of complete absorption in his topic, and yet, an ability to communicate that absorption . . . You felt that there's a real love for the work and that he has good ideas about it and that he knows a damn lot about it." The same esteemed historian quoted earlier, who was also a member of this panel, describes one of the top candidates as having great passion for his work, as well as great intellectual honesty and integrity. "It was clear that he was someone who had attracted extraordinary attention . . . But what really was remarkable [was the] sense that this is a young man who works on a rarefied topic, but he was somebody you'd love to talk to." Of a third candidate, he says:

> What we found in talking to him was that there was a real kind of depth and interest in what he said, a real passion, which was very impressive . . . [He had] incredible intellectual commitment, which had driven him in really a very short time to be an extraordinary Slavic expert . . . [He had] a kind of non-career-oriented fanatical energy.

When I asked this historian "To what extent do you feel that you are rewarding a moral self or a different intellectual identity?" he responded, "We're unquestionably doing that. Unquestionably. A substantial part of the way the committee works is by its response to the person, and what you very nicely call the 'moral self.' That is, these are not quantifiable reactions. These are not reactions that you could necessarily document. But there's no question."

Conclusion

This chapter explored the many meanings given to excellence by panelists, as well as the relative salience of formal and informal criteria of evaluation. Here I focused on differences between disciplinary clusters—the humanities, the social sciences, and history—as opposed to differences between and within individual disciplines (the focus of Chapter 3). At the level of disciplinary cluster, such differences seem much less accentuated. This may be because differences get washed out when considered in the aggregate, or because there are cross-cutting differences that make overall patterns less easily discernable.

We saw that among the respondents, significance and originality stand out as the most important of the formal criteria used, followed at a distance by clarity and methods. Informal standards are also a factor in evaluation and play a significant enough role to be considered part of the normal order of things. This is particularly the case for cultural capital and morality, two considerations that are extraneous to merit per se. The panelists admire intellectual virtuosos, risk-takers who offer a counterpoint to the duller, more staid image of the scholar that prevails in the American collective imagination. They praise applicants with "deft" and "elegant" minds—traits that are sometimes read through class signals or evidence of cultural capital. Panelists are enamored by those who are able to do intellectual somersaults, in part by creating repeated challenges throughout their careers, even after they have been able to build fairly comfortable positions for themselves.

Panelists' self-identity figures significantly in the evaluation process. While some panelists appreciate the role of subjectivity in the production and evaluation of knowledge, others try to bracket it out because they view it as a corrupting force. Also, some panelists are eager to reward scholars who demonstrate specific moral traits. These traits, which are considered separately from the content of their bearers' proposals, appear to be tied directly to the evaluators' idealized view of what makes academic life a worthy pursuit—the determination, humility, and authenticity that reveal a real depth of commitment to one's vocation.

By analyzing the specific meanings that panelists assign to evaluation criteria, I have also demonstrated here that in the vast and multifaceted universe of academic evaluation, criteria such as "originality" or "quality" are defined in a great many ways. One normative conclusion to be drawn from this observation is that it is pointless to attempt to collapse the many considerations that factor into funding decisions into a single matrix, whether it be grounded in positivist or in interpretive epistemologies. Academia is a highly variegated world, one where qualitatively incommensurate proposals cannot be subsumed under a single standard. Methodological rigor is defined somewhat differently whether one wishes to produce theoretical generalizations, or demonstrate what specific cases tell us about broader social processes. Similarly, significance can be measured in social or in intellectual or theoretical terms. Each and all of these standpoints enrich our understanding of what makes research a meaningful endeavor—and, likewise, shape the value we assign to the work of others.

Finally, we saw that evaluators' personal tastes and areas of expertise—as seen, for instance, in their preferences for more or less theory and more or less emphasis on social and intellectual significance—are interlaced in ways that the experts themselves do not always acknowledge. Such preferences appear to be unavoidable, and the technology of deliberation that is at the center of grant peer review is not fitted with mechanisms for countering idiosyncrasies or even capriciousness. The influence of such variables stands in sharp contrast to the view that "cream rises," that cognitive contextualism always applies, or that criteria are consistent.

Academic evaluation is fraught with imperfections, despite the strongest commitment to customary rules of evaluation. As we have seen here and in Chapter 4, the meanings and weight given to a variety of formal and informal criteria of evaluation constrain and orient the process, but ultimately, reasoned judgments are buffeted by unpredictable human proclivities, agency, and improvisation. These countervailing forces define the coexisting strengths and weaknesses of grant peer review as it is practiced in American higher education. Even if one were able to erase all particularistic considerations from the evaluation process, there would still be culturally and socially embedded assessments. The goal of a consistent and unified process is utopian: perspectives shift and the weight given to each criterion varies as the characteristics of the group of proposals being considered prime evaluators to consider different facets of each proposal in turn. How will these idiosyncrasies of the grant-review process accommodate considerations of interdisciplinarity and diversity?

6/Considering
Interdisciplinarity
and Diversity

We are clearly without any kind of mystery about it: criteria other than excellence are being used.

Political scientist

lthough the criteria of interdisciplinarity and diversity are used to distinguish one proposal from another, they do not speak to quality per se. Instead, they concern characteristics of proposals and applicants that may push a very good but not perfect project or candidate over the proverbial bar. As such, diversity in particular can act as an additive, rather than as an alternative, standard of evaluation.

The discussion focuses first on the distinct challenges raised by the evaluation of interdisciplinary proposals and explores how panelists define "good interdisciplinarity" given the general lack of consensus in this area. That the necessary types of expertise are rarely combined within a single person partly accounts for the difficulties of evaluating interdisciplinary research. Falling back on disciplinary standards is the path of least resistance.

We will see that in the world of funding panels, as in the world of American higher education, diversity takes many forms and comes in many hues. Yet while public debates center mainly on the place of racial and gender diversity in higher education, panelists assign the most weight to institutional and disciplinary diversity. Various types of diversity are valued as an intrinsic good that contributes to the overall quality of the research environment. Concerns for representation and efficacy (being truthful to the organizational mission) are factored into arguments in favor of diversity, but diversity is also valued as a component of excellence and as a means of redressing past injustices, leveling the playing field, and shaping the academic pipeline.

The five competitions under consideration are multidisciplinary in the sense that they aim to fund proposals emanating from a range of disciplines and their panel members are drawn from various disciplines (see Chapter 2). But these competitions all fund, in varying proportions, both disciplinary and interdisciplinary proposals. Only three of the sponsors explicitly encourage interdisciplinary scholarship.[1] As for diversity, while some competitions, such as that of the American Council for Learned Societies, specify that "minorities and other groups are encouraged to apply," others do not mention diversity criteria in their guidelines to panelists or applicants. Such considerations have become part of the taken-for-granted standards used for evaluation across a range of settings in American higher education; and most of the funding organizations I studied promote diversity as part of their broader organizational mandate. Not surprisingly, then, when reporting arguments made in favor and against proposals, the interviewees routinely refer to the influence of various kinds of diversity.

Critics of affirmative action believe that factoring in diversity poses challenges related to fairness. As explained by the political theorist Michael Walzer in his classic *Spheres of Justice*, justice is not one idea but several, because there is no single criterion by which justice should be assessed.[2] Principles of justice such as merit, need, and distributive fairness are not all of the same order and they often clash with one another. The French sociologists Luc Boltanski and Laurent Thévenot, however, suggest that "compromise" can often be reached between competing principles of legitimation.[3] How panelists balance excellence and diversity is a case in point, as we will see.

Tensions between excellence and diversity, and meritocracy and democracy, remain at the center of debates about peer review. The spatial dispersion of the American higher education system over a very large territory, its institutional diversity (covering public and private universities, as well as research universities, small liberal arts colleges, and community colleges), and the sociodemographic diversity of administrators, faculty, and students all keep these tensions alive. Against such a diverse landscape, winners should be chosen from a variety of groups and regions, and panelists should be somewhat representative of the broader population. For instance, winners cannot all come from a few select institutions in the Northeast—this would undermine the legitimacy of peer review as a meritocratic and democratic system. Such a result would likely be viewed as an organizational failure and/or as the outcome of elitism (opportunity hoarding) or poor procedures. The democratic impulse attenuates the steep institutional hierarchies that characterize American higher education, but it does not impede an unconditional celebration of excellence and meritocracy, which is viewed elsewhere as the expression of a certain social Darwinism.[4]

Rewards and Challenges of Interdisciplinary Evaluation

Interdisciplinarity has many manifestations, including the degree to which disciplinary boundaries are permeable and the extent to which disciplines are conceptually integrated.[5] More specifically, interdisciplinarity typically involves (1) developing conceptual links by using a perspective in one discipline to modify a perspective in another discipline, (2) using research techniques developed in one discipline to elaborate a theoretical model in another, (3) developing a new theoretical framework that may reconceptualize research in two or more separate domains as it attempts to integrate them, and (4) modifying a theoretical framework characteristic of one domain and then applying it to another.[6]

Interdisciplinarity has been a priority in the funding world for several years. It is favored by the leaders in federal funding (the National Institutes of Health and the National Science Foundation), by universities eager to stake out new territory that will raise their profile, and by a number of private foundations.[7] Thus the funding competitions I studied are not exceptional in promoting interdisciplinarity. Program officers take organizational guidelines seriously; in putting together funding panels, they factor in potential members' interdisciplinary orientation. Consequently, during interviews, many panelists were vocal in their appreciation for interdisciplinary research. An English professor's comments capture this enthusiasm: "The more subjects you canvas, the more likely you are to approach your topic fairly . . . Putting things together that are not usually put together is a good thing to do, an [innovation] that might produce useful knowledge." In addition to its role in producing "useful knowledge," interdisciplinarity is valued because it improves one's "ability to speak to different sets of people," thus broadening a project's intellectual reach. Yet as we will see, panelists also acknowledge that "true" or "good" interdisciplinarity is often elusive.

Doing It Well

After briefly establishing his identity as an interdisciplinary scholar ("I read things in anthropology, sociology, probably less in political science and literature"), a historian notes that interdisciplinarity "is a challenging thing to do effectively," and concedes that "there are valid criticisms about the way historians have sometimes adopted tools and ideas from other fields." Indeed, some critics dismiss interdisciplinary research as a fad, and as a form of scholarship that is not easily amenable to evaluation.[8] Others have argued that the very notion of "peer review" cannot be validly applied to interdisciplinary research.[9] It is in this context that social scientists have begun thinking systematically about the challenges of evaluating interdisciplinarity—an underexplored topic.[10] They have identified some criteria specific to the assessment of interdisciplinarity (for example, consistency with previous research, balance between interdisciplinary perspectives, and potential effectiveness).[11] There is also some agreement on the potential pitfalls of interdisciplinary scholarship. The panelists speak to both aspects, describing some of the positive as well as negative attributes of interdisciplinary work (and those who undertake it).

The best interdisciplinary proposals successfully combine breadth, parsimony, and soundness. Here is how a geographer goes about identifying applicants who meet these stringent standards:

> To be an artful and talented researcher, [what] one has to do is actually master several fields . . . You have to be able to talk the talk of several disciplines, but to be able to see where cutting edges are and take certain gambles in terms of advancing an idea . . . I take a risk on [proposals that have] interesting ideas, even if they're bumping into different fields. I look very carefully at the training [of the applicant], who they're working with, the scholarship of the person they have worked with, to assess whether I think this person is actually capable of raising some big questions.

A historian focuses on the dialogic character of successful interdisciplinary proposals.[12] "To hit a basic threshold of significance," he explains, the proposal must speak to different disciplines simultaneously: "If you can reach people outside your field, you're interdisciplinary . . . A proposal that is able to speak across disciplinary idioms to a majority of people on the panel is going to be a suitable proposal." The best interdisciplinary proposals are also integrative, that is, they bring together ideas and approaches from different disciplines.[13] Thus, unsurprisingly, among the pitfalls and drawbacks that respondents identify, a primary concern is overreaching or overambitiousness. As an English professor points out, "Projects that have a lot of ambition to reach beyond the person's initial field; they're risky. The person might not be able to do what they want to do. Over-ambitiousness was what was both attractive and fatal for some of the projects." A historian couples superficiality with overreach, maintaining that "if you are interdisciplinary, the burden is upon you, the candidate, to be aware of that discipline and not do shoddy work." This same panelist offers the following telling comparison of two applicants from literary studies, each of whom proposed to use a historical approach:

She did what he failed to do. She's not an historian, but she didn't get the history wrong, and she grounded [the proposal] correctly in context. And I could see how the work would contribute to this sort of interdisciplinary approach where she's trying to look at this literature historically within that context. The few literature proposals that I've gotten have just been very bad for the very reasons that I'm describing—they're all over the map. They have no real grounding in context. They bandy theory that isn't well integrated. I . . . ranked them quite harshly.

Flashiness, too, is often associated with overreach. Another historian, contrasting flashy and real interdisciplinarity, says of flashiness:

There is a . . . way of doing things in which you use your knowledge of the other things, the things outside your discipline, more as a rhetorical strategy than as something in which you really steep yourself in. It's always a danger in interdisciplinary work.

An English professor offers a similar criticism when she describes as "fast and loose" an interdisciplinary project concerning capitalism and the economic and political power of native Americans: "A fast and loose project would be throwing around some interdisciplinary vocabulary . . . It would pull in Gayatri Spivak and Benedict Anderson and throw them into some kind [of] theoretical soup, maybe just be tagging phrases and not really applying their theories in any kind of deep way." Although many have clear ideas about what makes for bad interdisciplinary research, the greatest difficulties it poses concern how to assess it fairly and with consensus.

Evaluating It Well

The standards used to evaluate interdisciplinary research are not a simple combination of the standards of single disciplines. They are a hybrid, and an emergent hybrid at that—one that has developed through practice and deliberation. Because the criteria have these emergent qualities, some panelists believe that interdisciplinary panels are more open-minded than regular, single-discipline panels, that there is a greater willingness to "listen to other people's criteria and sort of question your own . . . to change their minds or to reconsider." Others believe that such panels are more conservative than their disciplinary counterparts.[14] This conservative bias may be influenced by the members' age; panelists tend to be older than the average applicants to most competitions. Older scholars have been less socialized to appreciate interdisciplinary work. Mentioning a controversial tenure case at her elite institution, an English scholar remarks that "especially older colleagues are very unwilling even to approach judging [this scholar's] work. They just want to say, 'We shouldn't have this kind of work because we can't judge it. We can't tell whether it's good or bad.' And that seems to me a terrible reason to fire someone." As in tenure decisions, the challenge of fairly evaluating interdisciplinary proposals is not helped by the fact that typically no panelist has mastered all the knowledge needed to assess competently all of their aspects.[15] Sometimes no consensus emerges about whose disciplinary sovereignty should be deferred to, which means that evaluating interdisciplinary research can be an especially risky venture.

Interdisciplinarity often brings about a broadening and multiplication of evaluation criteria, which makes both individual judgment and group agreement much more difficult. The same English professor quoted earlier notes that in her field, the traditional criteria used with regard to close reading is whether the author can perform a "subtle, accurate reading" of a sonnet, for instance. In the case of interdisciplinary work, the criteria become whether the argument is "plausible, persuasive, how is evidence used." And although the use of evidence is a constant, it is often difficult or impossible for panelists to know whether an applicant is proposing to use the most appropriate evidence available. Only those extremely familiar with the specific case are in a position to evaluate this aspect—and even across academia in general, the number of such competent judges is likely to be very small. This same English professor, whose scholarship is well known and highly regarded, illustrates the dilemma by describing her own experience undertaking an interdisciplinary research project:

> You take your theoretical frame from some existing source. If
> you're writing about sexuality, you would follow the rules laid
> down by Foucault, so that it would be possible to judge whether
> someone was pursuing a Foucaultian reading in a proper way.
> [However], I felt that I certainly knew more about these journalis-

tic accounts [I was studying] than anybody else did, and that
meant that nobody really ever could say that I was wrong, and
that made me worried . . . They would inevitably be impressed by
the fancy footwork that I performed with these sources, but it
would be difficult for someone to say that I had read them wrong.

As this quote suggests, the lack of canonized agreement about how
to evaluate interdisciplinarity gives researchers more leeway concerning how to go about their work, but it also creates greater uncertainty about how to establish the resulting project's quality. A historian emphasizes the importance of using "other fields' toolkits" in
a disciplined way. This approach he contrasts with "the kind of
interdisciplinarity that Stanley Fish once complained about, which is
basically the person who makes up his own standards and therefore
is bound by no one. I am interested in consciously trying to sort of
broker useful relations between disciplinary toolkits."

Combining traditional standards of disciplinary excellence with
interdisciplinarity presents a potential for double jeopardy. This is
because expert and generalist criteria (what one respondent defines
as "virtuosity and significance") have to be met at the same time. Because interdisciplinary research is a hybrid form, the usual criteria of
evaluation—originality and significance, for instance—may end up
being weighted differently. A historian of China says it is important
to have

the endorsement of specialists who feel that . . . this [is] going to
satisfy needs in your particular discipline. I mean only after we
got a "yes" to that would I want to go on. Now we apply the second tier of criteria, which is, "Is it going to do anything for anybody else?" The first thing in the sequence . . . certifies people as
competent in their, as it were, local expertises. But to me, that's
not the ultimate criteria. The ultimate criterion is, is it going to do
anything for the rest of us.

Not surprisingly, given the emergent quality of the standards of evaluation for interdisciplinary genres, panelists readily fall back on existing disciplinary standards to determine what should and should not be funded. This may mean that at the end of the day, interdisciplinary scholarship is evaluated through several disciplinary lenses. That is the conclusion my colleagues and I reached in our study of cognitive contextualization and the production of fair judgments within interdisciplinary panels.[16] Of course, more research is needed in this area, particularly concerning the creation and evaluation of shared interdisciplinary cognitive platforms.[17] We also need to understand better the weak institutionalization of interdisciplinary criteria of evaluation in the face of considerable available funding, governmental mandates for interdisciplinary research, and industry's appreciation of it. Is ambiguity inherent to the genre?

While "good" interdisciplinary evaluation calls for a very distinct, if rare, combination of expertise, "good" diversity evaluation raises questions of a different order. These have to do with fundamental principles—how to reconcile evaluation based on merit, on the one hand, and evaluation based on needs and distributive justice, on the other.

Including Diversity Criteria

Many studies demonstrate the relatively few women and minority faculty members in the most prestigious levels of academia—in particular, tenured positions at research universities that have high levels of influence and productivity.[18] Although faculty diversity is increasing, unequal access to higher education continues to affect the pipeline.[19] It is against this background that diversity considerations affect all forms of selection in American higher education, ranging from law school admissions and department tenure decisions, to the awarding of fellowships.

Just as with interdisciplinarity, some of the funding agencies included in this study explicitly require that panelists do not discriminate. For instance, the website for the American Council for Learned Societies asserts:

> In the administration and awarding of its fellowships and grants, the ACLS does not discriminate on the basis of race, color, sex, sexual orientation, national origin, age, religion, disability, marital/family status, or political affiliation. Applications are particularly invited from women and members of minority groups. Younger scholars and independent scholars who do not hold academic appointments are also encouraged to apply.[20]

Other funding organizations are less specific. For instance, the website of the Woodrow Wilson National Fellowship Foundation, sponsor of the Women's Studies competition, simply states, "Since its earliest days, the Woodrow Wilson Foundation has broken barriers and opened doors for students whose access to the best educational opportunities had been limited. Woodrow Wilson continues to meet the nation's needs to cultivate young leaders who truly represent all Americans."[21] Two of the funding agencies do not mention diversity. Nevertheless, it is reasonable to expect that all panelists take it into consideration when making awards; diversity's relevance to academic evaluation is widely acknowledged in settings where panel members typically perform their day-to-day work as evaluators of colleagues and students. While they are generally asked only not to discriminate, diversity is often actively factored into decision making.

Promoting Many Diversities: Why and How

Panelists appear to favor an expansive definition of diversity that does not privilege race or gender, and that aims to promote diversity within academia because it is perceived as an intrinsic good, leading

Table 6.1 Percent of panelists per disciplinary cluster who mention diversity as a criterion

Types of diversity	Humanities (N = 22)	History (N = 20)	Social sciences (N = 29)	Total (N = 71)
Institutional	9 (41%)	8 (40%)	8 (28%)	25 (35%)
Disciplinary	7 (32%)	9 (45%)	8 (28%)	24 (34%)
Topics	6 (27%)	9 (45%)	5 (17%)	20 (28%)
Gender	0 (0%)	5 (25%)	6 (21%)	11 (15%)
Ethno-racial	4 (18%)	3 (15%)	3 (10%)	10 (14%)
Geographic	1 (5%)	0 (0%)	0 (0%)	1 (1%)
Total	27 (1.2*)	34 (1.7**)	30 (1.03**)	91**

Note: A "mention" occurs when a criterion is used during the interview.
* This number represents the ratio of mention per panelist. While some respondents mentioned each type of diversity more than once, their concern is registered only once for each diversity type.
**Some panelists mentioned two types of diversity. Thus, the total number of mentions is greater than the total number of panelists.

to a richer academic experience for all and to a broader production of talent for society as a whole.[22] Panelists do consider the racial and gender diversity of the awardees, but they also weigh their geographical location, the types of institutions where they teach (public/private, elite/nonelite, colleges/research universities), and the range of disciplines they hail from. Which kind of diversity is privileged from case to case is an object of negotiation among panel members. As shown in Table 6.1, around 34 percent of the interviewees mention institutional diversity and disciplinary diversity as criteria of evaluation, compared to only about 15 percent who mention ethno-racial or gender diversity. Diversity in topics is also a popular criterion. Only one respondent mentions geographic diversity.

Historians are most concerned with diversity in topics and disciplinary diversity (this may reflect noblesse oblige, given that historians reap the lion's share of the awards and submit a very large number of proposals). Social scientists are the least concerned with these two dimensions. Surprisingly, the humanists do not mention gender diversity, while, as the table shows, this is a relatively strong factor among historians and social scientists. Mentions of ethno-racial diversity are roughly equal across disciplinary clusters. Overall, the concern for diversity is strongest among historians (with a ratio of 1.7 mentions per respondent in this cluster, compared to 1.2 among humanists, and 1.03 among social scientists). It should be mentioned that while panelists have access to information concerning applicants' disciplinary affiliation, gender, institutional affiliation (and its geographic location), and research topic, they often have to guess ethno-racial identity based on applicants' past awards (for example, having received minority fellowships) and affiliations (such as membership in the Association of Black Sociologists).

Given the many forms of diversity and the relatively low salience of ethno-racial diversity as compared to disciplinary and institutional diversity, it is not surprising that when asked how much importance should be attached to diversity as a criterion of selection, an African-American scholar responds by referring to projects emanating from private and public universities as well as to competitions that target "younger scholars or ethnic minorities." He explicitly views policies aiming to promote racial diversity as exemplifying the promotion of a much broader principle of diversity. Some respondents go even further. A history professor says, "I do believe in having a mix, as much of a mix as possible, as much diversity of whatever kind. And that includes diversity of background or training or interest or maybe even age or personality." Framing the funding of women and people of color as the extension of a broader principle minimizes what could be perceived as an antinomy between promoting excellence and fairness. Since the 1980s, a similar trend has developed in other fields, such as organizational management, partly in response to federal cutbacks in affirmative action and equal opportunity regulations.[23]

Pro-diversity arguments are made by evoking not only the intrinsic value of diversity, but also the need to level the playing field and overcome biases (rationales that are often combined) in order to bring out the best work. "It's important for foundations such as these to encourage the production of as wide a range of knowledge as possible," one English scholar asserts, explaining that this process "helps us check some of the biases that we as evaluators may bring in. And I think it also allows us to 'level the playing field.' That's a metaphor that gets used often in terms of racial or class diversity, which I totally think is important." An African-American panelist also defends factoring in diversity by appealing to fairness in light of this uneven playing field. As he notes, "You've got people applying who teach at institutions where they have much heavier teaching loads and haven't had opportunities to publish as much. It is often the case that their proposals may not look as slick and polished—I should say 'polished,' I shouldn't say 'slick.' They may not have been able to maintain connections to leaders in the field whose names carry some kind of weight or who may have some kind of facility with letters of recommendation."

Still other panel members are concerned with the role that fellowships play in shaping the academic pipeline and in determining what the professoriate will look like in the next decades. According to a self-identified liberal historian:

> Since [the competition] is a gateway to the academy, I'm interested in seeing the academy have more than just white, upper-middle-class, careerist professionals [who] essentially come at this with a kind of dogged, mandarin-like desire to reproduce themselves in the academy . . . It's nice to see somebody [who] did different work, older candidates and young candidates . . . if at the end of the day you've essentially given a license to a group of people [to] fill out the academy with very different personalit[ies] and different backgrounds, that's . . . a massive plus.

As Lani Guinier and Susan Sturm point out, critics of affirmative action today find it easy to pit meritocracy against diversity, arguing that some "get in by merit," while others do so "by quota."[24] The case of peer review suggests another perspective, one where considerations of quality and diversity are combined to identify potential awardees. Awards are made to applicants who shine in both dimensions, even if in varying proportions; thus, I argue that merit and diversity often act as complementary criteria, rather than as alternative standards of evaluation. Consider how the promotion of diversity is typically accomplished in funding decisions. Arguments about diversity are rarely salient when the first awards are made—the awards around which strong consensus emerges rapidly. Such arguments are more likely to be advanced when the "maybe" proposals are discussed. In these cases, diversity, in its various forms, may act as a tie-breaker between two somewhat faulty—but each differently faulty and thus not easily commensurable—proposals, and thereby help "move things along." An evaluator who describes the self-monitoring process in which her panel was engaged gives an example. After members noted that they seemed to be funding a disproportionately large number of proposals by historians, the panel took corrective action: "Certain projects were included in our top list by taking into consideration field diversity as well as other kinds of [criteria, such as] institutional range, geographical range, all of which I think are very important categories." As an African-American English professor summarizes the situation: "Some [winners] are there because of questions having to do with field diversity and a diversity of kind of institutions, because [there is] less of a consensus about the qualities of the proposal. In other cases, there's more of a consensus that the project is suitable."

Note that those who benefit from diversity considerations may have had to overcome additional hurdles and stigmas based on their institutional affiliation, class, race, or nativity to join the pool of contestants. That these applicants' trajectory may have been steeper suggests perhaps their greater determination and potential to succeed compared to applicants from more privileged backgrounds.

Panelists are aware that they apply different standards as the group's deliberations progress beyond the few proposals for which a consensus is reached rather quickly. An English scholar states:

We all talked about weaknesses in [the last six] in ways we hadn't talked about [the others] . . . This is one where the topic may have been the criterion that made the difference, and this speaks to the affirmative action business. I'm comfortable with saying, "The top six are decided on this academic excellence, and then there are other factors that have more weight with the others" . . . Taking the other criteria into account [is important] . . . We're talking about relevance of study, how important a study is to a particular field, or many fields at this particular point in time, how much it's needed.

Thus consistency in the use of rules competes with other considerations as the panelists assess and reassess what constitutes a fair process for the group of proposals as a whole.

"Excellence versus Diversity"

Whether it is appropriate to "factor in" diversity criteria remains a contentious question among many academics, because many are unaware that most decisions are de facto based on a combination of excellence and diversity considerations. Purists argue that only excellence should be considered in the distribution of awards.[25] An economist, for instance, is skeptical of panels' ability to accommodate diversity considerations ("it's only under a very unlikely roll of the dice that you would get talent"). He argues that

Academia is intrinsically an elitist enterprise. We don't let everybody into college in this country; we don't let everybody into grad school; we don't give everybody a tenure track job; we don't tenure everybody. And that's a good thing . . . It's kind of like a popular feel-good urge to say, "Let's root for the underdog and hope they win." I think you should fund underdogs if they've got a good proposal.

Anticipating such objections, "progressive" panelists introduce nuances in the collective conversation around these issues. For instance, an English professor argues that producing diverse knowledge fosters excellence and should not be equated with a lowering of standards. Others take a strong stance in favor of combining types of criteria. Thus a political scientist explains, "Well, it's healthy when there are competing criteria put forward vigorously in dialogue with one another. And I think it's healthy to temper your own criteria with consideration of alternative criteria. I think where we get into trouble is where one set of criteria, whether it's excellence or diversity or what have you, are used to the exclusion of all other criteria." Still others seem to want to promote diversity, but within limits, and on a case-by-case basis, as this English professor suggests:

> We shouldn't run a place on some abstract idea, or a contextualist idea of academic excellence, because that would privilege one class of people and it wouldn't do anything for diversity. How far one strays from academic excellence to meet the other goals, you probably have to do that pragmatically, case by case, moment by moment. But I think it should be done.

In promoting greater racial and gender diversity among awardees, some panelists purposefully aim to break down the opposition between "standards of excellence" and "diversity standards." A prominent feminist who has served for many years on panels at the National Endowment for the Humanities and the American Association of University Women recalls promoting women academics and women's studies proposals at a time when these organizations were not inclined to fund them. She explains that she "would not argue for them as women's studies projects, but as being excellent," stating that over time general standards of excellence and standards pertaining to feminist scholarship have converged, so that now they are nearly indistinguishable. Speaking of the Woodrow Wilson Women's Studies competition, she says:

> To me, to win one of these [fellowships], you can't have one without the other . . . Women's studies scholars . . . really do have to master more. Because you could be very good, say, in seventeenth-century literature, and not pay any attention to women . . . But to win in this competition, you would have to not only master that field, but also master the feminist theory that speaks to that field. And I think they're absolutely crucial, they've got to have both.

Speaking of her own past, she recalls, "I had to be excellent in the standard fields and then be excellent in women's studies . . . Some of the people who had done more conventional work [in the past] chalked it up to, 'Oh, well, she does feminist stuff and that's really hot.'" That this panelist and others have experienced strong tensions between (not to mention discrimination over) being appreciated for high-quality scholarship and doing innovative work that contributes to the institutionalization of a new field speaks to the pervasive and far-reaching drama of diversity in academic evaluation.

Perspectives on Diversity: Panelists of Color

I conducted nine interviews with nonwhite panelists—seven African-American and two Asian evaluators. As in the larger group of respondents, here too I found significant variation in the approach to diversity as a criterion of selection. At one end of the spectrum, one panelist explicitly aims to ensure that diversity in all its manifestations is represented among the winners: "My agenda was to make sure that the list reflected some diversity in terms of demographics, you know, the representation of different kinds of schools, different fields, and ideally, scholars of color." At the opposite extreme, another panelist mentions that her panel did not explicitly apply diversity criteria: "We were pretty much going through and randomly judging each application on its own merits. There was no discussion of 'Well, we have too many history or we have too many of this.' There seemed to be no reason then to discuss race if you're just going through and making a determination just based on the individual projects and not other considerations." This same panelist, however, reports that during her second year on the panel, when the discussion turned to which of the proposals ranked "2" (the "maybe" category) should receive funding, she sought to promote underrepresented topics and applicants of color. "[I supported] topics that spoke to interests that I thought were not well represented in a pool of applications we had already supported . . . [and whose authors] themselves are in underrepresented groups."

It is nearly impossible to determine whether white and nonwhite panelists are equally likely to interpret diversity questions as pertaining to race, given the considerable variation that exists within each group. Moreover, because academics in the social sciences and the humanities are, overall, progressive, the promotion of diversity may very well be so taken for granted among panelists that there seems to be no need to explicitly discuss it. (As a sociologist puts it, "The people on the committee were nice and progressive people, so in our minds there was no [need for a] straightforward discussion of that.")[26] Nevertheless, we find positions among whites that are absent among nonwhites. For instance, one white panelist, an anthropologist, opposes any consideration of race because doing so seems patronizing toward nonwhites and to promote privileged people of color:

In my university, we are about to make an offer to someone, a woman from India who's from a high caste and probably grew up with twelve servants and so on, but she's considered under a special minority hiring. We can hire her without any search for a position that doesn't otherwise exist. I find that totally baffling. Certainly, if there were any evidence again of bias against minorities, that would be something to root out, but I just haven't encountered that . . . In other words, if we're not using the same standard, whatever that is, I'd be worried about being patronizing—you know, "Well, I've got to lower the standard, it's a black candidate."

Very few panelists mention class diversity. They do not appear to question that middle-class students, who are generally better endowed culturally for academic success through various forms of transmitted cultural capital, will be privileged in most academic selections. One interviewee, however, notes:

[Class diversity] is a deep problem for the American university in that gradually and [despite] many different kinds of efforts, the pool of people going into the humanities is becoming less diverse, wealthier, and more established—I don't know the situation in the social sciences. When you make a selection like this, you're already selecting from what is mostly [a] bourgeois group of very privileged people who have gone to elite universities and colleges, even if they didn't come from the elite . . . There were people from Harvard and Wellesley, but there was also a kid from Berkeley who supported himself managing a Barnes and Noble. So it was very good to see that we had a real range.

Awareness of Gender Bias

Social science research has contributed important findings on gender discrimination in scholarly performance evaluations.[27] For instance, a widely cited study of peer-reviewed evaluations of post-doctoral research applications shows that reviewers consistently gave female applicants lower average scores than male applicants, despite similar levels of productivity.[28] More broadly, we know that men's traits are generally viewed as more valuable than women's, and that men are generally judged as more competent.[29] In addition, women academics are often perceived as "less productive and/or incapable of succeeding in full-time, tenure-track positions," which results in women's performances being subject to both more scrutiny and higher standards than the performances of comparable men.[30] "Attribution biases" are frequent; these occur when "people tend to attribute the behavior of members of their in-group to stable causes, while they attribute the behavior of out-groups to situational causes: he's brilliant, but she just got lucky."[31] Such biases are especially likely in situations of tokenism, for example, when there are only a few women in a department or within a rank. Social categorization and same-group ("in-group") biases that lead to attribution biases are part of normal cognition, and they occur regardless of people's conscious feelings toward other groups.[32] Only continual self-evaluation, time, and systems of accountability can redirect these cognitive tendencies.

These findings inform the scholarship of some of the panelists, several of whom are well versed in the literature on gender inequality in academia. For instance, a political scientist explains that men may be more likely to dismiss the work of women colleagues as "not interesting," and that such appraisals "would obviously be a case of kind of bias . . . it would be rare that you'll find that the people who are different from you are doing things that you rate more highly." Also aware of the literature on bias, a historian, when asked how he deals with questions of diversity as he evaluates proposals, answers: "I [don't] foreground them, but I try to take them into serious consideration . . . After I've gone through a batch of proposals I look for a pattern. Are the ones that I'm scoring higher distinguished by gender, by discipline, [by being] at research universities, and so forth?" This panelist also recalls the panel as a whole being sensitive to bias. He provided the example of a time when "someone remarked, 'Hey, two of the last three were not at major universities.' And suddenly somebody attended to that matter, and we said, 'Yes, that is true.' We wanted to make sure we were not blindly ignoring those kinds of things."

Others focus on some of the more subtle ways that gender influences evaluation. For instance, one sociologist, citing the work of Pierre Bourdieu and Jean-Claude Passeron on "strategies of relegation" (or self-tracking) among working-class students, suggests that women may be less likely to win fellowships because they deliberately choose more traditional topics and "safer" professional strategies.[33] Another woman, an anthropologist serving on the Society of Fellows panel, notes that men interview much better than women; they are more at ease. "[There is the] male interview style, [which is more] persuasive, and the certain female interview style, not quite as pushy. It's not necessarily apologetic, but just not as strong. They seem not good and that's something we have to watch out for." Alternatively, she notes that women often lose points because they are perceived as too aggressive, in line with findings that ambitious women are penalized if they claim rewards for their achievements.[34] Indeed, studies indicate that when men are assertive, their behavior is perceived as evidence of great talent, but when women exhibit the same behavior, they are seen as being too aggressive. Similarly, men and women who engage in "self-promotion" are often viewed in different ways, with the men admired for their accomplishments, while the women are seen as arrogant.[35]

Finally, indirect biases arise from the fact that women often privilege qualitative research and constructivist epistemological approaches. Elisabeth Clemens and her colleagues show that in sociology, women are proportionately more likely than men to write books, especially books that use qualitative data.[36] A panel that favors quantitative work over qualitative work could thus put women at a disadvantage. In comparing the epistemological styles valued by panelists, my colleagues and I found that women were more likely to use a constructivist style than men.[37] A panel that values more a positivist epistemological style would thus also put women at a slight disadvantage. In these cases, discrimination results not from direct gender bias but from adopting criteria of selection that are slanted in favor of men.[38] Considered together, these factors suggest a possible "cumulative advantage" that works in favor of men—a possibility heightened by the presence of additional influences, such as those discussed in Chapter 5 (for example, letters of recommendation for male applicants appear to be more detailed and make a stronger impression on panelists).[39] Similar factors may also increase the likelihood of tenure for men as compared to women. A comparative study of young men and women academic stars could potentially reveal contrasting patterns in the role played by mentors, the passing on of privileges, and the advantages provided by having a stay-at-home partner and other informal resources.

Institutional Affirmative Action

As its name indicates, the American Council for Learned Societies is an organization of national associations. It serves a highly diverse membership. The participating associations represent those working in public and private universities, elite and nonelite universities, research universities and liberal arts colleges, institutions with heavy or light teaching loads, and universities located in less central areas. For those serving on the ACLS's panel, therefore, diversity concerns are salient. This umbrella organization wants its distribution of awards to reflect the diverse morphology of American higher education, including its geographical dispersion and the various categories of institutions. A representational logic is not strictly applied, but it is a factor. In this organization, distributing awards across the associations' various constituencies is a matter not only of fairness, but also of organizational efficacy.

Other competitions also ask their panelists to take institutional diversity into consideration when making awards, as this panelist indicates:

> We had the usual injunction from the program officer that we should be careful to consider underrepresented institutions as one extra plus in a proposal's favor, though not to [the extent that it would] cancel out [other negative attributes] if we thought the proposal was weak. And equally, if we saw that we were over-rewarding to any given institution, to recall that. He said the way we should think about it is, we don't want all the Michigan or Columbia people in one year; we want the best of their cohort. And that means, of course, in a way, [that] the person [who's] fifth in line at Columbia in our imaginations might [have turned] out to be first in line if they [had been] at, you know, SUNY–New Paltz.

During post-deliberation interviews, more than a third of the panelists mentioned institutional "affirmative action" as a criterion of evaluation. Much as panelists are encouraged to follow the rule of cognitive contextualism by applying the epistemological style most appropriate to the applicant's field (see Chapter 4), funding program officers urge them to apply different standards depending on the resources available at the applicant's institution and the applicant's career stage. An English scholar working in women's studies describes how she factors in institutional criteria:

> I'm going to cut someone less slack if they're at Rutgers or some other institution that has a lot of women's studies, or at Maryland, but [if she's] stuck at Northern Illinois or is out in Utah where there is a lot of hostility to feminist issues . . . where it's

open hostility that may even sometimes involve violence, I think, man, this person has really worked to get as far as she has. And if what she has done is excellent and there's promise that it will continue to be, then I say, that's a good affirmative action.

Panelists practice institutional affirmative action because they believe that private, elite, and research-focused universities are privileged in the competition process. For instance, an English professor observes: "When we finally looked at our final ten awards, we were chagrined that they were almost all to people at major research universities, or at places where the teaching load was probably relatively low . . . We didn't judge ourselves, but I think we had some talk about that as the proposals went by." Similarly, a political scientist says about funded projects in her field:

> It didn't please me so much that three of the four political science ones went to Berkeley. I have nothing against that. I actually think Berkeley's a great place; I went there . . . I think that Berkeley does train fabulous comparative political scientists . . . But . . . you'd like to see a number of schools succeeding.

Top institutions often put an array of resources at the disposal of applicants—including internal graduate research fellowship competitions, closer mentoring, and more extensive graduate course offerings. One panelist notes, "Occasionally you get a proposal from someone that is really off the beaten track of these research universities. Clearly, they are at a big disadvantage both in not having colleagues around to help and not having the help to talk about the proposal, just not being well-informed about the kind of research method that goes on." This same person adds:

> Once a student enters a second- or third-rate program and works with someone who's totally unknown, you know, even though

they might in fact have as good qualities as anybody else, they're going to be at a major disadvantage. Partly because for graduate students, it's very hard to evaluate their training other than by these kinds of institutional means.

Demonstrating the Matthew effect, according to which capital goes to capital, being affiliated with a prestigious university can keep a proposal above the bar.[40] A sociologist describes this phenomenon while discussing a project by a scholar of China who teaches at the University of Pennsylvania:

> I know that Chinese literature at Penn is very highly regarded, and she can't be a dummy doing this particular kind of work, and it was a beautiful proposal . . . This is a subject that if she had been from some tiny little hole-in-the-wall college, it's not likely, I don't think. For me, I mean. I don't know about the others because we didn't really talk about these subtleties. But I know in my case, when I see where she is, and she's a professor, which they don't give out so much, I assume that this must be a very good person.

Scholars working at elite universities have a more nuanced view of differences among institutions at the top, particularly with respect to how they prepare students for competitive fellowships. A historian of China says:

> People from Harvard get no advice of any kind, whereas at Stanford they have to submit draft after draft and they get all these comments . . . It's like teaching people to the test; it's not necessarily something we want to encourage . . . in the end, I want our first emphasis to be along excellence. But we have to sort of add points for certain kinds of diversity because in the end that promotes more excellence than allowing this to devolve into the control of just a few institutions.

For an English scholar, the solution is to fund "people from other than Ivy League or Research I institutions, people from sort of smaller colleges, who might not have had access to research support and might be read as 'under-published.' Also people from different parts of the country, people from ethnic studies, if possible, that kind of thing."

Panelists also sometimes suggest limiting fellowships for applicants who have already received them in the past. This is a sensitive issue, in part because track record is read as indicating excellence, and in part because it raises the issue of need. Assessing need is largely framed as illegitimate—panelists do not even mention it as a consideration. Still, tensions exist around whether it should be factored in. The legitimacy of need, like that of institutional affirmative action, turns on distributive justice, which is a different principle of allocation than that of merit.[41] At the center of the debates is whether scholars who have access to many resources should get more, or whether those who have access to very little should be advantaged. One panelist, a sociologist, argues strongly against institutional affirmative action because he believes that the distribution of the cultural and social capital that come with institutional affiliation cannot easily be manipulated:

> The chair of our panel seemed to be quite keen on [promoting] underrepresented institutions. I tend not to be all that sympathetic to that argument. It's stupid to be prejudiced against, say, people who are pursuing advanced graduate work at Oklahoma State. But it may very well be that, for example, just to pick a topic out of the hat, if you want to do a study of [a] nineteenth-century French critique of bureaucracy, . . . maybe it's not the best place to pursue that kind of work, given that there aren't adequate faculty members, you know, infrastructures or what not. So by and large, [it's] an unfortunate fact of life that other things being equal, someone who went to Stanford and studied with Keith Baker or

whoever would probably be better off, and it's kind of silly to try to amend that.

Self-interest influences the position that some scholars take on the question of institutional affirmative action. A panelist who teaches at UCLA believes that the funding competitions are biased against public school students:

> At UCLA you see a lot of bright people, but they're coming out of miserable school systems . . . They are not going to rise to the top in a competition like SSRC . . . [neither will] somebody who goes through a program that doesn't have a rigorous sort of theoretical background. So that sort of biases it against like Big Ten type schools, the UC system as a public school system. But it puts a lot more emphasis I think on the very schools that keep getting funded—Chicago, Harvard, the Ivy League schools, as well as Berkeley.

Affirmative Action Regarding Research Topics

Two of the funding competitions privilege specific types of research: that emanating from the field of women's studies (the WWNFF competition); and comparative work (the SSRC's International Dissertation Field Research competition). These competitions instruct panelists to consider potential contributions to these specific areas when evaluating proposals. But beyond these explicit and organizationally specific foci, some panelists favor topics of scholarship that they particularly value, and which they believe are neglected. This is what I call "substantive affirmative action." A political scientist who promotes it in the name of originality says:

> Non-Western subjects, we felt an obligation to give those a kind of extra advantage . . . Opening up scholarship in relatively un-

touched areas seems to me a good thing to do. Some of the applications that I remember being very beautifully crafted fell lower in the rankings, either overall or just in my view, because they were going over such familiar ground. And even if the person was brilliant and had something somewhat original to say about it, I would end up feeling that this is less important work overall than scholarship in some area that Western scholars just don't have any exposure to.

Feminist scholarship and "non-Western topics" frequently are portrayed as having been historically neglected or "marginalized." Feminist research has been circumscribed by a tradition of gender-neutral scholarship that ignores the gendered character of all aspects of social life; non-Western topics have been hampered by a Eurocentric scholarly tradition that privileges "the West" over all other areas.[42] Both also are likely to be identified by more conservative forces as politically correct pet topics of the academic left, along with critical subaltern studies, antipositivist research, and work that addresses antiglobalization and environmentalism.

The earlier work of Everett Carl Ladd Jr. and Seymour Martin Lipset, as well as the more recent work of sociologists Neil Gross and Solon Simmons, shows how politically progressive academics are overall, especially in the social sciences and the humanities.[43] Thus it is hardly surprising that quality and social justice are conflated at times. Academics who see their research as contributing in very significant ways to the production of social representations are concerned with giving voice to subordinate, neglected, or marginal groups. This type of social contribution has become particularly valued since the 1980s, with the growing influence of "history from below" in cultural history; of the Birmingham School (with its focus on resistance) in English, cultural studies, sociology, and anthropology; and with parallel developments in political theory (where the influence of critical theory remains pronounced). Of course, the development of women's studies has also had an important, independent influence as an extraordinarily dynamic interdisciplinary and disciplinary field.[44]

Panelists offer a wide range of reasons for privileging scholarship emanating from women's studies or from feminist perspectives. Some appeal to homophilic preferences—where excellence is what looks most like one's own work (see Chapter 4)—but the "social usefulness of knowledge" is mentioned as well. An English professor well-known for her feminist scholarship explains:

> I certainly followed my own scholarly enthusiasm; I gave high marks to "feminist" projects or projects focusing on gender . . . Gender is a very important way in which the world and cultures are organized. Even though gender scholarship has been in the academy for twenty or thirty years, I still think that it's insufficiently integrated into many scholars' understanding of the world. So I'm very happy when I see projects that incorporate gender as part of their analytic equipment.

Feminist scholarship also is sometimes promoted on the grounds that in some quarters this type of work is the target of ridicule and discrimination. One anthropologist notes, "I've served on a lot of committees now with political scientists in my own institution, and in a couple of cases cross-institutionally, and [they were] very hostile to feminist work and women's work." An English scholar who noted little opposition to gender proposals on her panel reasons that other panelists may have felt "guilty" or been "embarrassed to admit" that they had little interest in feminist work. She contrasts this with the situation in her department, where "people make no bones about disparaging feminist scholarship. They do that very freely."

Precisely because some panelists explicitly privilege feminist scholarship, proposals that receive such support can be construed as substandard by unsympathetic panelists. A political scientist describes his reaction to a women's studies proposal:

> This proposal that I thought was really badly done might have gone through because they were giving this woman a break. It was related to a women's studies question, her thesis. She was a woman. She was coming from a real second-tier institution. But it was a project in an area of women's studies that clearly needed more research and everything. So . . .

Feminist research is valued in part because it serves practical purposes and is meant to have a transformative social role. This standard of evaluation, however, is rejected by those panelists who value the production of knowledge as an end in itself (typically, the same panelists who espouse comprehensive or positivist epistemological styles). These opposing understandings of the purpose of research create tension. An anthropologist who directed a program in women's studies for several years notes that "women's studies people" frequently are in "a defensive battle [where] they are having to say that 'feminist' doesn't mean that academic excellence is lowered." Despite the field's increased legitimacy, "Some people are still going to bridle at the preface 'feminist' because they're going to think, 'Well, if it's related to a cause, then it can't be necessarily trustworthy.'"

The tension is not only over the aim of knowledge, but also over conceptions of objectivity and of "positionality" in the production of high-quality research. Because positivism as an epistemological style requires bracketing the relationship between the researcher and her topic, it is incompatible with developments in feminist research, whereas standpoint theory emphasizes that one's relationship with the object of study defines the lens through which the research is conducted—a position that gives greater latitude to feminist-oriented scholarship.[45]

A different logic is applied to substantive affirmative action directed toward non-Western subjects. While preferences for certain topics and perspectives in these areas could be seen as idiosyncratic, panelists legitimize them on substantive grounds (for example, by referring to breadth, originality, or scholarly significance), and do so using the language of expertise. A historian of China, for instance, emphasizes intellectual breadth when she defines diversity in opposition to Eurocentrism: "I would really welcome people who knew there was something besides the Euro-American, Western tradition and could work on it . . . I feel it's my job to make those points, and I don't feel that they're necessarily very strongly influential. It's more like a little tweak or a nag."

She adds to the formal criteria used by the funding program a criterion of her own:

Awareness of the [intellectual] world beyond their focus . . . It's not just international. Many people are extremely either . . . usually Eurocentric . . . or Americano-centric . . . It's very common in the academy, but I like to point it out when I find it and I consider it a sign of narrowness . . . [I dislike] the pomposity of people who make sweeping [statements] always . . . based on Europe. As a person who's been in the China field for thirty or forty years, it's very annoying. It just shows their ignorance.

Another panelist, a sociologist, admits that for him, "There are absolutely some areas which are pet areas." He favors proposals that address these topics and geographic areas not for personal reasons, but because they make accessible materials that are otherwise "hard to find."

At the same time, some panelists refuse to engage in substantive affirmative action because doing so seems ill-advised, like favoring proposals that emanate from one's own field. One respondent firmly rejects factoring this diversification of topics into his own thinking about what to fund:

> There's no way I will be able to figure that into my reading . . . I don't have information [to make such judgments]. Even if I have the information, would I say, "OK, there are already ten people who study South Korea and this proposal is well written, but there are already ten people, and therefore I will grade it low?" [Doing that] just doesn't make sense to me.

This scholar prefers to grade on quality only, but he admits that later in the deliberative process, other factors are taken into consideration: "Then we shuffle them and put them together . . . At that level, I'm not judging them on the basis of quality, I'm just judging them on the basis of representation, and I would feel extremely fine [about it]." Separating the "real evaluation" from the negotiated rankings is a conceptual framework that allows panelists to protect the sanctity of the process (see Chapter 4).

Similarly, as a political scientist's comments suggest, by combining evaluative rationales—those related to expertise as well as to social justice—panelists can preserve legitimacy while incorporating diversity criteria. He describes his support for a proposal in archeology this way:

> [The proposal] was the only one I read in archeology, and so part of it was simply trying to widen the spectrum of people [whom] we funded. But it wasn't just simply a quota system, getting an archeologist in the group photo. He made a pretty reasonable case that when anthropologists and cultural historians have studied Islam, they tended to derive most of their understandings about

medieval Islam from the urban environment. By looking at this particular spatial location . . . in terms of the mixture of different influences, cultural influences, one could have a very different understanding about the nature of medieval Islam . . . I liked the multi-dimensionality of the project.

Partly because they are interdisciplinary disciplines that concern "diverse" populations, fields such as women's studies, African-American studies, and ethnic studies struggle to keep from being pushed to the periphery, or to the bottom of the academic totem pole. The same is true of other interdisciplinary fields, such as cultural studies.[46] That so much uncertainty remains about how to insert considerations of diversity and interdisciplinarity into scholarly evaluation underscores the fact that older, more established disciplines continue to define the rules of the game, contributing to the fragility of these fields.

Conclusion

Interdisciplinarity and diversity are among the main challenges that American higher education faces at the beginning of the twenty-first century. While interdisciplinarity has been a permanent feature of tertiary education ever since disciplines began to compete with one another to maximize their jurisdictional claims, the challenge of diversity has become even more pronounced since the 1960s, as various groups have piggy-backed on the hard-won gains that African Americans have made toward greater inclusion.[47] While elite institutions have become more diverse, conflicting visions persist, and these reverberate in panel dynamics.

Because of the very elite character of academic research, tensions around diversity may be intrinsic to American higher education, which itself is pulled between its democratic mission, the pursuit of knowledge, and market pressures.[48] Because so many social scientists and humanists are liberal or progressive, they are also concerned that the elite not be favored at the expense of meritocracy. As an anthropologist puts it, "Those who have famous advisers and are at [the] top three or four universities will be ranked higher than people who aren't, even if the quality of the proposal is the same. It seems to me there's far too much elitism and just [a] sort of favoritism."

Perhaps there is something distinctively American in how these tensions are experienced, something that is linked to the sheer size of the higher education system, to its spatial dispersion, and to its institutional diversity and its uniquely wide-ranging sociodemographic variations. That American panelists deploy so much energy to elaborate positions with regard to diversity that are nuanced and compatible indicates how aware they are of the sheer complexity of the academic world they inhabit. Their attentiveness to the issue contrasts with the situation in most European countries, where higher education systems are smaller and more homogeneous, and thus less subject to a complicated weighing of nontraditional considerations like diversity when academic achievements are evaluated. In these countries, considerations such as spreading the riches across types of institutions do not arise to the same degree. For example, the British reform of evaluation processes imposed during the 1980s promoted a straightforward application of meritocratic standards that allowed no consideration of needs and distributive fairness, in response in part to the historically ascriptive system of distribution that favored elite institutions such as Oxford and Cambridge.[49]

Despite its democratic impulse, the sheer size of the American system, along with the entrenched hierarchy of institutions that characterize it, may doom efforts to free it of ongoing elitism. A British panelist notes how American students from better universities are privileged:

> They've got all the best professors anyway. For example, people talk about, "Well, you know, so and so is our supervisor, so that would give me confidence that the work will be done even despite the doubts about it," and that's so inside-knowledge. But it's also an assumption about the role between the supervisor and the student.

Nevertheless, the claims regularly made by lower-rank universities for privileging justice-inflected alternative principles of distribution are certainly a force for social change. This is the case notably within professional associations such as the American Sociological Association, where elections to important committees make room for various subcategories of candidates, including sociologists working in four-year institutions, as well as applied sociologists. The response to a push from within the American Political Science Association for a similar approach, however, is a vivid reminder that dilemmas of democracy are handled very differently across disciplines. Segments of the APSA's top leadership resisted this suggestion, preferring to maintain the status quo, whereby members simply rubber-stamp a list of nominees chosen by members of the discipline's elite—although this list does include individuals teaching in a range of types of institutions. These two different disciplinary responses, which continue to generate much angst within segments of each discipline, clearly demonstrate how meritocracy and democracy often operate as antinomic principles within the context of American higher education. That academics are struggling so hard—or not struggling at all—to reconcile them speaks volumes about their importance as buttresses to the structure of our academic world. In addition, that these two principles exist in tension helps us understand why so often excellence and diversity do not function as alternative criteria of evaluation, but as additive, complementary factors—despite popular perceptions and rhetorical attacks against affirmative action and other policies aimed at promoting diversity within higher education. Like excellence, diversity appears to have become a moral imperative of the system—another manifestation of what is sacred in American academia.[50]

7/Implications in the United States and Abroad

n American higher education, excellence, merit, and quality are often captured by quantitative measures such as GRE and SAT scores (if you are a student) or number of citations (if you are a researcher). But when it comes to evaluating the proposed work of academics across disciplines, simple measures like these usually will not do. Instead, scholars are brought together to deliberate the merits of these proposals. As historians, political scientists, anthropologists, and literary scholars weigh in with their particular expertise, they also learn from one another, improvise, opine, convince, and attempt to balance competing standards. They strategize, high-ball, and follow scripts shaped by their academic disciplines, but they also contextualize and compromise. They respect alternative perspectives and expect reciprocity. They try to impress other panelists, save face, and help others do the same. They set the agenda, flex their muscles, see if they measure up, and enjoy intellectual barter. They invest themselves in decisions and share excitement with others. They reach "good enough" solutions instead of ideal ones, because they have to get the job done in the time allotted. They go home usually feeling that they have risen to the occasion, betraying neither "the system" nor themselves. They have stood for principles, but not so rigidly that they could not reach consensus. For them, panels are an opportunity to be influential, and to be appreciated.

Within practical constraints, panelists aim to "produce the sacred" of fair evaluation, while respecting institutional, disciplinary, and other diversities. In particular, disciplinary cultures are tempered by the exigencies of multidisciplinary evaluation. Evaluators aim for consistency in standards across disciplines even as they use standards appropriate to the discipline of the applicant. They both engage in consensual and egalitarian decision making and defer to expertise. In addition, evaluators attempt to balance meritocracy and diversity, seeing these as complementary ideals, not alternatives.

The panelists' experience reflects many of the system's tensions, and the doubts these tensions create. Just how biased is academia? Do people get what they deserve? Am I getting what I deserve? Their collective evaluation mobilizes and intertwines emotions, self-interest, and expertise. Moreover, it requires coordinating actions and judgments through a culture of evaluation that has been established long before the panelists set foot in the deliberative chambers.

This story is fundamentally about fairness and the attempt to achieve it. What is presented as expertise may sometimes be merely preference ("taste"), described in depersonalized language. The reciprocal recognition of authority is central to the process, but it may lead to explicit horse-trading, which produces suboptimal results. Despite these potential hazards, however, panelists think the process works, in part because they adopt a pragmatic conception of "truth" (or at least of what constitutes a "fair evaluation") as something inevitably provisional and defined by the best standards of the community at the time.[1] Indeed, the constraints on the evaluative process—particularly the considerable time that panelists spend preparing for deliberations and their dedication to convincing their peers of the merit of their point of view—go a long way toward creating the conditions for a more meritocratic system. The performative effects of positing a meritocratic system are comparable to those of having "faith in the market": the belief creates the conditions of its own existence—within limits.[2]

Some academics have a propensity to assume that quality is intrinsic to the work and that some scholars have a natural talent for finding it. But in fact the "cream" does not rise naturally to the top, nor is it "dug out" in unlikely places: it is produced through expert interaction, with the material provided by applicants. Neither the work nor the people are socially disembedded. Panelists' definitions of excellence are rooted and arise from their networks of colleagues and ideas. They aim for fairness, but the taken-for-granted aspects of social life—the cognitive structures they use routinely, the multiple networks of which they are a part—may lead them to assume that what appeals to them is simply best.

So evaluation is contextual and relational, and the universe of comparables is constantly shifting. Proposals demand varied standards, because they shine under different lights. In some cases, the significance of the proposed work is determined by the likely generalizability of its findings. In others, how a topic informs our understanding of broader processes is more important. In yet other cases, significance is assessed by the deeper understanding that results from a particular interpretation. In panel deliberations, the ideal of a consistent or universalist mode of evaluation is continually confronted with the reality that different proposals require a plurality of assessment strategies.

This plurality manifests itself starkly when disciplinary evaluative cultures are exposed in the kinds of arguments that individual panelists make for or against proposals, and in how these arguments are received—factors that together influence which proposals will be funded. In evaluating excellence, formal and informal criteria of evaluation are weighed differently by humanists, social scientists, and historians. Yet across fields, excellence is viewed as a moral as well as a technical accomplishment. It is thought to be a result of determination and hard work, humility, authenticity, and audacity. Other "evanescent qualities" count too, even if, as is the case for elegance and the display of cultural capital, they run counter to the meritocratic ideal that animates the system.

The self-concept of evaluators is central to the process of assessment, especially to the perception that the decision making is fair. Panelists evaluate one another as they evaluate proposals. Their respect for customary rules sustains their identity as experts and as fair and broadminded academics, who as such deserve to serve on funding panels. Yet if their self-concept orients knowledge production and evaluation, panelists downplay its role, often viewing it as an extraneous and corrupting influence.[3]

For most panelists, interdisciplinarity and diversity are aspects of excellence, not alternatives to it. Because there is a lack of agreement on the standards of evaluation for interdisciplinary genres, panelists readily fall back on the tools they have available—existing disciplinary standards—to determine what interdisciplinary research should be funded. While debates about diversity in higher education have focused mostly on gender and racial and ethnic diversity, the scholars I talked to were most concerned with institutional and disciplinary diversity. They see diversity as a good that can lead to a richer academic life for all and to a broader production of talent for society as a whole.

Like the panelists in my study, many American academics take for granted the legitimacy of the peer review system. Yet estimates of the fairness of the meritocratic process may ebb and flow with one's own academic successes and level of ambition. Empirical research should establish whether outsiders have the least faith. The peer review process is deeply influenced by who gets asked to serve as a panelist and what viewpoints and intellectual habitus those individuals bring to the table. Biases are unavoidable. In particular, program officers tend to extend invitations to the most collegial (who may be the least objectionable and most conventional) scholars and those whose careers are already established. Thus peer review is perceived to be biased against daring and innovative research—an explanation I have often consoled myself with when my own research proposals have been denied funding. And it is true that, at the end of the day, we cannot know for sure whether the "cream rises." But if panelists believe that it does, and make considerable sacrifices to do a good job, they contribute to sustaining a relatively meritocratic system. A system where cynicism prevailed at all levels would most likely generate much greater arbitrariness, and would result in less care being put into the decision-making process and into the preparation of applications.

Exporting the U.S. Evaluation Model Abroad

The peer review system I have described is often associated with American higher education, although it is of course practiced elsewhere. Particularly in Europe, this system has become an explicit point of reference for the teaching reforms of the "Bologna Process" put in place by the member states of the European Union.[4] Named after a 1999 Bologna Declaration, this process "puts in motion a series of reforms needed to make European Higher Education more compatible and comparable, more competitive and more attractive for Europeans and students and scholars from other continents . . . to match the performance of the best performing systems in the world, notably the United States and Asia."[5] Under the impetus of this declaration, the higher education systems of several European countries (including France and Germany) are undergoing major transformations aimed at bringing about greater standardization by 2010. References to peer review figure prominently in these efforts—

along with calls for other forms of rationalization, measurement, rankings, accreditations, standardization, and so on.[6]

These national conversations often have as a background idealized, vague, or ill-informed views concerning the actual practice of peer review in the United States today. Moreover, rarely is there a systematic reflection on the conditions that sustain such a system. For instance, conspicuous collegiality is essential in a vast, largely anonymous system where trust and tight social control through interpersonal contacts cannot be assumed; blind review is facilitated by the large number of universities and the sheer size of the academic community; and the geographic dispersion of universities makes centralized panel deliberation a necessity. These aspects do not apply to most European societies, and European policymakers do not always consider these conditions for the implementation of grant peer review. It is my hope that this book will inform these European conversations. Consideration of the roles played by unions of academics, the state, professional organizations, national funding agencies, and foundations in the evaluation of research and the distributed of resources is important. But so too is consideration of the legacy of different evaluative cultures, including whether meritocracy is considered a grand illusion, an impossibility, or a goal that can be approximated.

Consider the case of France. Today, many French scholars are skeptical of their colleagues' ability to have informed and disinterested opinions regarding the work of their peers.[7] Pierre Bourdieu's *Homo Academicus*, for example, used survey data to analyze the criteria of evaluation operating in university departments and research institutes.[8] Bourdieu argued that the criteria privileged in various institutions correspond to the type of endowment that their members are most likely to have. Traditional institutions such as the Sorbonne and the Ecole Normale Supérieure d'Ulm privilege traditional criteria of evaluation, such as mastering the philosophical foundation of a discipline and having a general culture, as opposed to acquiring a deep understanding of recent developments within substantive subfields. Cynicism toward meritocracy is often taken for granted, as is the view that evaluation is closely and directly tied to interpersonal networks, to localism.[9] The strong competition for a small number of positions in France may lead French applicants to delegitimize the system, dismissing those who "win" as simply better strategists or as benefiting from better support by their networks—not as more deserving.

In her comparison of university hiring decisions in France, Germany, and the United States, Christine Musselin has argued that Bourdieu exaggerated the extent to which the field position of academic institutions affects the criteria of evaluation used by scholars. She found that institutional location accounts for less than 15 percent of the variance in criteria. She concludes, however, that "personal connections" play a particularly crucial role in hiring for administrative and teaching positions in France. It turns out that the prime concern of hiring commissions is not ensuring fairness but reducing uncertainty concerning the different types of hires.[10]

This type of empirical study is exactly what is needed if we are to understand better how peer review is practiced across contexts and how its characteristics are the product of distinct national conditions. In particular we need to understand whether and how fairness is produced differently across systems of higher education. How do the French and American cultures of excellence, and the meanings attributed to the term, influence the evaluative practices of academics in both countries? The cult of success is found across a range of universities in the United States—from the smallest to the largest. What alternative grammars do we find in France?

Toward an Even More Social View of Peer Review

In line with rhetoricians and sociologists of science who address the coproduction of intersubjectivity, I have been concerned with how scholar-evaluators serving on peer review panels come to agreements through interactions.[11] My study examined not only how panelists justify their judgments, but also how the processes and rules of practice set the stage for a sense of legitimacy. This approach is in stark contrast to what remains the dominant approach in the study of peer review, with a focus on the abstract norms of science that are said to govern peer review, particularly norms regarding universalism and disinterestedness.

Panelists do not simply enact the rule of meritocracy (as functionalism would have it); they engage in a genuinely social—that is, interactional—micro-political process of collective decision making. They draw emotional and cognitive boundaries between the work they appreciate and the work they do not, and they do so within relationships of exchange and deliberation. The relationships they form during the negotiation process, based largely on shared "taste," influence the outcome, as do their preexisting networks, the epistemological and cultural similarities and differences between the fields they hail from, and their own temperaments and idiosyncrasies.

The older as well as the more recent literature on peer review focuses on issues of partiality and fallibility, as well as on risk avoidance, the Matthew effect, bias in favor of research that confirms commonly accepted theory, gender and ideological bias, and other external factors that may influence the possibility that a particular project will be labeled "of quality."[12] Authors have shown that the characteristics of scientists have very little effect on the evaluation of proposals, due to a lack of consensus among reviewers and self-selection among applicants.[13] This literature focuses on factors that can be viewed as somewhat exogenous and anomalous, but which may come to disturb the ordinary order of things. I maintain that such influences are fundamental to the peer review process, because evaluation is embedded in social and cognitive networks. Elements intrinsic to the evaluation process should not be construed as corrupting that process.[14] Trying to remove subjectivity entirely from evaluation is doomed to failure, because the evaluation process is intersubjective. The panelists' sense of the legitimacy of the process is as tied to unwritten customary rules that they themselves produced (and reproduce), as it is to broader norms of universalism and professionalism.

The literature on peer review proposes remedies such as double-blinding (or deleting from proposals bibliographic references that could lead to identification of researchers) in order to overcome known pitfalls. Yet given the contextual nature of evaluation, this strategy would not remove the possibility of bias. Although imperfect safeguards can still have value, it would be more useful to educate panelists about how peer evaluation works. It is particularly important to emphasize the dangers of homophily and how it prevents the identification of a wide range of talents. My hope is that the content of this book and the conversations it generates will make evaluators more aware of the influence of their personal "tastes" and, particularly, more concerned with actively countering their own idiosyncratic judgments.

In addition, at a minimum, peer review processes themselves should be subject to further evaluation, in order to determine, for instance, the most effective size of panels, the order in which panelists should look at elements of proposals, how often panelists should be rotated, and the criteria (formal and informal) by which they should be chosen. We may also need a more systematic approach to training screeners and to advising and supervising program officers. Overall, our collective aim should be to make the review process more transparent, while maintaining the privacy of the deliberations. And we must always acknowledge the inevitable element of randomness, chance, and plain dumb luck.

The panelists I interviewed might be said to be aiming for what

Jürgen Habermas describes as ideal speech conditions.[15] The fact that these evaluators are not part of a closely connected community probably increases their ability to keep their personal interests at bay. In this context, the book contains implications for scholars interested in deliberation and in decision theory.[16] Decision theory, strongly influenced by utility theory, posits that decisions are driven by the information required to assess the utility of various outcomes.[17] My analysis questions the notion of culturally disembedded evaluation and the view that some outcomes would be more rational than others.

My analysis is not, however, based exclusively on the discourse of justification. Nor do I claim to formulate an analysis of fields regarding position and discourse, à la Bourdieu.[18] Instead, I show how panelists create a sense of justice, an undertaking that I argue is not only a compromise between conflicting norms, but also an outcome of following customary rules within specific constraints.[19] Thus I identify a number of pragmatic constraints and customary rules that emerge from the requirements of the evaluative process: a need to finish the job within a certain time while maintaining the evaluators' commitment to the justice of the enterprise (as well as outsiders' view of the process as fair). These rules act as constraints on and regulators of behavior, but also function as justifications that create commitments in the justice of the enterprise.[20]

Implications for Other Types of Evaluation

The implications of my analysis of peer review may be helpful for understanding evaluation across a range of contexts, such as peer review journals, university presses, tenure review committees, or college admission, as well as athletic, artistic, and financial fields.[21] It could also enrich a much broader discussion of the group processes involved in producing legitimacy and conferring elite status in many different kinds of organizations. Screening and ranking play a role in selecting members of elite professional organizations and hiring and promotion decisions in high-prestige occupations. In each case, actors have to reach a consensus between competing definitions or instantiations of excellence. Like peer review panels, these contexts often are characterized by strong tensions, especially those between evaluation and self-interest, and between democratic principles and expertise.

The next step is to produce a general theory of valuation and the pragmatics of evaluation, with a focus on the constraints on the actions and success of evaluators across domains of activity and institutions.[22] We need a deeper understanding of the rules that evaluators follow to accomplish what they set out to do—especially rules concerning the intersubjective conventions and criteria of evaluation that escape individual control, and that are important to legitimating particular cultural products.[23] And we need to consider the increasingly complicated apparatus that produces the applicants—from the world of prep schools to graduate schools and beyond.[24]

Belief in the legitimacy of the system is essential to preserving the vitality of research and of higher education in the United States and beyond. At the same time, a Pollyannaish support for this system, as opposed to a full recognition of its contradictory character, will ultimately weaken it. So it is crucial to recognize its necessary embeddedness in human action and its frequent conflation of judgments of quality with judgments of taste. In the end, having a better understanding of peer evaluation and its imperfections may help academics to attempt to practice it with greater self-awareness as well as increased conviction.

Appendix: Methods and Data Analysis

The organizations that participated in this research are the American Council for Learned Societies, the Social Science Research Council, the Woodrow Wilson Society of Fellows, an anonymous foundation in the social sciences, and a Society of Fellows at an elite university. They were chosen based on a combination of the following criteria: (1) centrality in the world of social science and humanities funding, (2) diversity in types of panels, (3) convenience (personal contacts who would facilitate involvement), and (4) willingness to participate. The last two factors are particularly important because the data I aimed to obtain are highly confidential and very rarely made available to researchers. I had to engage in lengthy negotiations with some of these organizations before I was given access; I also had to sign a formal agreement covering the conditions of participants' involvement and protection of confidentiality.

The conditions for the recruitment of panelists varied. Two funding agencies strongly encouraged panelists to volunteer to be interviewed and three made my access contingent on panel members' unanimous agreement to participate. In all cases, I wrote to panel members to secure their individual consent, provide them with background information on the project, and invite them to discuss the research and their concerns. These letters of invitation stated unambiguously the purpose of the research and assured recipients that in the presentation of results all information that might lead to their identification would be safeguarded.

Respondents

A total of 81 interviews were conducted, including 66 interviews with 49 different panel members (17 panelists were interviewed twice, because they served on panels for the two years of the study period). Fifteen additional interviews were conducted with relevant program officers and chairpersons for each panel, who provided details about what had happened during the panel deliberation in the absence of direct observation. Panelists are distributed across a range of disciplines. The disciplines most represented are, in descending order, history (14); literature and anthropology (7 each); political science and sociology (6 each); anthropology (5); musicology (3); art history, economics, classics, and philosophy (2 each); and geography and evolutionary biology (1 each).

In addition to their disciplinary affiliation, some respondents identified themselves as having more than one field. For instance, a dozen individuals described themselves as involved in women's studies or in African-American studies. Thus, in the interviews, these two fields emerge as booming interdisciplinary areas that are significantly reshaping the social sciences as well as the humanities.[1] They also present some of the characteristics of "weak" disciplines as described by Thomas Bender—they are fields that do not display rigid external boundaries or strong internal consensus.[2]

I interviewed slightly more males than females. Respondents included seven African American and one Asian scholar. Almost two-thirds of the panelists taught in private institutions, with 27 teaching in an Ivy League university. This figure is particularly high in part because the Society of Fellows is located in such a university. All the panelists were tenured and the vast majority had previous experience serving on funding panels. They were not offered an honorarium for the service they provided, except in the case of one funding competition.

Interviewing

This research builds directly on my past work in cultural sociology, in particular, the study of evaluation criteria. Drawing on classics such as Robert Weiss's *Learning from Strangers,* I used a similar open-ended and inductive interviewing technique here to identify and explore the taken-for-granted criteria that panel members rely on to draw boundaries between deserving and undeserving research projects.[3]

Interviews generally lasted around ninety minutes. I decided to forgo face-to-face interviews in most cases because I was eager to collect insights from the panelists shortly after they had completed their deliberations. Thus the majority of the interviews were conducted over the phone a few hours or a few days following the panelists' meeting. Face-to-face interviews were conducted with panelists located within driving distance of my university. We typically met in a café or in the respondent's office. I read a large sample of proposals prior to the interviews and was able to ask specific questions about the arguments made in favor and against funding them.

Observing

I was able to observe three panels. The panelists had been informed of my presence ahead of time and had agreed to it. I was able to discuss my project with them prior to the deliberations. I also socialized with panelists during coffee breaks and at lunch, so as to attempt to blur the boundary between them and myself. In all cases, I believe I was treated more as a colleague than as an outsider. This was facilitated by the welcoming attitude that program officers and panel chairs manifested toward me from the onset. During the course of deliberation, I tried to be as inconspicuous as possible as I sat quietly at the end of a table. I took ample written notes and avoided betraying my reactions to arguments made by evaluators.

Reactivity and Confidentiality

I acknowledge that reactivity (the impact of the identity of the interviewer on the object of study) probably characterized both the dynamics of the panels I observed and the content of the interviews I conducted. It is likely that in anticipation of being interviewed, panelists were more reflexive about the criteria they used and about their behavior as evaluators. They may have been more aware of possible biases, and more likely to go the extra mile to try to limit their impact. Thus, their emphasizing that "cream rises" was certainly accentuated by the interview situation. But the in-depth interviews I conducted convinced me that this view is so pervasive (as illustrated by the data quoted in this book) that it cannot be explained solely by the communicative act that the interview represents.

One of the panels I observed in Year 1 was quite contentious. The funding organization refused to let me observe deliberations in Year 2 in part because the chairperson was concerned about reactivity, and also perhaps because of the discomfort panelists experienced from having heated debates in front of an outside observer.

The relationships I had with the panelists had a small impact on the interviews. I had close connections with only two respondents (one is a personal friend; the other, a close colleague in my field). I had a more distant relationship with three other panelists; their areas of research being somewhat related to mine. This relatively low degree of connectedness probably weakened the impact of reactivity on my results.

Because I am committed to preserving the anonymity of panel-ists and removing information that could lead to their identification, I do not provide a detailed analysis of the ways in which their em-beddedness within networks may shape their evaluations. Neither do I provide specific information concerning how distinctive organiza-tional features influence evaluation. Per my agreement with the par-ticipating organizations, the study explicitly does not concern the functioning of specific funding agencies. Instead, I treat the agencies as entry points to the world of peer review, channels through which to tap the discourse on excellence that prevails in American universi-ties and provide instantiation of this discourse. In a separate analysis, focused on the criteria of originality, my colleagues and I considered differences in the evaluative criteria used across panels. We did not find significant differences.[4]

Data Analysis

Interviews were tape-recorded and transcribed. I began by perform-ing a qualitative analysis of the transcripts that was inductive and thematic in nature, using analytic matrices that enable a systematic identification of criteria of evaluation.[5] The analysis centered on the differences and commonalities between and within disciplines by focusing on criteria used by people within the fields under study. I also paid particular attention to how people in different disciplines assessed the quality of the same proposal or candidate, as well as to how people in the same field assessed them. In addition, I consid-ered the formal categories of evaluation and criteria provided by the funding institutions, whether and how these were used by panelists, and what other categories and criteria they used.

I also asked two research assistants to independently content-analyze the interviews using the popular software Atlas.ti.[6] This soft-ware package increases inter-coder reliability by making it possible to standardize the set of codes to be used, track the codes assigned by each coder, and subject each transcript to coding by one coder and checking by another. The coding scheme took the following form: each descriptive word used by a respondent was classified within various categories and criteria of evaluation, many of which had been identified from the observations and interviews using analytic matrices. The codes were also derived inductively, with each coder initially coding the same two transcripts and developing their own coding scheme. The coding scheme was then standardized and the transcripts split randomly between coders. After this initial round of coding, the coders exchanged transcripts and verified and improved each other's work. For greater reliability, a third coder who was not involved in the development of the coding key recoded all the transcripts. Any conflicts were discussed with me and resolved. The coding key is available upon request.

Note that the interviews I conducted with program officers are not included in our analysis of the frequency of use of formal and informal criteria of evaluation and of epistemological styles. The five interviews I conducted with three different panel chairs are included, since they also served as peer reviewers and were asked about their criteria of evaluation.

The last phase of data analysis was to connect the thematic analysis of the transcripts with an analysis of the frequencies of themes and criteria produced with the assistance of Atlas.ti. Combining these two methods allows for depth in interpretation and for systematic quantitative analysis of themes and patterns within the data.

Limitations of the Study

In all phases of this study, I have been very aware of the many ways in which I am indebted to work of researchers who have come before, even while I am critical of some of their blind spots. This awareness has strengthened my view of research as a truly collective (and intergenerational) endeavor. It is against this background that I pinpoint some of the weaknesses of the book:

This study concerns only multidisciplinary panels. Our interviewees suggested that interdisciplinary panels are less contentious than disciplinary panels, to the extent that panelists tend to be less critical of proposals that speak to areas of research that they are less familiar with. Moreover, interdisciplinary panels are perceived to be less stringent from a methodological perspective than disciplinary panels because of the norm of cognitive contextualization. As a political scientist put it, "the National Science Foundation panel I was on was very concerned about being good science, being at the cutting edge of methodology and that was not a criterion for me on the present panel." As originally conceived, this book was to compare multidisciplinary panels with disciplinary panels. I have tried to take a stab at the differences between disciplinary and multidisciplinary panels elsewhere.[7]

This study considers only quality as defined in grant peer review panels. Instead of focusing on the panelists' representation of quality, I could have considered the decision-making process in academic hiring and promotion, peer review in scholarly journals and academic publishing, or historical changes in standards of evaluation. Or I might have interviewed veteran panelists about their past experience or assembled qualified focus groups to evaluate proposals. I believe the strategy I adopted is preferable for two main reasons: (1) Focusing on national funding programs, as opposed to local hiring and promotion decisions, enables greater generalizability of the findings about institutionalized categories and criteria of evaluation. Moreover, promotion decisions are based on factors such as teaching and service to the university, and are less exclusively about competing definitions of scholarly excellence. Finally, analyzing peer review panels at several funding institutions presents the advantages of being economical, of facilitating a systematic approach, and of drawing on data collected in roughly comparable sites—although the funding panels considered distribute research grants as well as dissertation, research, and scholars-in-residence fellowships; and (2) A historical approach would largely preclude drawing on interviews with evaluators, as well as taking unsuccessful proposals into account, since journals generally discard reviews of rejected manuscripts.

This study is based on a limited number of interviews. Negotiating access to funding panels required surmounting important obstacles. I did the best I could given the availability of funding organizations willing to participate in the study. I can only wish that other scholars will find here inspiration and will take on related research projects that will go beyond what I have accomplished.

Notes

1. Opening the Black Box of Peer Review

1. A general analysis of the system of peer review and of other means of allocating resources within academia can be found in Chubin and Hackett (2003). On various reward systems and gatekeepers, see also Crane (1976).

2. Cognitive psychologists and organizational behavior experts also focus on the identification of success, intelligence, creativity, and the development of excellent individuals. See, for example, Csikszentmihalyi (1996); Gardner (1999); Goleman, Boyatzis, and McKee (2002); and Ericsson (1996).

3. This approach is akin to that described in Latour (1988), Hennion (2004), Heinich (1996), and Rosental (2003) on the recognition of intellectual and cultural outputs. See also Frickel and Gross (2005) and Lamont (1987). On conventions, see Becker (1982).

4. My approach to evaluative cultures builds on Fleck's classic book *Genesis and Development of a Scientific Fact* (1979), which brought attention to the importance of "thought style" produced by "thought collectives." He also wrote about the "disciplined shared mood of scientific thought" (144).

5. Social scientists use the term "cultural scripts" to refer to widely available notions that individuals draw on to make sense of reality. On "scripts" in higher education, I draw on the work of John Meyer and his associates (2006),

which emphasizes the role of individual rationalist models diffused by Western higher education.

6. These evaluative cultures are embedded in epistemic cultures, such as peer review, which are not simply modes of evaluating work, but also technologies or mechanisms for producing and determining truth claims. The concept of epistemic culture is borrowed from Knorr-Cetina (1999).

7. The literature on gender discrimination and evaluation tends to downplay such variations to emphasize consistencies. See especially Schiebinger (1999).

8. On learning by monitoring in organizations, see Helper, MacDuffie, and Sabel (2000).

9. Deliberations, rather than abstract formulations, both produce and uncover common standards of justice in real situations. More specifically, as students of jury deliberation put it, "temporary situated recourse, common sense, lively, and contingent determinations" of justice occur through deliberation, as actors attempt to convince one another. See Maynard and Manzo (1993, 174).

10. For instance, the *Journal of the American Medical Association (JAMA)* has sponsored a conference on peer review every four years since 1989 to study it and monitor its reliability.

11. This preference for face-to-face meetings speaks volumes about the value that academics place on the role of debate in fostering fairness and reducing bias. Deliberations contrast with more mechanistic techniques of evaluation, such as quantitative rating, that have built-in protections against the vagaries of connoisseurship and subjectivity. On the difference made by quantification, see for instance Porter (1999) and Espeland and Sauder (2007). Quantification has also been applied to anticipate and avoid insolvency and credit failure, and to regularize trust; see Carruthers and Cohen (2008). On the management of information and uncertainty in organizations, see Stinchcombe (1990). Many believe that when it comes to grant peer review, instituting rigid, technical decision-making rules of evaluation would generate only the illusion of objectivity.

12. The concept of group style is developed by Eliasoph and Lichterman (2003, 738): "We define group style as recurrent patterns of interaction that arise from a group's shared assumptions about what constitutes good or adequate participation in the group setting . . . Everyday experience makes the concept of group style intuitively plausible. When people walk into a group

setting, they usually recognize the style in play. They know whether the setting calls for participants to act like upstanding citizens or iconoclasts. They know some settings call for joking irreverence, while others demand high-minded seriousness. Settings usually sustain a group style; different settings do this differently."

13. My thinking on this subject is influenced by recent writings on the place of the self in evaluation and objectivity, especially the work of Daston and Galison (2007) and Shapin (1994).

14. In science studies and economic sociology, these effects are described as "performative effects." As Michel Callon writes (1998, 30), the economy "is embedded not in society but in economics," because economics brings the market into being and creates the phenomena it describes. Thus the discipline creates the rational actor it posits. Donald MacKenzie and Yuval Millo have refined this approach by analyzing performativity as a "stabilizing" self-fulfilling prophecy that results from conflictual and embedded processes; see MacKenzie and Millo (2003).

15. For a critique of the classical dichotomy between the cognitive and the social, see Longino (2002). A concern for how the social corrupts the cognitive is typical of the institutional approach to peer review developed by Robert K. Merton, Jonathan Cole and Stephen Cole, Harriet Zuckerman, and others—see, for example, Cole and Cole (1981); Cole, Rubin, and Cole (1978); and Zuckerman and Merton (1971). Others, such as Mulkay (1976), have been concerned with the noncognitive aspects of evaluation. For their part, Pierre Bourdieu and Bruno Latour have analyzed how criteria of evaluation reflect social embeddedness; see Bourdieu (1988) and Latour (1987). My critique of the literature on peer review is developed more fully in Chapters 4 and 5.

16. See Jenkins (1996), a study of social identity as a pragmatic individual achievement that considers both group identification and social categorization.

17. Hochschild (1979).

18. See Stevens, Armstrong, and Arum (2008) for a probing analysis of the current state of the literature on American higher education.

19. Kanter (1977) uses the concept of homophily to refer to recruiters who "seek to reproduce themselves in their own image"; see also Rivera (2009). Homophily often affects the candidate pool when informal networks are used for recruitment and job searches, which results in more men being hired; see

Ibarra (1992) and Reskin and McBrier (2000). For an analysis of claims based on arguments about cultural descent—particularly sacred properties of tradition—see Mukerji (2007). For a measure of homophily in the panels discussed in this book, see Guetzkow et al. (2003).

20. On the conservative bias, see Eisenhart (2002).

21. In proposing this concept, Merton drew on the Gospel according to Matthew: "For unto everyone that hath shall be given and he shall have abundance: but from him that hath not shall be taken away even that which he hath"; see Merton (1968).

22. While Bourdieu (1988) suggests that the *habitus* of academics promote criteria of evaluation that favor their own work due to the competitive logic of fields, I suggest that this tendency results from their necessary cultural and institutional embeddedness. Because he leaves very little room for identity, Bourdieu ignores the types of pushes and pulls that I discuss here.

23. See for example Ben-David (1991); Fuchs and Turner (1986); Collins (1994); Braxton and Hargens (1996); and Hargens (1988).

24. Galison and Stump (1996); Knorr-Cetina (1999).

25. On this topic, see Guetzkow, Lamont, and Mallard (2004) and Chapter 5.

26. Many authors have noted this. See, for instance, Brint (2002); Slaughter and Rhoades (2004); Kirp (2003). For a theoretically sophisticated account of the relationship between science and society, see also Jasanoff (2004).

27. Hall and Lamont (2009) is an attempt to intervene in this tug-of-war around the question of what may define "successful societies."

28. Hargens (1988).

29. Hayagreeva, Monin, and Durand (2005).

30. Some advocate the use of citation counts as a means for measuring quality while avoiding biases. A large literature criticizes bibliometric techniques. For a discussion, see Feller et al. (2007).

31. Lustick (1997).

32. Feagin (1999).

33. On conditions that sustain coproduction, see Jasanoff (2004), particularly pp. 1–12.

34. McCartney (1970).

35. Shenhav (1986).

36. Cole and Cole (1973).

37. In this, I add to the work of Daryl Chubin, Edward Hackett, and many others. See in particular Chubin and Hackett (2003).

38. In order to protect the participants' anonymity, I do not specify the years. Likewise, I have altered certain identifying details in some respondents' answers to interview questions in order to ensure the anonymity of all panelists and applicants.

39. This approach contrasts that provided in Weinberg (1963), which normatively defines criteria (such as social and technical utility) that should be used to assess the value of a scientific endeavor.

40. I did not aim to establish whether respondents' accounts of their actions corresponded to their observed behavior. Instead, I analyzed their representations of their behavior, together with statements about the quality of scholarship, as part of their broader construction of excellence. I also consider what they told me in the context of the interview a performative action or a speech act.

41. For details see Lamont (1992, appendix 3); and Lamont (2000, introduction).

42. This contrast between attitudes and beliefs and meaning is developed in White (2007).

43. Brenneis (1999).

44. The psychological benefits that are conferred by the awards are emphasized by recipients of the women's studies dissertation grants who were interviewed in Kessler-Harris, Swerdlow, and Rovi (1995).

45. On the role of third parties in the production of status, see Sauder (2006).

46. My unpublished dissertation (written in French) concerned rapid shifts in disciplinary prestige across the social sciences and the humanities. I also have studied the intellectual and institutional conditions behind the success of theories and have compared the role and social position of cultural specialists, intellectuals, and sociologists in France and the United States (Lamont 1987; Lamont and Witten 1989; Lamont and Wuthnow 1990). Recent coauthored articles have concerned the criteria of excellence at work in fellowship competitions in American higher education: I have analyzed how prize-winning students define personal and academic excellence—see Lamont, Kaufman, and Moody (2000)—and changes in criteria of excellence used in letters of recommendation written between 1950–1955 and 1968–1972; see Tsay et al. (2003). These works contribute to my long-term interest in the study of boundary formation—e.g., Lamont and Molnár (2002); Pachucki, Pendergrass, and Lamont (2007); Wimmer and Lamont (2006).

47. Merton (1972).

48. In this sense, the book shares a kinship with the work of others who have been influenced by these traditions, such as Karin Knorr-Cetina and Bruno Latour.

49. Bénatouïl (1999); Boltanski (2007b); Boltanski and Thévenot (1991); DiMaggio (1997); Garfinkel (1967); Geertz (1973); Goffman (1990); Thévenot (2007b).

50. Latour and Woolgar (1979); Collins and Evans (2007). On expertise and controversies, see the 2003 debate in *Social Studies of Sciences* (June and August 2003), vols. 3 and 4; also Gieryn (1983); Abbott (2001).

51. Cole (1978; 1992); Cole, Cole, and Simon (1981); Liebert (1976); Merton (1996); Mulkay (1991).

52. Bell (1992); General Accounting Office (1994); Roy (1985). The most exhaustive study directly inspired by Merton is that of Stephen Cole, who examined the evaluation of grant proposals submitted to the National Science Foundation in 1975 in the fields of chemical dynamics, solid-state physics, and economics—see Cole (1978); Cole and Cole (1981). Cole found a low level of consensus among the reviewers concerning which proposals should be funded and little effect of most investigators' characteristics on the success of the proposal. He concluded that successful proposals were those that were of the highest "quality." A more recent study of the peer review process at the National Science Foundation, National Endowment for the Humanities, and National Institutes of Health supported many of Cole's findings, but also concluded that "the intrinsic qualities of a proposal (such as the research design and the importance of the question it addressed) were important factors in reviewers' scoring." See General Accounting Office (1994). None of these studies, however, focuses on the question of how the peer review panelists assess the quality of the proposals (captured by categories such as "originality," "significance," "feasibility," etc.).

53. Ilse Hartmann and Friedhelm Neidhardt provide the foundation for a model of how to accomplish this (1990). Using content analysis, they study which categories of evaluation (for example, qualifications/reputation of the principal investigator, preparatory work that had already been done, and scientific significance of the proposal) affect funding of grant proposals submitted to the Deutsche Forschungsgemeinschaft—the German equivalent of the National Science Foundation. They find more consensus in the grant-making process than did Cole and show the process to be less random than his analysis suggested: the categories of evaluation they identify accounted for 55 per-

cent of the variance, with the rest being explained by "elements 'behind the curtain'" (425).

54. Harry Collins and Robert Evans argue that panelists produce a fair evaluation by engaging in "cognitive translations" between different viewpoints, that is, by displaying the "special ability to take on the style of the 'other' and to alternate between different social worlds and translate between them" (Collins and Evans 2002, 262; also Callon 1994). My approach complements theirs. But whereas Collins and Evans argue that translation automatically leads to fair evaluations, I am interested in the full range of customary rules. Note, too, that other science studies authors have analyzed more specifically the cognitive dimension of evaluation, without significant attention to the question of fairness—see, for example, Gilbert and Mulkay (1984); Latour (1987); Latour and Woolgar (1979); and Travis and Collins (1991). Their goal was to demonstrate how scientists present their results by abstracting them from their context of production. Influenced by ethnomethodology, they have focused on cultural schemas and on the negotiation of cognitive content. For instance, Gilbert and Mulkay (1984, 56) shows that although biochemists can use a "contingent repertoire" to describe how they produce results in the privacy of their laboratory (stressing the importance of social interests and serendipitous processes of research), in public, they strategically mobilize an "empiricist repertoire" to describe their work, a repertoire according to which the theory "follow[s] unproblematically and inescapably from the empirical characteristics of an impersonal natural world." Elsewhere, Latour (1988) explains that when presenting their research to their peers in publications, biologists use a "reductionist" rhetoric that provides a linear description of the research process. Scientists also mobilize various epistemological styles to obtain the support of colleagues for a paper under review—see Gilbert and Mulkay (1984); Latour and Woolgar (1979)—or a grant proposal (see Travis and Collins [1991]). These authors are not concerned, however, with how this strategic orientation relates to the issue of fairness. For more details see Mallard, Lamont, and Guetzkow (2009); Gilbert and Mulkay (1984).

55. Gladwell (2005); also Gigerenzer (2007).

56. Michael Mulkay's criticism of the Mertonian approach to the institution of science (1976) underscores how emotional commitment is pervasive within this institution—certainly as much as the notion of emotional neutrality. Mulkay argues that the norms of science identified by Merton are part of a

vocabulary of justification produced by an occupational group, rather than being actual, functioning norms of science. My analysis builds on Mulkay's, but I also argue that the shared definition of reality makes certain things possible that otherwise would not be. For instance, belief in the fairness of the process contributes to the recruitment of new entrants. Buying into the norm of meritocracy is very costly to evaluators, because this belief leads them to spend countless hours assessing the work of others. On "emotion work," see Hochschild (1979).

57. Whitley (1984) and Bourdieu (1996).

58. Whitley (1984).

59. Bourdieu and de St. Martin (1975); also Bourdieu (1996, 30–53).

60. His concept of habitus offers a rather thin analysis of subjectivity—see Ortner (2005). The alternative, proposed by Boltanski, Thévenot, and their associates, is to produce a sociology of critical judgment and other modes of engagements. See Boltanski (2007a). On other modes of engagement, see Thévenot (2007a). For a critique of Bourdieu's approach to the self, see Alexander (1995). For a critique of the zero-sum assumptions built into his concept of field, see Lamont (1992).

61. Bourdieu (1988).

62. On self-concept as a crucial but neglected dimension of the sociology of knowledge, see especially Gross (2008). As argued by Gross, concerns with self and self-concept are absent in the work of Bourdieu (1988) and Collins (1998). For an earlier formulation, see Lamont (2001) and Szakolcai (1998). The role of the self is explored in Chapter 4.

63. Heinich (1997); Thévenot (2006). See also Bénatouïl (1999).

64. Dewey (1985). See also Ansell and Gash (2007). On the differences between my perspective and that of Bourdieu, see Lamont (2009). On the differences between my perspective and that of Boltanksi and Thévenot, see Lamont (2008).

2. How Panels Work

1. Knorr-Cetina (1999).

2. Meyer and Rowan (1977).

3. Elsewhere I take up differences [0]between the competitions under consideration and other funding organizations, as well as their implications for customary rules of evaluation and other topics. For a comparison

with three panels from the Finnish Academy of Science, see Lamont and Huutoniemi (2007). For a comparison with seven disciplinary and interdisciplinary funding panels of the Standard Research Grants Program of the Social Sciences and Humanities Research Council of Canada (SSRC), see Lamont et al. (2006). Also see Guetzkow, Lamont, and Mallard (2004) and Mallard, Lamont, and Guetzkow (forthcoming).

4. See Cohen, March, and Olsen (1972); March and Olsen (1976). For an illuminating analysis of academic evaluation and decision making, see Powell (1985).

5. I am grateful to Mitchell Stevens for these suggestions. He considers some of these topics in his *Creating a Class* (2007).

6. The ACLS also contributes funds to support fellowships in this SSRC program.

7. The dissolution of eleven SSRC area-studies committees, and the creation of the IDRF program, occurred under the direction of Kenneth Prewett. For a detailed description of the debates that surrounded this decision, see Worcester (2001).

8. See the IDRF website at http://programs.ssrc.org/idrf.

9. See the Woodrow Wilson Foundation website at www.woodrow.org/fellowships/women_gender/index.php (accessed July 8, 2008).

10. Weisbuch (1999, 4).

11. American Council of Learned Societies (n.d.).

12. On repair work, see Garfinkel (1967).

13. On indirect power, see Lukes (1974).

14. Social Sciences Research Council (n.d.).

15. D'Arms (1998).

16. For a comparative perspective, see Walter Powell's analysis of how editors in the book publishing industry select reviewers (1985, esp. chaps. 3 and 4).

17. On this topic, see also ibid.

18. The role of networks is described in Chapter 4.

19. On this topic see, for instance, Brint and Karabel (1989).

20. I am grateful to Claude Rosental for this observation. See his own work on evaluation of logarithms in Rosental (2008).

21. Collins (1998; 2004) on effervescence and the sharing of norms.

22. Bourdieu (1997).

23. Collins (1998).

24. Gross (2008).

25. On identity maintenance, see Goffman (1990). On opportunity hoarding, see Tilly (1998).

26. Stevens (2007).

27. On how much time academics spend working, see Jacobs (2004); also Jacobs and Winslow (2004).

28. Specifically, this panelist recalls thinking, "Here was a project which was going to really say something different about that period. I remember pulling down this basic, what's his name? Jim Doe, who has the basic Mideast history, I'm not a Mideast historian, but I have him on my shelf. And [I] pulled it down and looked at what he had to say. This is the sort of text that someone like me who is not a specialist would go and look to, to find something out. And what this person had there was completely different and had the potential of really reshaping what the standard text was, so I was very high on that." When asked whether he went to such trouble with many proposals, he replied, "I did that, I think, with a few. One does what one can."

29. On incommensurables, see Galison (1997); also Espeland and Stevens (1998).

30. In his study of peer review at the National Science Foundation, Don Brenneis noted that "participation in panel reading events plunges one into . . . a normalization process—or 'norming,' as it is sometimes referred to in in-house dialect." (1994, 32). On learning how to evaluate, see Walker et al. (2008); Gumport (2000b).

31. In one of the competitions I studied, proposals are not read by all the panelists, only by a subset of them. For a discussion of differences between panels that make final decisions and those that make only recommendations, see Lamont and Huutoniemi (2007).

32. Garfinkel (1967).

33. Much could be learned from studying age, race, and gender dynamics on panels. Panel deliberations would, for example, provide fertile terrain for those conversation analysts interested in the gendered patterns of interruptions during group conversations (Kollack, Blumstein, and Schwartz [1985]); likewise, they would offer a rich venue for investigating the gendered distribution of power and status within small groups. See Ridgeway (1997); also Berger et al. (1993).

34. The analysis of Collins and Evans (2002; 2007) on warrants of expertise and experience applies.

35. On performance of the self, see Goffman (1963).

36. Eliasoph and Lichterman (2003).

37. The term "satisficing" was coined by Herbert A. Simon (1957). It refers to making a choice or judgment that is good enough given cognitive and situational constraints.

38. Dewey (1985). For a contemporary approach that builds on Dewey's view of the role of dialogue in successful deliberation, see Ansell and Gash (2007).

39. In Abbott (2001), the focus on fractals in the dynamics of disciplinary conflicts does not consider epistemic cultures as machineries for building bridges.

40. Jury deliberations also involve a collective forging of the rules. This is why these deliberations are described as a collaborative achievement, with conversations being integral to the application of the rules. In so doing, members of juries go beyond abstract reasoning to draw on personal experience. See Manzo (1993), as well as Maynard and Manzo (1993).

41. For a study of a mechanized form of evaluation—credit-rating—see Carruthers and Cohen (2008).

42. See Dubet (2006). On academic recruiting in France, see also Musselin (2005).

43. On the influence of uncertainty on moral signaling among professionals and managers, see Jackall (1988) and Lamont (1992).

44. Meyer (1986).

45. On the recent elitist character of American higher education, see Karabel (2005), as well as Wilson (1942) and Lewis (1998). On changes in criteria of evaluation, see Tsay et al. (2003).

3. On Disciplinary Cultures

1. For a published (and revised) version of Snow's 1959 Rede Lecture, see Snow (1993).

2. On the broader topic of disciplinary cultures, see, for instance, Bender and Schorske (1998) and Becher and Trowler (2001); also Steinmetz (2005). Bourdieusian analysis of the "structuration" of academic fields also contains many observations on differences in disciplinary orientation, for example, in Bourdieu (1988). See also Abbott (2001) for an analysis of disciplinary dynamics.

3. See Knorr-Cetina (1999). Epistemology refers to theories of knowledge that are part of the philosophy of science tradition. Standard epistemological positions include positivism, realism, constructivism, etc. The epistemological styles I describe are related to these positions, but are also "spontaneous philosophies" adopted by respondents.

4. Abbott (2001); Bourdieu (1988); Merton (1972); Weber (1984).

5. For the former view, see DeVault (1999) and Smith (1990a); for the latter, see Nagel (1961).

6. On the value of formal models and hypothesis testing, see, for example, Nagel (1961); Ragin (1987); Singleton and Straits (1999); Stinchcombe (2005); and Tilly (1984). Clifford and Marcus (1986) offer what has become a classic argument against such approaches.

7. For a study of inquiry beliefs in psychology, see Martin (1994); for sociology, see Abend (2006). For an excellent analysis of the literature on research practices within sociology, see Leahey (2008).

8. Fiske (2002). On the relational dimensions of identity, see Jenkins (1996).

9. Whitley (1984).

10. The fields not discussed here are art history (two respondents), geography (two respondents), musicology (three respondents), natural sciences (one respondent), and sociology (six respondents). I have omitted sociology because all interviewees from this field knew me personally. Their representations of sociology were directly influenced by their understanding of my own identity as a sociologist and an academic—factors that seemed of little or no interest to respondents from other disciplines. I do draw on these sociologists' views of other disciplines.

11. I gained access to several social science panels at the National Science Foundation, but was ultimately denied access by the general counsel's office. Lawyers evoked the Privacy Act to justify the decision.

12. This comparison concerns how panelists describe the arguments they made during deliberations, as well as the criteria they use to evaluate research in general. For details, see Mallard, Lamont, and Guetzkow (2007). A systematic comparison of the epistemological styles at the discipline level did not reveal statistically significant differences, although the population of respondents is too small to support conclusive statistical analysis.

13. Munch (1975).

14. In this study, "social scientists" include anthropologists, economists, political scientists, sociologists, a geographer, and an evolutionary biologist.

"Humanists" include art historians, English professors, musicologists, and philosophers. While some historians are committed to producing a narrative and descriptive history, others are more engaged with theory and with social explanation.

15. Guillory (1993, chapter 2).

16. Lamont (2004b) discusses indicators of the vitality of fields. See also Feller et al. (2007). For an illustration of a more encompassing study of indicators of the health of a field, see http://www.asanet.org/cs/root/leftnav/research_and_stats/health_of_sociology_fact_sheets (accessed July 8, 2008).

17. The literature on the conditions for consensus is voluminous. See, for instance, Cole, Cole, and Simon (1981); also Hargens (1988).

18. See for instance, Knorr-Cetina (1999) on the role played by context in the production of knowledge for molecular biology and high energy physics. For quantitative social science, see Ragin's important book (2000) on fuzzy sets.

19. Sewell (2005).

20. Chapter 4 discusses cognitive contextualization as well as the other customary procedural practices of panelists. See also Mallard, Lamont, and Guetzkow (2009). Science studies such as Callon (1994), Callon, Lascoumes, and Barthe (2001), and Collins and Evans (2007) have considered procedural fairness in evaluation. Collins and Evans (2002, 262) suggests that procedural fairness is achieved when panelists demonstrate the generalized applicability of idiosyncratic criteria through an intersubjective process of translation, defined as the "special ability to take on the style of the 'other,' to alternate between different social worlds and translate between them." Future work should consider academic judgments in the context of broader literatures on injustice, such as Dubet (2005), and corruption—see Bezes and Lascoumes (2006).

21. Nehamas (1997, 232).

22. A trend toward "naturalism" within philosophy in recent decades aims to "adopt and emulate the methods of successful sciences . . . or to operate in tandem with the sciences, as their abstract and reflective branches"; see Leiter (2004, 3). Naturalism has made philosophy more compatible with interdisciplinary evaluation, because it incites philosophers to collaborate with psychologists, computer scientists, linguists, and economists. This trend did not facilitate the work of the panels I studied, however, perhaps because few if any of their members were drawn from most of these fields.

23. Pointing to the variety of approaches and substantive issues within contemporary American philosophy, Leiter (2004) notes that analytical philosophy remains widely influential mostly as "a style that emphasizes 'logic,' 'rigor,' and 'argument.'" The *Philosophical Gourmet Report,* which provides information on disciplinary ranking, suggests that substantive work in analytical philosophy had largely ended by the 1970s, so that "analytical simply demarcates a style of scholarship, writing, and thinking: Clarity, precision, and argumentative rigor are paramount." http://www.philosophicalgourmet.com (accessed October 20, 2006). Pragmatism and continental philosophy appear to be marginal to the field of philosophy today, so much so that the study respondents did not even mention either one.

24. See the American Philosophical Association's "Statements on the Profession" at http://www.apa.udel.edu/apa/governance/statements/research .html.

25. As Chapter 4 explains, well-functioning panels adhere to "customary rules," including deference to disciplinary expertise. The kind of behavior that this philosopher attributes to the geographer violates this important guideline, and so signals the panel's troubled dynamics.

26. A widely publicized letter to the executive director of the American Philosophical Association, written by John Lachs (Vanderbilt University) after he had served on philosophy panels for the National Endowment for the Humanities, notes that the contentiousness of panelists often translates into fewer grants for this discipline—Lachs was a leader of a "pluralist revolt" within the American Philosophical Association. As a Santayana scholar, he is rather at odds with the analytical tradition. See http://www.apa.udel.edu/apa/ governance/edletters/.

27. The decline of philosophy as a discipline is often discussed on the blog Philosophy Talk. See, for example, theblog.philosophytalk.org/2006/08/ the_future_of_p.html (accessed May 29, 2008). On the increasing rigidity of standards in philosophy, see Putnam (1997).

28. On canonization and the canon war, see especially Bryson's (2005) analysis of the controversy's framing in English departments. Also see Guillory (1993), Graff (1992), and Palumbo-Liu (1995). One driving force behind the canon war is the push to teach literature so that it reflects the diversity of the American college population.

29. Lamont (1987); also Lamont and Wuthnow (1990). French literary

studies scholars did not question the existence of the canon as much as rede-fine it—in strong contrast with their American counterparts. On this topic, see Duell (2000) and Mallard (2005).

30. On the declining centrality of close reading in English, see Turner (1991).

31. Jeffrey Williams (2004).

32. On the recent changes in literary studies, including the decline and transformation of its public, see Moser (2001), as well as Lamont and Witten (1989) and Lamont (1987).

33. On the emergence of the phenomenon of "stars" in literary studies, and the role of theory in that development, see Shumway (1997). I thank Leah Price and Jonathan Arac for sharing their reflections on this topic.

34. Also pointing to respect for craftsmanship of various types, a medieval historian recognizes disciplinary cleavages but also says, "Even if people can-not stand a particular approach or methodology, they might be able to recog-nize a good example of this when they see it and recognize that it's the stron-gest of what's being considered."

35. Iggers (1997, 144).

36. For details, see Frank, Schofer, and Torres (1994).

37. See http://www.historians.org/info/Data_Jobs_PhDs.pdf. A 2004 sur-vey by the American Historical Association reports an increase in the number of full-time and part-time history faculty. The majority teach in European and American history and "the remaining fields all account for less than 10 percent of the faculty." See "The State of the History Department: The 2001–2002 AHA Department Survey," http://www.historians.org/perspectives/is-sues/2004/0404/rbtfaculty0404.cfm, which also shows that in the year 2002–2003 there was an 8 percent increase in the number of history majors. Ac-cording to data from the *Books in Print* database, the number of history titles published rose significantly in 2002–2003 (from 7,929 to 10,439)—with an increase of 60.3 percent between 1993 and 2003. Historical titles represent al-most 10 percent of new university press titles. See http:// www.historians.org/ Perspectives/issues/2004/0410/0410new2.cfm (accessed November 1, 2006).

38. Novick (1988, 362).

39. Ibid., 593.

40. On this topic, see ibid.

41. Sewell (2005); Burke (2004); Iggers (1997).

42. The culture section of the American Sociological Association has the second largest membership of all sections, and the largest number of graduate student members. See Erskine and Spalter-Roth (2006).

43. Givens and Jablonski (1996). A 1996 survey conducted by the American Anthropological Association showed that the number of bachelor of arts degrees (BAs) in anthropology declined sharply from the mid-1970s into the 1980s. This slide halted by the late 1980s; in 1995, a record number of BAs (7,555) and PhDs (464) were conferred. Unlike the turnaround at the undergraduate level, however, PhD figures have remained relatively flat.

44. On the theme of crisis, see also Borofsky (1994), who outlines what holds the field of cultural anthropology together and what pulls it apart. He argues that many factors work against the accumulation of knowledge and a stable disciplinary identity: disagreements over whether the discipline properly belongs among the humanities or among the natural sciences; the postcolonial critique of the discipline; challenges to the notion of culture as homogenous and stable; and the interdisciplinary orientation of many cultural anthropologists, who turn either toward the humanities (for example, literary studies) or toward the social sciences (like Marxism and political economy).

45. Geertz (1985, 623).

46. On disciplinary boundary work, see Gieryn (1994). On anthropology and disciplinary boundaries, see Lederman (2006).

47. See, for instance, Keane (2003). Disciplinary questioning about representation was also stimulated by postcolonial writers such as Talal Asad (1973).

48. On multi-sited research, see Martin (1994).

49. It should be noted that some authors have proposed syntheses that combine rational choice theory with other approaches. See, for instance, Hall and Soskice (2001), as well as Carlsnaes, Risse, and Simmons (2002).

50. Green and Shapiro (1994) and Shapiro (2005) provide a substantive critique of rational choice theory as well as an analysis of the changes that it has brought to the discipline. On the lack of coherence within political science, see also Mansfield and Sisson (2004), a volume whose introduction traces how over the past half century, political science has become increasingly specialized around subfields. Laitin (2004) provides a detailed analysis of the ways in which coherence has dissipated, as manifested by the lack of agreed-upon standards in introductory courses, for instance.

51. Tarrow (2007).

52. On this movement, see Stewart (2003).

53. Shapiro, Smith, and Masoud (2004).

54. On consensus as an indicator of evaluation and status, see Cole (1992).

55. King, Keohane, and Verba (1994).

56. See, for instance, http://www.asu.edu/clas/polisci/cqrm/Qualitative MethodsAPSA.html.

57. For an illustration, see http://www.asu.edu/clas/polisci/cqrm (accessed July 8, 2008).

58. Breslau and Yonay (1999). Nevertheless, the definition of the disciplinary consensus of economics varies across countries. See in particular Fourcade-Gourinchas (2001) and Fourcade (2009).

59. Personal communication, February 19, 2007.

60. On this process, see Fourcade (2006). The author's analysis stresses the universalism of economic knowledge, the rhetoric of quantification, and mathematical formalism as bases for disciplinary homogenization and consensus building. On divisions within economics, see Breslau in Steinmetz (2005); on formalism, see Lawson in Steinmetz (2005).

61. National Opinion Research Center (2006).

62. Scott (2001).

63. Cole (1992).

64. Fish (1980).

4. Pragmatic Fairness

1. Of these panelists, 97 percent explicitly or implicitly affirmed the integrity of the review process. Only two respondents voiced major reservations. But 54 percent qualified this positive judgment with minor reservations, pertaining most frequently to procedural fairness, the intrinsic fallibility of the process ("we may overlook something"), and epistemological bias. These "minor objectors" also described problems tied to (in decreasing order) ideological fairness, elitism, hesitancy, and lack of quality. Concern for procedural fairness seemed to occur when unfair results were explained by procedural failures or domineering personalities.

2. The Bourdieusian approach to academic discourse shows how seemingly disinterested positions are in fact interested (for example, Bourdieu 1984) and denounces these hidden interests (Bourdieu and Wacquant 1992). My approach, in contrast, draws on Goffman's analysis of frames to prob-

lematize subjective orientation to action—see Goffman (1974); Polletta and Ho (2005). For a similar approach and critique of Bourdieu's work, see Guaspare et al. (2005), as well as Boltanksi and Thévenot (1991).

3. See Armstrong (1999); Bakanic, McPhail, and Simon (1987); Chubin and Hackett (1990); Cole (1978); Cole and Cole (1981); Cole, Rubin, and Cole (1978); General Accounting Office (1994); Liebert (1982); Roy (1985); and Zuckerman and Merton (1971). See also Bornmann and Daniel (2005), which examines the extent to which a Swiss foundation gave awards to the "best" scientists.

4. Merton (1973) in particular is associated with this view. The functionalist vision of culture appealed intuitively to the notion that funding (or publishing) decisions in scientific fields should be based on the evaluation of research projects (or research results) *independently* of the social characteristics of the researchers. Subjectivism, cooptation, and in-group favoritism stood in opposition to open scientific debate, free inquiry, and unbiased discussion of results and scientific quality of proposals. The empirical literature found that reviewers follow universalistic norms more often than not; see Cole (1978); Cole and Cole (1981); Cole, Rubin, and Cole (1978); General Accounting Office (1994); and Zuckerman and Merton (1971).

5. My approach draws on insights from several sources, including the rhetorical approach proposed in Gilbert and Mulkay (1984); Cicourel's point that rules and mores are not things for definition by sociological analysis but are available for definition by actions in everyday life (1974); works by science studies scholars—such as Fujimura (1988); Gerson (1983); Clarke (1990); Clarke and Gerson (1990); and Star (1985)—that examine the cooperative pursuit of tasks in science and the role of claim-making in this process.

6. For Weber, legitimacy varies according to the "type of obedience [it claims], the kind of administrative staff developed to guarantee it, and the mode of exercising authority." See Weber (1978, 213).

7. For Emile Durkheim, religious systems provide a general interpretation of how the world is organized and how its elements relate to one another and to the sacred. This cosmology acts as a system of classification and its elements are organized according to a hierarchy (for example, high/low, pure/impure, us/them). The belief invested in this "order of things" structures people's lives to the extent that it limits and facilitates their action. See Durkheim (1965, chapter 7).

8. On customary rules, see Burbank (2004). On how academics learn to do their job, see Walker et al. (2008). On the accomplishment of research training, see Gumport (2000b).

9. In contrast, see Musselin (1996) on the recruitment of colleagues in French academia. See also Fournier, Gingras, and Mathurin (1988) for an analysis of tenure promotion.

10. Rational-legal legitimacy is grounded in the "legitimacy of enacted rules and the right of those elevated to authority under such rules to issue commands" (Weber 1978, 215).

11. In other words, I asked respondents to perform "boundary work" in the context of the interview. This technique is useful for revealing not only the taken-for-granted categories with which interviewees operate, but also how they understand similarities and differences among respondents, as well as differences in the subjective criteria of evaluation they use. For other applications of this technique, see Lamont (1992; 2000).

12. On "presentation of self," see Goffman (1990).

13. Wilson (1942) and Lewis (1998).

14. On the role of morality and emotion in the functioning of peer review, and how they have been ignored in the literature in favor of cognitive factors, see Guetzkow, Lamont, and Mallard (2004) and Mallard, Lamont, and Guetzkow (2007).

15. On "ideal speech situation," see Habermas (1982). See also Habermas (1984). Some political theorists have suggested that certain principles should guide democratic deliberation and determine the criteria by which it should be judged. Those who advance general conditions for democratic deliberation identify reciprocity (mutual respect), publicity (as opposed to secrecy), and accountability as important. They suggest that participants should be free, have an "equal voice," be rational (as opposed to emotional), and that deliberation be consensual and focused on the common good. See Gutmann and Thompson (1996); also Cohen (1989).

16. On this topic, see also Stark (2007).

17. There is a large literature on cultural authority and on how scientists go about establishing their expertise. See, for instance, Shapin and Schaeffer (1985), which focuses on the alternative cultural universes of Hobbes and Boyles and the collective accomplishment of science. See also Abbott (1988) on how occupational groups lay claims to legitimate knowledge and juris-

diction. On the negotiation of authority between science and politics, see Jasanoff (1990).

18. The term "universalism" is used differently across literatures. The functionalist literature in sociology compares cultural orientations cross-nationally along a number of dimensions of the "universalistic/particularistic" pattern variable. A universalistic orientation consists in believing that "all people shall be treated according to the same criteria (e.g., equality before the law)" while a particularistic orientation is predicated on the belief that "individuals shall be treated differently according to their personal qualities or their particular membership in a class or group" (Lipset 1979, 209). This is the definition adopted here.

19. On the notion of elective affinity, see Weber (1978).

20. On the importance of context for cognition, see Engel (1999). On embeddedness, see Granovetter (1985), in which the author argues, against overly individualistic interpretations, that human beings are embedded in networks. On the relationship between the production of value and embeddedness in the economy, see Uzzi (1999).

21. On this topic, see Burt (2005) and Cook (2005).

22. Guetzkow, Lamont, and Mallard (2004) discusses the types of originality that panelists attribute to their own work and how these tend to overlap with the types of originality they attribute to other proposals—even as they remain open to recognizing and valuing other forms of originality. Liking what resembles oneself is a social phenomenon that sociologists label "homophily." The "homophilic principle" states that similarity breeds connection. "Homophily limits people's social worlds in a way that has powerful implications for the information they receive, the attitudes they form, and the interactions they experience"—according to McPherson, Smith-Lovin, and Cook (2001, 415). See also Kanter (1977). Travis and Collins (1991, 336) points to a "cognitive particularism" that resonates with the notion of cognitive homophily: cognitive particularism is a form of favoritism based on shared schools of thought. While the authors suggest that it is more likely to happen in "interdisciplinary research, frontier science, areas of controversy, and risky new departure" than in mainstream research, I argue that this kind of cognitive homophily is endemic to research in general.

23. Despite the concern over biases related to "political correctness" that have animated congressional debates about the future of the National Endow-

ment for the Humanities and other funding agencies, this comment is one of the very few examples across all of my interviews that could be interpreted as explicitly reflecting an "identity politics" bias.

24. On subjectivity and connoisseurship, see Daston and Galison (2007).

25. This is not unlike the logicians described by Claude Rosental in his sociology of taste in logic. See Rosental (2008).

26. Smith (1990b); Marcus and Fischer (1986). See Mallard, Lamont, and Guetzkow (2009) on the association between disciplines and epistemological styles, including the constructivist style.

27. See the influential work of Dorothy Smith, especially Smith (1990a).

28. See Mallard, Lamont, and Guetzkow (2009).

29. On what diversity brings to collective decision making, see Page (2007).

30. In Durkheimian terms, the panelists are engaged in rituals that are essential for the production of the sacred.

31. Contra Bourdieu, scarcity introduces important variations in the degree to which disinterested behavior is interested.

32. Focusing on the breaking of rules as a means to reveal the taken-for-granted nature of the social order is one of ethnomethodology's main contributions to the sociological tradition. See Garfinkel (1967).

33. For a detailed description of these panels, see Mallard, Lamont, and Guetzkow (2009).

34. See Mallard, Lamont, and Guetzkow (2007) for an illustration of competing claims of expertise.

35. Lakatos (1974).

36. On anti-racist strategies developed by elite African Americans, which may also apply to black academics, see Lamont and Fleming (2005).

37. On priming, see Bargh (2006).

38. See Gruenfeld, Martorana, and Fan (2000) on the psychology of power.

39. For a summary of expectation state theory, see Webster (2003); also Berger, Wagner, and Zelditch (1985).

40. Ibid.

41. Common referents and jokes are part of the development of an idioculture, as described in Gary Alan Fine's (1979) article on the development of group culture in Little League baseball.

42. See Tilly (2006).

43. Collins (2004).

44. Engel (1999).

45. For a preliminary analysis of the differences between disciplinary and multidisciplinary panels, see Lamont and Huutoniemi (2007).

5. Recognizing Various Kinds of Excellence

1. Readings (1996, chapter 2).

2. The concept of intellectual habitus is borrowed from Bourdieu, who studied theoretical culture as habitus, that is, as a set of structured dispositions. On the notion of intellectual habitus, see Brubaker (1993).

3. Jencks and Reisman (1977, 18–19).

4. Goffman (1981, 171) uses the concept of script to make sense of the conventional ordering of social interaction and the definition and maintenance of social worlds.

5. On the weighting of criteria, see, for instance, Langfeldt (2001), which notes that in the social sciences and the humanities, the greatest weight is put on the project description.

6. Following Princeton philosopher Harry Frankfurt, I define bullshit as "a lack of connection to a concern with truth—an indifference to how things really are." See Frankfurt (2005, 30).

7. Sixteen panelists cited the letters as important to their decision making; the remainder did not express an opinion.

8. On bandwagons in science, see Fujimura (1988).

9. I do not alter the identity of the academics whom panelists say they admire or trust because this information is not prejudicial to the named scholars, and because the real names help readers understand why these academics are respected.

10. To the extent that male students benefit from longer and more detailed letters of recommendation, they are likely to be advantaged by these same evaluators. Frances Trix and Carolyn Psenka identified these gender schemas in their analysis of 300 letters of recommendation for faculty at a large American medical school in the mid-1990s—see Trix and Psenka (2003).

11. Whereas Goffman (1990) and Garfinkel (1967) present signaling and the establishment of trust as a collective achievement, more recent literature on signaling draws on a rational choice perspective to consider how to reduce vulnerability. See, for instance, Gambetta and Hamill (2005).

12. Merton (1968).

13. Merton (1973, 293).

14. Latour (1987).

15. Guetzkow, Lamont, and Mallard (2004).

16. Mallard, Lamont, and Guetzkow (2007).

17. Levinson (2002).

18. A British panelist was pleased that social significance did not figure prominently among the criteria that she was asked to consider. In her words, she was "kind of relieved that it wasn't like so many of the British [competitions], with a [focus] on what kind of value for money, social usefulness, social significance, significance to the development of the country, etc. I thought they'd escaped all of those really, really well." In the United Kingdom, since the beginning of the 1980s, scholars have been required to consider the social utility of research. A large cross-disciplinary survey of research performance across disciplines guides the allocation of resources for all university research, in an effort to increase the influence and social relevance of research projects (Lamont and Mallard 2005). Cambridge anthropologist Marilyn Strathern has remarked that the diffusion of an audit culture in the academic world is difficult to criticize insofar as it promotes values of openness, transparency, and democracy, but she also notes that the government's evaluative work results in greater standardization and normalization of research practices: audits and performance assessment posit commensuration, i.e., the need to compare different units by using a single standard. Thus, an audit culture has a direct effect on the range and diversity of research being conducted. See Strathern (2000). On a similar point, see Espeland and Sauder (2007).

19. Lamont (1989); Lamont and Wuthnow (1990); Cusset (2003).

20. Bourdieu (1988).

21. For standards of empirical rigor as they apply to qualitative research, see National Science Foundation (2004). See also the 2008 National Science Foundation report on shared standards across the social sciences, documented in Lamont and White (2008).

22. Camic and Gross (1998).

23. Gerhard Sonnert's 1995 quantitative study of the criteria by which American biologists evaluate the quality of their peers' overall scientific contribution shows as the most powerful predictor annual publication productivity rate (which explains 40 percent of the variance). This factor, the existence of solo-authored publications, and graduate school prestige explain 59 percent of the variance in quality rating.

24. Geertz (1973).

25. Lamont and Lareau (1988).

26. This pattern is hardly surprising. Stephen Jay Gould pointed out that "humanists rightly stress the virtues and felicities of stylistic writing," while "scientists tend to assert that although brevity and clarity should certainly be fostered, verbal style plays no role in the study of material reality." See Gould (2003). Similarly, in *Homo Academicus*, Pierre Bourdieu compared the relative cultural capital of various disciplines and described the humanities as "canonical" disciplines, and ones where familiarity with elite culture is particularly important. See Bourdieu (1988, 176, 255–256, 339).

27. At the same time, this philosopher acknowledges that in his discipline, elegance "goes with manner, appearance, superficiality. It's a way both of admiring and of putting someone down."

28. Bourdieu (1988).

29. On this point, see Bourdieu (1984).

30. Recent work has documented more refined domains of classism, such as interpersonal classism via separation, devaluation, discounting, and exclusion, as well as institutionalized classism and stereotype citation. Regina Day Langhout, Francine Rosselli, and Jonathan Feinstein found that 43 to 80 percent of the working-class college students they surveyed had experienced at least one form of classism. See Langhout, Rosselli, and Feinstein (2007).

31. As a group, the respondents do not seem so much to view working-class student applicants as less accomplished as they seem unaware that signals of brilliance often resemble signals of upper-middle-class upbringing, or of having grown up in an academic household. On working-class students, see Granfield (1991); also Stuber (2006). These class dynamics have not been studied for graduate student populations. Autobiographical essays of working-class academics, however, provide numerous examples of instances where an uneasy cultural fit leads to lower academic evaluation. See Dews and Law (1995); also http://www.workingclassacademics.org.

32. Davis (1971).

33. This is in line with Daston and Galison (2007).

34. Latour (1987; 1988).

35. On the closing of controversies, see Epstein (1996). Also Martin and Richards (1995).

36. Guetzkow, Lamont, and Mallard (2004).

6. Considering Interdisciplinarity and Diversity

1. The SSRC competition aims to promote "work that is relevant to a particular discipline while resonating across other fields"; the Society of Fellows is committed to "innovative interdisciplinary approaches"; and the Women's Studies fellowship competition encourages "original and significant research about women across disciplinary, regional, and cultural boundaries." The ACLS's website simply states that "interdisciplinary proposals [for the fellowship competition] are welcome"; the anonymous social science foundation makes no mention of interdisciplinarity.

2. Walzer (1983).

3. Boltanski and Thévenot (2006); also Lamont and Thévenot (2000).

4. Dubet (2006).

5. The first reported mention of the term "interdisciplinarity" occurred in 1929. See Balsiger (2004).

6. This definition is proposed in Fuller (1988), which builds on Bechtel (1986).

7. See Brainard (2002). For data on the multiplication of publications on interdisciplinarity, see Jacobs (forthcoming-a).

8. On the absence of widely agreed-on criteria to ensure quality control in interdisciplinary research (as opposed to disciplinary research), see Klein (2003; 2005); Mansilla and Gardner (2004); and Weingart (2000).

9. Porter and Rossini (1985, 33).

10. See in particular the special issue of *Research Evaluation* (Spring 2006) edited by Grit Laudel and Gloria Origgi. See also the workshop "Quality Assessment in Interdisciplinary Research and Education" (2006), organized by Veronica Boix Mansilla, Irwin Feller, and Howard Gardner, at the American Association for the Advancement of Science, Washington, D.C., February 8, 2006.

11. Boix Mansilla (2006).

12. Dialogic work carries on a continual dialogue with other works of literature and other authors; see Bakhtin (1981).

13. Klein (1996). In contrast, an alternative approach argues that three distinctive logics guide interdisciplinary research: accountability, innovation, and ontology. See Barry, Born, and Weszkalnys (2008); also Rhoten (2003).

14. This point is also made by Langfeldt (2006).

15. Veronica Mansilla and Howard Gardner point out other difficulties in assessing interdisciplinary work: variety of criteria, lack of conceptual clarity, and the challenge of developing germane criteria from the subject matter itself as the inquiry proceeds (evaluators often tend to rely on disciplinary proxy criteria instead). Their study—Mansilla and Gardner (2004)—is based on sixty interviews with researchers working at interdisciplinary institutes.

16. Mallard, Lamont, and Guetzkow (2009).

17. Lamont, Boix Mansilla, and Huutoniemi (2007).

18. In the case of African-American faculty, for instance, Walter Allen and his colleagues show "serious, persistent obstacles to their recruitment, retention, and success"; see Allen et al. (2000, 112). See also Jacobs (forthcoming-b) and Perna (2001).

19. On the improving situation in academia, see, for instance, Smith and Moreno (2006). Differences in salary and promotion by gender are less pronounced in the humanities than in other disciplines due to the increased proportion of female humanities faculty. Both men and women in the humanities, however, earn on average less than academics in the hard sciences; see Ginther and Hayes (2003). On problems affecting the presence of women in the academic pipeline, see especially National Academy of Sciences (2006).

20. See http://www.acls.org/fel-comp.htm (accessed November 1, 2006).

21. See the WWNFF website at http://www.woodrow.org/diversity.php.

22. In this approach, the panelists' views are congruent with the University of Michigan Law School admissions policy that led to *Grutter v. Bollinger* (litigation that itself built on the 1978 case of the *Regents of the University of California v. Bakke*). This policy aspired to "achieve that diversity which has the potential to enrich everyone's education and thus make a law school class stronger than the sum of its parts" (118). This policy does not restrict the types of diversity contributions that are eligible for "substantial weight" in the admissions process, but instead recognizes "many possible bases for diversity admissions" (118, 120). The policy does, however, reaffirm the law school's longstanding commitment to "one particular type of diversity," that is, "racial and ethnic diversity with special reference to the inclusion of students from groups which have been historically discriminated against, like African-Americans, Hispanics and Native Americans, who without this commitment might not be represented in our student body in meaningful numbers" (120). Thus, the policy does not define diversity "solely in terms of racial and ethnic status" (121). See *Grutter v. Bollinger*, 539 U.S. 306 (2003); http://

www.supremecourtus.gov/opinions. This argument has been made repeatedly, including by former Harvard President Neil Rudenstine; see Rudenstine (2001).

23. In research for their 2001 paper "Diversity Rhetoric and Managerialization of Law," Lauren B. Edelman, Sally Riggs Fuller, and Iona Mara-Drita used a content analysis of nineteen professional managerial journals to study the meanings of diversity in the managerial models adopted by a wide range of organizations. They show that the meaning of diversity has expanded to embrace categories beyond those which are protected legally. Corporate diversity rhetoric has shifted away from the notion of righting historical wrongs (a conception embedded in such legislation as the Civil Rights Act) to a new emphasis on efficiency and productivity. Regarding the timing of this change and the consequences of Reagan's cutbacks, see Kelly and Dobbin (1998; 2001).

24. Guinier and Sturm (2001).

25. Glazer (1976). For a critique of the argument that affirmation action is discrimination, see Dobbin (2009). Glazer's argument posits that the hiring and promotion system in corporations is based on proven excellence, ability, and school performance. In fact, hiring and promotion was completely informal prior to the 1970s for most managerial positions, and almost all firms relegated women and minorities to the worst jobs.

26. On the generally progressive outlook of academics in the social sciences and humanities, see Gross and Simmons (2006).

27. See, for instance, Castilla (2006).

28. Wenneras and Wold (1997).

29. Ridgeway (1997).

30. Perna (2001); Joan Williams (2004).

31. Lamont (2004a; 2000, 321).

32. Reskin (2000, 321); Fiske (1998, 364).

33. Bourdieu and Passeron (1990).

34. Fels (2004).

35. Joan Williams (2004).

36. Clemens et al. (1995).

37. Mallard, Lamont, and Guetzkow (2009).

38. Sonnert (1995; 2002). This type of indirect bias would apply to the pure sciences at large, given that definitions of what constitutes "good science" seem to vary significantly between male and female scientists.

39. Trix and Psenka (2003).

40. For more on the Matthew effect, see Merton (1968; 1988).

41. Walzer (1983).

42. For a sociology-based elaboration of this argument about the gendered character of social life, see Ferree, Khan, and Morimoto (2007).

43. Ladd and Lipset (1975); Gross and Simmons (2006).

44. Gumport (2002); Messer-Davidow (2002). One example of the influence on sociology of the development of women's studies is that today the section on sex and gender, with more than one thousand members, is one of the three largest sections within the American Sociological Association (along with those pertaining to medical sociology and cultural sociology). See http://www.asanet.org.

45. Smith (1990a).

46. Hall (1990). On women's studies, see Bird (2001). On African-American studies and its fragile status, see the essays assembled in Gordon and Gordon (2006).

47. On the territorialism of various disciplines, see Abbott (1988); on the work of different groups to achieve equal standing in American culture and academia, see Skrentny (2002).

48. Brint (2002); Kirp (2003).

49. Lamont and Mallard (2005).

50. See also the notion of "diversity imperative" proposed in Roksa and Stevens (2007).

7. Implications in the United States and Abroad

1. This is much in line with the concept of truth in James (1911).

2. MacKenzie and Millo (2003); also Dobbin (1994).

3. See, e.g., Shapin (1994) and Daston and Galison (2007).

4. On the Bologna process, see Ravinet (2007).

5. A description of the Bologna Process is on the European Union's website Europa; see http://ec.europa.eu/education/policies/educ/bologna/bologna_en.html.

6. See, for instance, the European Union's website Europa at http://ec.europa.eu/education/index_en.html.

7. See Lamont and Mallard (2005).

8. Bourdieu (1988).

9. Olivier Godechot and Alexandra Louvet, "Le localisme dans le monde académique: Une autre approche." April 22, 2008. http://www.laviedesidees .fr/Le-localisme-dans-le-monde,315.html (accessed July 8, 2008).

10. Musselin (2005).

11. On intersubjectivity, see Bazerman (1988); also Lynch (1993). My analysis here is influenced by the work of my French collaborators Boltanski and Thévenot, whose 2006 book *On Justification* concerns the intersubjective production of agreement.

12. See Campanario (1998a; 1998b). A broad overview of the pitfalls of partiality and fallibility is provided by Hojat, Gonnella, and Caelleigh (2003). Laudel (2006) points to factors such as a country's level of investment in research funding that affect what can be labeled "of quality."

13. Cole and Cole (1981).

14. Travis and Collins (1991, 336) points to a "cognitive particularism" that resonates with the notion of cognitive homophily: cognitive particularism is a form of favoritism based on shared schools of thought. While they suggest that it is most likely to happen in "interdisciplinary research, frontier science, areas of controversy, and risky new departures" than in mainstream research, I argue that this kind of cognitive homophily is endemic to research in general.

15. Habermas (1984).

16. Stout (2004); Chambers (1996); Mansbridge (1983).

17. Hastie (2001).

18. Bourdieu (1984).

19. On achieving a compromise between conflicting norms, consult the work of Boltanksi and Thévenot (2006). For a detailed discussion of the similarities and differences between my approach and theirs, see Lamont (2008).

20. While for Lévi-Strauss rules are unconscious, and while for Bourdieu they are strategic codes used by actors, I describe rules that are pragmatically created by actors as they participate in a given situation. See Lévi-Strauss (1983); Bourdieu (1977).

21. Chambliss (1988); Stevens (2007); Espeland and Sauder (2007); Baumann (2007); Frickel and Gross (2005).

22. This theory should build on the work of Boltanski and Thévenot, and that of Bourdieu, but also borrow from recent developments in economic sociology, organizational sociology, and cultural sociology in the United States.

23. See Lamont and Zuckerman (in preparation).

24. See, for instance, Gaztambide-Fernandez (2009).

Appendix

1. Klein (1996).

2. Bender (1998).

3. Weiss (1994). On my approach to conducting interviews, see Lamont (2004b).

4. Guetzkow, Lamont, and Mallard (2004).

5. Miles and Huberman (1994).

6. On Atlas.ti, see Kelle, Prein, and Beird (1995).

7. Lamont and Huutoniemi (2007).

References

Abbott, Andrew D. 1988. *The System of Professions: An Essay on the Division of Expert Labor.* Chicago: University of Chicago Press.

———. 2001. *Chaos of Disciplines.* Chicago: University of Chicago Press.

Abend, Gabriel. 2006. "Styles of Sociological Thought: Sociologies, Epistemologies, and the Mexican and U.S. Quests for Truth." *Sociological Theory* 24 (1): 1–41.

Alexander, Jeffrey C. 1995. *Fin-de-siècle Social Theory: Relativism, Reduction, and the Problem of Reason.* London: Verso.

Allen, Walter R., Edgar G. Epps, Elizabeth A. Guillory, Susan A. Suh, and Marguerite Bonous-Hammarth. 2000. "The Black Academic: Faculty Status among African Americans in U.S. Higher Education." *Journal of Negro Education* 69 (1–2): 112–127.

American Council of Learned Societies. N.d. "A.C.L.S. Fellowship Program Peer Review Process." Report prepared for the American Council of Learned Societies, New York.

Ansell, Chris, and Alison Gash. 2007. "Collaborative Governance in Theory and Practice." *Journal of Public Administration Research and Theory Advance Access.* November 13.

Armstrong, J. Scott. 1999. "Forecasting for Environmental Decision-Making."

Pp. 192–225 in *Tools to Aid Environmental Decision Making*, ed. Virginia H. Dale and Mary R. English. New York: Springer-Verlag.

Asad, Talal, ed. 1973. *Anthropology and the Colonial Encounter*. London: Ithaca Press.

Bail, Christopher. 2008. "Diverse Diversities: Symbolic Boundaries against Immigrants in Twenty-one European Countries." *American Sociological Review* 73 (1): 37–59.

Bakanic, Von, Clark McPhail, and Rita J. Simon. 1987. "The Manuscript Review and Decision-Making Process." *American Sociological Review* 52 (5):631–642.

Bakhtin, Mikhail. 1981. *The Dialogic Imagination: Four Essays*. Trans. Caryl Emerson and Michael Holquist. Austin: University of Texas Press.

Balsiger, Philip W. 2004. "Supradisciplinary Research Practices: History, Objectives and Rationale." *Futures* 36: 407–421.

Bargh, John A. 2006. "What Have We Been Priming All These Years? On the Development, Mechanisms, and Ecology of Nonconscious Social Behavior." *European Journal of Social Psychology* 36 (2): 147–168.

Barry, Andrew, Georgia Born, and Gisa Weszkalnys. 2008. "Logics of Interdisciplinarity." *Economy and Society* 37 (1): 20–49.

Baumann, Shyon. 2007. "A General Theory of Artistic Legitimation: How Art Worlds Are Like Social Movements." *Poetics: Journal of Empirical Research on Literature, Media, and the Arts* 35:47–65.

Bazerman, Charles. 1988. *Shaping Written Knowledge: The Genre and Activity of the Experimental Article in Science*. Madison: University of Wisconsin Press.

Becher, Tony, and Paul Trowler. 2001. *Academic Tribes and Territories: Intellectual Enquiry and the Cultures of Disciplines*. Philadelphia: Society for Research into Higher Education.

Bechtel, William, ed. 1986. *Integrating Scientific Disciplines*. Boston: Kluwer Academic.

Becker, Howard. 1982. *Art Worlds*. Berkeley: University of California Press.

Bell, Robert. 1992. *Impure Science: Fraud, Compromise, and Political Influence in Scientific Research*. New York: John Wiley and Sons.

Ben-David, Joseph. 1991. *Scientific Growth: Essays on the Social Organization and Ethos of Science*. Berkeley: University of California Press.

Bénatouïl, Thomas. 1999. "A Tale of Two Sociologies: The Critical and the Pragmatic Stance in Contemporary French Sociology." *European Journal of Social Theory* 2 (3): 379–396.

Bender, Thomas. 1998. "Politics, Intellect, and the American University, 1945–1995." Pp. 17–54 in *American Academic Culture in Transformation: Fifty Years, Four Disciplines*, ed. Thomas Bender and Carl E. Schorske. Princeton: Princeton University Press.

Bender, Thomas, and Carl E. Schorske, eds. 1998. *American Academic Culture in Transformation: Fifty Years, Four Disciplines*. Princeton: Princeton University Press.

Berger, Joseph, David G. Wagner, and Morris Zelditch Jr. 1985. "Expectation States Theory: Review and Assessment." Pp. 1–72 in *Status, Rewards, and Influence*, ed. Joseph Berger and Morris Zelditch Jr. San Francisco: Jossey-Bass.

Berger, Joseph, Murray Webster Jr., Cecilia Ridgeway, and Susan J. Rosenholtz. 1993. "Status Cues, Expectations, and Behavior." Pp. 1–22 in *Social Psychology of Groups: A Reader*, ed. Edward J. Lawler and Barry Markovsky. Greenwich, Conn.: JAI Press.

Bezes, Philippe, and Pierre Lascoumes. 2006. "Percevoir et juger la 'corruption politique' Enjeux et usages des enquêtes sur représentations des atteintes à la probité publique." Manuscript from Centre de Sociologie des Organisations: Fondation nationale de Sciences Politique, Paris.

Bird, Elizabeth. 2001. "Disciplining the Interdisciplinary: Radicalism and the Academic Curriculum." *British Journal of Sociology and Education* 22 (4): 463–478.

Boix Mansilla, Veronica. 2006. "Assessing Expert Interdisciplinary Work at the Frontier: An Empirical Exploration." *Research Evaluation* 15 (1): 17–31.

Boix Mansilla, Veronica, Irwin Feller, and Howard Gardner. 2006. "Proceedings from Workshop on 'Quality Assessment in Interdisciplinary Research and Education.'" Submitted February 8 to the American Association for the Advancement of Science.

Boix Mansilla, Veronica, and Howard Gardner. 2004. "Assessing Interdisciplinary Work at the Frontier: An Empirical Exploration of Scientific Quality." Cambridge: Interdisciplinary Studies Project, Project Zero, Harvard Graduate School of Education. http://www.interdisciplines.org/interdisciplinarity/papers/6 (accessed February 26, 2004).

Boltanski, Luc. 2007a. "La domination revisitée: De la sociologie française critique des années 1970 à la sociologie contemporain." Unpublished manuscript. Paris: Ecole des Hautes Etudes en Sciences Sociales.

———. 2007b. "L'inquiètude sur ce qui est: Pratique, confirmation, et cri-

tique comme modalités du traitement social de l'incertitude."
Anthropologie et pragmatique. Papier preparé pour la journeée d'études
du Laboratoire d'anthropologie sociale.

Boltanski, Luc, and Laurent Thévenot. 1991. *De la justification. Les économies
de la grandeur.* Paris: Gallimard.

———. 2006. *On Justification: Economies of Worth.* Trans. Catherine Porter.
Princeton: Princeton University Press.

Bornmann, Lutz, and Hans-Dieter Daniel. 2005. "Selection of Research Fellowship Recipients by Committee Peer Review: Reliability, Fairness, and
Predictive Validity of Board of Trustees' Decisions." *Scientometrics* 63
(2): 297–320.

Borofsky, Robert. 1994. *Assessing Cultural Anthropology.* New York: McGraw-
Hill.

Bourdieu, Pierre. 1977. *Outline of a Theory of Practice.* Trans. Richard Nice.
New York: Cambridge University Press.

———. 1984. *Distinction: A Sociology of the Judgment of Taste.* Cambridge:
Harvard University Press.

———. 1988. *Homo Academicus.* Trans. Peter Collier. Cambridge, Eng.: Polity Press.

———. 1996. *The State Nobility.* Trans. Lauretta C. Clough. Stanford: Stanford University Press.

———. 1997. "Marginalia—Some Additional Notes on the Gift." Pp. 231–
241 in *The Logic of the Gift: Toward an Ethic of Generosity,* ed. A. D.
Schrift. New York: Routledge.

Bourdieu, Pierre, Jean-Claude Chamboredon, and Jean-Claude Passeron.
1968. *Le Métier de Sociologue.* Paris: EHESS Editions.

Bourdieu, Pierre, and Monique de St. Martin. 1975. "Les catégories de
l'entendement professoral." *Actes de la recherche en science sociales* 1 (3):
63–93.

Bourdieu, Pierre, and Jean-Claude Passeron. 1990. *Reproduction in Education, Society, and Culture.* Trans. Richard Nice. Newbury Park, Calif.:
Sage.

Bourdieu, Pierre, and Loïc Wacquant. 1992. *Invitation to Reflexive Sociology.*
Chicago: University of Chicago Press.

Brainard, Jeffrey. 2002. "U.S. Agencies Look to Interdisciplinary Science."
Chronicle of Higher Education 48 (40): A20–22.

Braxton, John M., and Lowell L. Hargens. 1996. "Variation among Academic
Disciplines: Analytical Frameworks and Research." Pp. 1–46 in *Higher*

Education: Handbook of Theory and Research, ed. John C. Smart. New York: Agathon.

Brenneis, Donald. 1994. "Discourse and Discipline at the National Research Council: A Bureaucratic *Bildungsroman.*" *Cultural Anthropology* 9 (1): 23–36.

————. 1999. "New Lexicon, Old Language: Negotiating the 'Global' at the National Science Foundation." Pp. 123–146 in *Critical Anthropology Now,* ed. George Marcus. Santa Fe: School of American Research Press.

Breslau, Daniel, and Yuval Yonay. 1999. "Beyond Metaphors: Mathematical Models in Economics as Empirical Research." *Science in Context* 12 (2): 317–332.

Breviglieri, Marc, Claudette Lafaye, and Daniel Trom, eds. 2005. *Sens de la critique, sens de la justice.* Paris: La Découverte.

Brint, Steven. 2002. *The Future of the City of Intellect: The Changing American University.* Stanford: Stanford University Press.

Brint, Steven, and Jerome Karabel. 1989. "American Education, Meritocratic Ideology, and the Legitimation of Inequality: The Community College and the Problem of American Exceptionalism." *Higher Education* 18 (6): 725–735.

Brubaker, Rogers. 1993. "Social Theory as Habitus." Pp. 212–234 in *Bourdieu: Critical Perspectives,* ed. Craig J. Calhoun, Edward LiPuma, and Moishe Postone. Chicago: University of Chicago Press.

Bryson, Bethany Paige. 2005. *Making Multiculturalism: Boundaries and Meaning in U.S. English Departments.* Stanford: Stanford University Press.

Burbank, Jane. 2004. *Russian Peasants Go to Court: Legal Culture in the Countryside, 1905–1917.* Bloomington: Indiana University Press.

Burke, Peter. 2004. *What Is Cultural History?* Malden, Mass.: Polity Press.

Burt, Ronald S. 2005. *Brokerage and Closure: Introduction to Social Capital.* Chicago: University of Chicago Press.

Callon, Michel. 1994. "Is Science a Public Good?" *Science, Technology, and Human Values* 4 (19): 395–424.

————. 1998. *The Laws of the Markets.* Malden, Mass.: Blackwell.

Callon, Michel, Pierre Lascoumes, and Yan Barthe. 2001. *Agir dans un monde incertain: Essai sur la démocratie technique.* Paris: Seuil.

Camic, Charles, and Neil Gross. 1998. "Contemporary Developments in Sociological Theory: Current Projects and Conditions of Possibility." *Annual Review of Sociology* 24:453–476.

Camic, Charles, Neil Gross, and Michèle Lamont. In preparation. *Knowledge Making, Use, and Evaluation in the Social Sciences.* New York: Russell Sage Foundation.

Campanario, Juan Miguel. 1998a. "Peer Review of Journals as It Stands Today: Part 1." *Science Communication* 19 (3): 181–211.

———. 1998b. "Peer Review of Journals as It Stands Today: Part 2." *Science Communication* 19 (4): 277–306.

Carlsnaes, Walter, Thomas Risse, and Beth A. Simmons, eds. 2002. *Handbook of International Relations.* Thousand Oaks, Calif.: Sage.

Carruthers, Bruce G., and Barry Cohen. 2008. "The Mechanization of Trust: Credit Rating in Nineteenth-Century America." Chicago: Department of Sociology, Northwestern University.

Castilla, Emilio. 2006. *Gender, Race, and Meritocracy in Organizational Careers.* Cambridge: Department of Organizational Behavior, Massachusetts Institute of Technology.

Chambers, Simone. 1996. *Reasonable Democracy: Jürgen Habermas and the Politics of Discourse.* Ithaca, N.Y.: Cornell University Press.

Chambliss, Daniel F. 1988. *Champions: The Making of Olympic Swimmers.* New York: William Morrow.

Chubin, Daryl E., and Edward J. Hackett. 1990. *Peerless Science: Peer Review and U.S. Science Policy.* Albany: State University of New York Press.

———. 2003. "Peer Review of the Twenty-first Century: Applications to Education Research." Report prepared for the National Research Council, Washington, D.C.

Cicourel, Aaron. 1974. *Cognitive Sociology.* New York: Free Press.

Clarke, Adele. 1990. "A Social Worlds Research Adventure: The Case of Reproductive Science." Pp. 15–42 in *Theories of Science in Society,* ed. S. Cozzens and Thomas Gieryn. Bloomington: Indiana University Press.

Clarke, Adele, and Elihu Gerson. 1990. "Symbolic Interactionism in Social Studies of Science." Pp. 179–214 in *Symbolic Interaction and Cultural Studies,* ed. Howard Becker and Michael McCall. Chicago: University of Chicago Press.

Clemens, Elisabeth S., Walter W. Powell, Kris McIlwaine, and Dina Okamoto. 1995. "Careers in Print: Books, Journals, and Scholarly Reputations." *American Journal of Sociology* 101 (2): 433–494.

Clifford, James, and George Marcus, eds. 1986. *Writing Culture: The Politics and Poetics of Ethnography.* Berkeley: University of California Press.

Cohen, Joshua. 1989. "Deliberation and Democratic Legitimacy." Pp. 17–34 in *The Good Polity: Normative Analysis of the State,* ed. Alan Hamlin and Philip Pettit. Oxford: Basil Blackwell.

Cohen, Michael D., James J. March, and Johan P. Olsen. 1972. "A Garbage Can Model of Organizational Choice." *Administrative Science Quarterly* 17 (1): 1–25.

Cole, Jonathan, and Stephen Cole. 1973. *Social Stratification in Science.* Chicago: University of Chicago Press.

————. 1981. *Peer Review in the National Science Foundation: Phase Two of a Study.* Washington, D.C.: National Academy Press.

Cole, Stephen. 1978. "Scientific Reward Systems: A Comparative Analysis." Pp. 167–190 in *Research in the Sociology of Knowledge, Science and Art,* ed. Robert A. Jones. Greenwich, Conn.: JAI.

————. 1992. *Making Science: Between Nature and Society.* Cambridge: Harvard University Press.

Cole, Stephen, Jonathan Cole, and Gary Simon. 1981. "Chance and Consensus in Peer Review." *Science* 214:881–886.

Cole, Stephen, Leonard Rubin, and Jonathan Cole. 1978. *Peer Review in the National Science Foundation: Phase One of a Study.* Washington, D.C.: National Academy Press.

Collins, Harry M., and Robert Evans. 2002. "The Third Wave of Science Studies: Studies of Expertise and Experience." *Social Studies of Science* 32 (2): 235–296.

————. 2007. *Rethinking Expertise.* Chicago: University of Chicago Press.

Collins, Randall. 1994. "Why the Social Sciences Won't Become High-Consensus, Rapid-Discovery Science." *Sociological Forum* 9 (2): 155–177.

————. 1998. *The Sociology of Philosophies: A Global Theory of Intellectual Change.* Cambridge: Belknap Press of Harvard University Press.

————. 2004. *Interaction Ritual Chains.* Princeton: Princeton University Press.

Cook, Karen S. 2005. "Network, Norms, and Trust: The Social Psychology of Social Capital." *Social Psychology Quarterly* 68 (1): 4–14.

Crane, Diane. 1976. "Reward Systems in Art, Science and Religion." *American Behavioral Scientist* 19 (6): 719–735.

Csikszentmihalyi, Mihaly. 1996. *Creativity: Flow and the Psychology of Discovery and Invention.* New York: Harper Perennial.

Cusset, François. 2003. *French Theory: Foucault, Derrida, Deleuze, and Cie et les mutations de la vie intellectuelle aux Etats-Unis.* Paris: Découverte.

D'Arms, John. 1998. "Press Conference Announcing Major Foundation Grants." New York: American Council of Learned Societies. February 5.

Daston, Lorraine, and Peter Galison. 2007. *Objectivity*. Cambridge: Zone Books.

Davis, Murray. 1971. "That's Interesting! Toward a Phenomenology of Sociology and a Sociology of Phenomenology." *Philosophy of the Social Sciences* 1:309–344.

Debray, Regis. 1979. *Le pouvoir intellectuel en France*. Paris: Ramsay.

DeVault, Marjorie L. 1999. *Liberating Methods: Feminism and Social Research*. Philadelphia: Temple University Press.

Dewey, John. 1985. *How We Think: A Restatement of the Relation of Reflective Thinking to the Educative Process*. Mineola, N.Y.: Dover Publications. (Orig. pub. 1933.)

Dews, C. L. Barney, and Carolyn Leste Law. 1995. *This Fine Place So Far from Home: Voices of Academics from the Working Class*. Philadelphia: Temple University Press.

DiMaggio, Paul. 1997. "Culture and Cognition." *Annual Review of Sociology* 23:263–287.

Dobbin, Frank. 1994. *Forging Industrial Policy: The United States, Britain, and France in the Railway Age*. New York: Cambridge University Press.

———. 2009. *Inventing Equal Opportunity*. Princeton: Princeton University Press.

Dubet, François. 2005. "Propositions pour une syntaxe des sentiments de justice dans l'experience du travail." *Revue française de sociologie* 46 (3): 495–528.

———. 2006. *Injustices: L'experiences des inegalites au travail*. Paris: Seuil.

Duell, Jason. 2000. "Assessing the Literary: Intellectual Boundaries in French and American Literary Studies." Pp. 94–126 in *Rethinking Comparative Cultural Sociology: Repertoires of Evaluation in France and the United States*, ed. Michèle Lamont and Laurent Thevenot. New York: Cambridge University Press.

Durkheim, Emile. 1965. *The Elementary Forms of Religious Life*. New York: Free Press.

Edelman, Lauren B., Sally Riggs Fuller, and Iona Mara-Drita. 2001. "Diversity Rhetoric and the Managerialization of Law." *American Journal of Sociology* 106 (6): 1589–1641.

Eisenhart, Margaret. 2002. "The Paradox of Peer Review: Admitting Too Much or Allowing Too Little?" *Research in Science Education* 32 (2): 241–255.

Eliasoph, Nina, and Paul Lichterman. 2003. "Culture in Interaction." *American Journal of Sociology* 108 (4): 735–794.

Engel, Susan. 1999. *Context Is Everything: The Nature of Memory.* New York: W. H. Freeman.

Epstein, Steven. 1996. *Impure Science: AIDS, Activism, and the Politics of Knowledge.* Berkeley: University of California Press.

Ericsson, Karl A. 1996. "The Acquisition of Expert Performance: An Introduction to Some of the Issues." Pp. 1–50 in *The Road to Excellence: The Acquisition of Expert Performance in the Arts and Sciences, Sports, and Games,* ed. Karl A. Ericsson. Mahwah, N.J.: Lawrence Erlbaum.

Erskine, William, and Roberta Spalter-Roth. 2006. "Profile of 2005 ASA Membership: Who Joined, Who Moved to the Top, and Who Is in What Subfield?" Report prepared for the American Sociological Association, Washington, D.C.

Espeland, Wendy N., and Michael Sauder. 2007. "Rankings and Reactivity: How Public Measures Recreate Social Worlds." *American Journal of Sociology* 113 (1): 1–14.

Espeland, Wendy N., and Mitchell L. Stevens. 1998. "Commensuration as a Social Process." *Annual Review of Sociology* 24:313–343.

Feagin, Joseph. 1999. "Soul-Searching in Sociology: Is the Discipline in Crisis?" *Chronicle of Higher Education* 46 (8): B4.

Feller, Irwin, Paul C. Stern, the National Research Council, and the Committee on Assessing Behavioral and Social Science Research on Aging. 2007. "A Strategy for Assessing Science: Behavioral and Social Research on Aging." Report prepared for the National Academies Press, Washington, D.C.

Fels, Anna. 2004. *Necessary Dreams: Ambition in Women's Changing Lives.* New York: Pantheon Books.

Ferree, Myra M., Shamus Khan, and Shauna Morimoto. 2007. "Assessing the Feminist Revolution: The Presence and Absence of Gender in Theory and Practice." Pp. 438–479 in *Sociology in America: A History,* ed. Craig Calhoun. Chicago: University of Chicago Press.

Fine, Gary A. 1979. "Small Groups and Culture Creation." *American Sociological Review* 44:733–745.

Fish, Stanley. 1980. "How to Recognize a Poem When You See One." Pp. 322–337 in *Is There a Text in this Class? The Authority of Interpretive Communities.* Cambridge: Harvard University Press.

Fiske, Susan T. 1998. "Stereotyping, Prejudice, and Discrimination." Pp. 357–

411 in *Handbook of Social Psychology,* ed. Daniel T. Gilbert, Susan T. Fiske, and Gardner Lindzey. New York: McGraw-Hill.

———. 2002. "What We Know about Bias and Intergroup Conflict, the Problem of the Century." *Current Directions in Psychological Science* 11:123–128.

Fleck, Lidwik. 1979. *Genesis and Development of a Scientific Fact.* Trans. Fred Bradley and Thaddeus Trenn. Chicago: University of Chicago Press. (Orig. pub. 1935.)

Fourcade-Gourinchas, Marion. 2001. "Politics, Institutional Structures, and the Rise of Economics: A Comparative Study." *Theory and Society* 30:397–447.

Fourcade, Marion. 2006. "The Construction of a Global Profession: The Transnationalization of Economics." *American Journal of Sociology* 112 (1): 145–194.

———. 2009. *Economists and Societies: Discipline and Profession in the United States, Great Britain and France.* Princeton: Princeton University Press.

Fournier, Marcel, Yves Gingras, and Creutzer Mathurin. 1988. "L'evaluation par les pairs et la définition legitime de la recherche." *Actes de la Recherche en Sciences Sociales* 74:47–54.

Frank, David John, Evan Schofer, and John Charles Torres. 1994. "Rethinking History: Change in the University Curriculum, 1910–90." *Sociology of Education* 67 (4): 231–242.

Frankfurt, Harry G. 2005. *On Bullshit.* Princeton: Princeton University Press.

Frickel, Scott, and Neil Gross. 2005. "A General Theory of Scientific/Intellectual Movements." *American Sociological Review* 70 (2): 204–232.

Fuchs, Stephen, and Jonathan H. Turner. 1986. "What Makes a Science 'Mature': Patterns of Organizational Control in Scientific Production." *Sociological Theory* 4 (2): 143–150.

Fujimura, Joan H. 1988. "The Molecular Bandwagon in Cancer Research: Where Social Worlds Meet." *Social Problems* 35 (3): 261–283.

Fuller, Steve. 1988. *Social Epistemology.* Bloomington: Indiana University Press.

Galison, Peter L. 1997. *Image and Logic: A Material Culture of Microphysics.* Chicago: University of Chicago Press.

Galison, Peter L., and David J. Stump, eds. 1996. *The Disunity of Sciences. Boundaries, Contexts, and Power.* Stanford: Stanford University Press.

Gambetta, Diego, and Heather Hamill. 2005. *Streetwise: How Taxi Drivers Establish Their Customers' Trustworthiness.* New York: Russell Sage.

Gardner, Howard. 1999. *Intelligence Reframed: Multiple Intelligences for the Twenty-first Century.* New York: Basic Books.

Garfinkel, Harold. 1967. *Studies in Ethnomethodology.* Englewood Cliffs, N.J.: Prentice Hall.

Gaztambide-Fernandez, Ruben. 2009. *Lives of Distinction: Ideology, Space, and Ritual in Processes of Identification at an Elite Boarding School.* Cambridge: Harvard University Press.

Geertz, Clifford. 1973. *The Interpretation of Cultures: Selected Essays.* New York: Basic Books.

———. 1985. "Waddling In." *Times Literary Supplement,* June 5.

General Accounting Office. 1994. "Peer Review Reforms Needed to Ensure Fairness in Federal Agency Grant Selection: Report to the Chairman, Committee on Governmental Activities, U.S. Senate." Washington, D.C.: General Accounting Office.

Gerson, Elihu. 1983. "Scientific Work and Social Worlds." *Knowledge* 4:357–377.

Gieryn, Thomas. 1983. "Boundary-work and the Demarcation of Science from Non-Science: Strains and Interests in Professional Ideologies of Scientists." *American Sociological Review* 48:781–795.

———. 1994. "Boundaries of Science." Pp. 393–443 in *Handbook of Science, Technology, and Society,* ed. Sheila Jasanoff, Gerald Markle, James Petersen, and Trevor Pinch. Beverly Hills, Calif.: Sage.

———. 1999. *Cultural Boundaries of Science: Credibility on the Line.* Chicago: University of Chicago Press.

Gigerenzer, Gerd. 2007. *Gut Feelings: The Intelligence of the Unconscious.* New York: Viking.

Gilbert, Nigel, and Michael Mulkay. 1984. *Opening Pandora's Box: A Sociological Analysis of Scientists' Discourse.* Cambridge, Eng.: Cambridge University Press.

Ginther, Donna K., and Kathy J. Hayes. 2003. "Gender Differences in Salary and Promotion for Faculty in the Humanities, 1977–95." *Journal of Human Resources* 38 (1): 34–73.

Givens, David B., and Timothy Jablonski. 1996. "AAA Survey of Anthropology PhDs." Report prepared for the American Anthropological Association, Arlington, Va.

Gladwell, Malcolm. 2005. *Blink: The Power of Thinking without Thinking.* New York: Little, Brown.

Glazer, Nathan. 1976. *Affirmative Discrimination.* New York: Basic Books.

Goffman, Erving. 1963. *Stigma.* Englewood Cliffs, N.J.: Prentice Hall.

―――. 1974. *Frame Analysis.* New York: Harper.

―――. 1981. *Forms of Talk.* Philadelphia: University of Pennsylvania Press.

―――. 1990. *The Presentation of Self in Everyday Life.* New York: Doubleday. (Orig. pub. 1959.)

Goleman, Daniel, Richard E. Boyatzis, and Annie McKee. 2002. *Primal Leadership: Realizing the Power of Emotional Intelligence.* Boston: Harvard Business School Press.

Gordon, Lewis R., and Jane Anna Gordon, eds. 2006. *A Companion to African-American Studies.* Oxford, Eng.: Blackwell.

Gould, Stephen Jay. 2003. *The Hedgehog, the Fox and the Magister's Pox: Mending the Gap between Science and the Humanities.* New York: Harmony Books.

Graff, Gerald. 1992. *Beyond the Culture Wars: How Teaching the Conflicts Can Revitalize American Education.* New York: Norton.

Granfield, Robert. 1991. "Making It by Faking It: Working-Class Students in an Elite Academic Environment." *Journal of Contemporary Ethnography* 20 (3): 331–351.

Granovetter, Marc. 1985. "Economic Action and Social Structure: The Problem of Embeddedness." *American Journal of Sociology* 91 (3): 481–510.

Green, Donald P., and Ian Shapiro. 1994. *Pathologies of Rational Choice Theory: A Critique of Applications in Political Science.* New Haven: Yale University Press.

Gross, Neil. 2008. *Richard Rorty: The Making of a Philosopher.* Chicago: University of Chicago Press.

Gross, Neil, and Solon Simmons. 2006. "Americans' Views of Political Bias in the Academy and Academic Freedom." Paper presented at the Annual Meeting of the American Association of University Professors, Washington, D.C., June 8–11.

Gruenfeld, Deborah, Paul V. Martorana, and Elliot T. Fan. 2000. "What Do Groups Learn from Their Worldliest Members? Direct and Indirect Influence in Dynamic Teams." *Organizational Behavior and Human Decision Processes* 82 (1): 45–59.

Guetzkow, Joshua, Michèle Lamont, Marcel Fournier, and Grégoire Mallard. 2003. "Originality and the Construction of Academic Worth: Substantive Qualities and Scholarly Virtue in Peer Review." Paper presented at the Annual Meeting of the American Sociological Association, Atlanta, Ga., August 16–19.

Guetzkow, Joshua, Michèle Lamont, and Grégoire Mallard. 2004. "What Is Originality in the Social Sciences and the Humanities?" *American Sociological Review* 69 (2): 190–212.

Guillory, John. 1993. *Cultural Capital: The Problem of Literary Canon Formation.* Chicago: University of Chicago Press.

Guinier, Lani, and Susan Sturm. 2001. *Who's Qualified?* Boston: Beacon Press.

Gumport, Patricia J. 2000a. "Academic Restructuring: Organizational Change and Institutional Imperatives." *Higher Education: An International Journal of Higher Education and Educational Planning* 39:67–91.

———. 2000b. "Learning Academic Labor." *Comparative Social Research* 19:1–23.

———. 2002. *Academic Pathfinders: Knowledge Creation and Feminist Scholarship.* Westport, Conn.: Greenwood.

Gutmann, Amy, and Dennis Thompson. 1996. *Democracy and Disagreement.* Cambridge: Harvard University Press.

Habermas, Jürgen. 1982. "A Reply to My Critics." In *Habermas: Critical Debates,* ed. John B. Thompson and David Held. Cambridge: MIT Press.

———. 1984. *The Theory of Communicative Action.* Trans. Thomas McCarthy. Boston: Beacon Press.

Hall, Peter A., and Michèle Lamont, eds. 2009. *Successful Societies: How Institutions and Culture Affect Health.* New York: Cambridge University Press.

Hall, Peter A., and David Soskice, eds. 2001. *Varieties of Capitalism: The Institutional Foundations of Comparative Advantage.* New York: Oxford University Press.

Hall, Stuart. 1990. "The Emergence of Cultural Studies and the Crisis of the Humanities." *October* 53:11–23.

Hargens, Lowell L. 1988. "Scholarly Consensus and Journal Rejection Rates." *American Sociological Review* 53 (1): 139–151.

Hartmann, Ilse, and Friedhelm Neidhardt. 1990. "Peer Review at the *Forschungsgemeinschaft.*" *Scientometrics* 19 (5–6): 419–425.

Hastie, Reid. 2001. "Problems for Judgment and Decision Making." *Annual Review of Psychology* 52:653–683.

Hayagreeva, Rao, Phillippe Monin, and Rodolphe Durand. 2005. "Border

Crossing: Bricolage and the Erosion of Categorical Boundaries in French Gastronomy." *American Sociological Review* 70 (9): 868–991.

Heinich, Nathalie. 1996. *The Glory of Van Gogh.* Princeton: Princeton University Press.

————. 1997. "Les frontières de l'art à l'épreuve de l'expertise: politique de la décision dans une commission municipale." *Politix* 38:111–135.

Helper, Susan, John Paul MacDuffie, and Charles Sabel. 2000. "Pragmatic Collaborations: Advancing Knowledge While Controlling Opportunism." *Industrial and Corporate Change* 9 (3): 443–488.

Hennion, Antoine. 2004. "Pragmatics of Taste." Pp. 131–144 in *Blackwell Companion to the Sociology of Culture,* ed. Mark Jacobs and Nancy Hankahan. Oxford, Eng.: Blackwell.

Hochschild, Arlie. 1979. "Emotion Work, Feeling Rules and Social Structure." *American Journal of Sociology* 85 (3): 551–575.

Hoffer, T. B., V. Welch Jr., K. Webber, K. Williams, B. Lisek, M. Hess, D. Loew, and I. Guzman-Barron. 2006. "Doctorate Recipients from United States Universities: Summary Report 2005." Report prepared for the National Opinion Research Center, Chicago.

Hojat, Mohammadreza, Joseph S. Gonnella, and Addeane S. Caelleigh. 2003. "Impartial Judgment by the Gatekeepers of Science: Fallibility and Accountability in the Peer Review Process." *Advances in Health Sciences Education* 8 (1): 75–96.

Ibarra, Herminia. 1992. "Homophily and Differential Returns: Sex Differences in Network Structure and Access in an Advertising Firm." *Administrative Science Quarterly* 37:422–447.

Iggers, Georg G. 1997. *Historiography in the Twentieth Century: From Scientific Objectivity to the Postmodern Challenge.* Middletown, Conn.: Wesleyan University Press.

Jackall, Robert. 1988. *Moral Mazes: The World of Corporate Managers.* New York: Oxford University Press.

Jacobs, Jerry A. 2004. "The Faculty Time Divide (Presidential Address)." *Sociological Forum* 19 (1): 3–27.

————. Forthcoming-a. "Interdisciplinarity: A Review of Research on Communication among Social-Science Disciplines." *Annual Review of Sociology.*

————. Forthcoming-b. *Women in Higher Education.* New York: Russell Sage Foundation.

Jacobs, Jerry A., and Sarah Winslow. 2004. "Overworked Faculty: Job Stresses and Family Demands." *Annals of the American Academy of Political and Social Science* 596 (1): 104–129.

James, William. 1911. "The Essence of Humanism." Pp. 121–135 in *The Meaning of Truth*. New York: Longman, Green.

Jasanoff, Sheila. 1990. *The Fifth Branch: Science Advisers as Policy Makers.* Cambridge: Harvard University Press.

———, ed. 2004. *States of Knowledge: The Co-Production of Science and Social Order.* New York: Routledge.

Jencks, Christopher, and David Riesman. 1977. *The Academic Revolution.* Chicago: University of Chicago Press.

Jenkins, Richard. 1996. *Social Identity.* London: Routledge.

Kanter, Rosabeth M. 1977. *Men and Women of the Corporation.* New York: Basic Books.

Karabel, Jerome. 2005. *The Chosen: The Hidden History of Admission and Exclusion at Harvard, Yale, and Princeton.* Boston: Houghton Mifflin Co.

Keane, Webb. 2003. "Self-Interpretation, Agency, and the Objects of Anthropology: Reflections on a Genealogy." *Comparative Studies in Society and History* 45(2): 222–248.

Kelle, Udo, Gerald Prein, and Catherine Beird. 1995. *Computer-Aided Qualitative Data Analysis: Theory, Methods, and Practice.* Thousand Oaks, Calif.: Sage.

Kelly, Erin, and Frank Dobbin. 1998. "How Affirmative Action Became Diversity Management: Employers' Response to Anti-Discrimination Law, 1961–1996." *American Behavioral Scientist* 41:960–984.

———. 2001. "How Affirmative Action Became Diversity Management: Employer Response to Anti-Discrimination Law, 1961–1996." Pp. 87–117 in *Color Lines: Affirmative Action, Immigration and Civil Rights Options for America.*, ed. John Skrentny. Chicago: University of Chicago Press.

Kessler-Harris, Alice, Amy Swerdlow, and Sue Rovi. 1995. "Evaluation of Woodrow Wilson National Fellowship Foundation." Report prepared for the Woodrow Wilson National Fellowship Foundation, Princeton.

King, Gary, Robert O. Keohane, and Sidney Verba. 1994. *Designing Social Inquiry: Scientific Inference in Qualitative Research.* Princeton: Princeton University Press.

Kirp, David L. 2003. *Shakespeare, Einstein, and the Bottom Line: The Marketing of Higher Education.* Cambridge: Harvard University Press.

Klein, Julie T. 1996. *Crossing Boundaries: Knowledge, Disciplinarities, and Interdisciplinarities.* Charlottesville: University of Virginia Press.

————. 2003. "Thinking about Interdisciplinarity: A Primer for Practice." *Colorado School of Mines Quarterly* 103 (1): 101–114.

————. 2005. "Interdisciplinary Teamwork: The Dynamics of Collaboration and Integration." Pp. 23–50 in *Interdisciplinary Collaboration: An Emerging Cognitive Science,* ed. S. J. Derry, C. D. Schunn, and M. A. Gernsbacher. Mahwah, N.J.: Lawrence Erlbaum.

Knorr-Cetina, Karin. 1999. *Epistemic Cultures: How the Sciences Make Knowledge.* Cambridge: Harvard University Press.

Kollock, Peter, Philip Blumstein, and Pepper Schwartz. 1985. "Sex and Power in Interaction: Conversational Privileges and Duties." *American Sociological Review* 50:34–46.

Ladd, Everett Carll, and Seymour M. Lipset. 1975. *The Divided Academy: Professors and Politics.* New York: Norton.

Laitin, David. 2004. "The Political Science Discipline." Pp. 11–40 in *The Evolution of Political Knowledge: Theory and Inquiry in American Politics,* ed. Edward D. Mansfield and Richard Sisson. Columbus: Ohio State University Press.

Lakatos, Imre. 1974. "History of Science and Its Rational Reconstructions." in *The Interaction between Science and Philosophy,* ed. Yehuda Elkana. Atlantic Highlands, N.J.: Humanities.

Lamont, Michèle. 1987. "How to Become a Dominant French Philosopher: The Case of Jacques Derrida." *American Journal of Sociology* 93 (3): 584–622.

————. 1989. "The Power-Culture Link in a Comparative Perspective." *Comparative Social Research* 11:131–150.

————. 1992. *Money, Morals, and Manners: The Culture of the French and American Upper-Middle Class.* Chicago: University of Chicago Press.

————. 2000. *The Dignity of Working Men: Morality and the Boundaries of Race, Class, and Immigration.* Cambridge: Harvard University Press.

————. 2001. "Three Questions for a Big Book: Collins' *The Sociology of Philosophies.*" *Sociological Theory* 19 (1):86–91.

————. 2004a. "Recruiting, Promoting, and Retaining Women Academics: Lessons from the Literature." Report prepared for the Committee on the Status of Women, Faculty of Arts and Sciences, Harvard University, Cambridge.

————. 2004b. "Theoretical Growth and Conceptual Foreplay." *Perspectives: Newsletter of the ASA Theory Section* 27 (3): 1.

————. 2008. "Critères d'évaluation et structures culturelles: réflections sur un parcours de recherches." in *Sens de la critique, sens de la justice,* ed. Catherine Guaspare, Marc Breviglieri, Claudette Lafaye, and Daniel Trom. Paris: La Découverte.

————. 2009. "The Challenges of Pierre Bourdieu." In *After Bourdieu,* ed. Elisabeth Silva and Alan Warde. London: Routledge.

Lamont, Michèle, Veronica Boix Mansilla, and Katri Huutoniemi. 2007. "Fostering Successful Interdisciplinarity through Shared Cognitive Platforms." Prepared for the Canadian Institute for Advanced Research, Toronto.

Lamont, Michèle, and Crystal Fleming. 2005. "Everyday Anti-Racism: Competence and Religion in the Cultural Repertoire of the African-American Elite and Working Class." *Du Bois Review* 2 (1): 29–43.

Lamont, Michèle, Marcel Fournier, Josh Guetzkow, Grégoire Mallard, and Roxane Bernier. 2006. "Evaluating Creative Minds: The Assessment of Originality in Peer Review." Pp. 166–181 in *Knowledge, Communication and Creativity,* ed. Arnaud Sales and Marcel Fournier. London: Sage.

Lamont, Michèle, and Katri Huutoniemi. 2007. "Comparing Customary Rules of Fairness: Evidence of Evaluative Practices in Various Types of Peer Review Panels." Paper presented at the conference Making, Evaluating, and Using Social Scientific Knowledge, Russell Sage Foundation, New York, December 7–8.

Lamont, Michèle, Jason Kaufman, and Michael Moody. 2000. "The Best of the Brightest: Definitions of the Ideal Self among Prize-Winning Students." *Sociological Forum* 15 (2): 187–224.

Lamont, Michèle, and Annette Lareau. 1988. "Cultural Capital: Allusions, Gaps, and Glissandos in Recent Theoretical Developments." *Sociological Theory* 6 (2): 153–168.

Lamont, Michèle, and Grégoire Mallard. 2005. "Peer Evaluation in the Social Sciences and Humanities Compared: The United States, the United Kingdom, and France." Report prepared for the Social Sciences and Humanities Research Council of Canada, Ottawa.

Lamont, Michèle, and Viràg Molnár. 2002. "The Study of Boundaries across the Social Sciences." *Annual Review of Sociology* 28:167–195.

Lamont, Michèle, and Laurent Thévenot, eds. 2000. *Rethinking Comparative Cultural Sociology: Repertoires of Evaluation in France and the United States.* London: Cambridge University Press.

Lamont, Michèle, and Patricia White. 2008. "Workshop on Interdisciplinary Standards for Systematic Qualitative Research: Cultural Anthropology,

Law and Social Science, Political Science, and Sociology Programs." Report prepared for the National Science Foundation, Washington, D.C.

Lamont, Michèle, and Marsha Witten. 1989. "Surveying the Continental Drift: The Diffusion of French Social and Literary Theory in the United States." *French Politics and Society* 6 (3): 17–23.

Lamont, Michèle, and Robert Wuthnow. 1990. "Betwixt-and-Between: Recent Cultural Sociology in Europe and the United States." Pp. 287–315 in *Frontiers of Social Theory: The New Synthesis,* ed. George Ritzer. New York: Columbia University Press.

Lamont, Michèle, and Ezra Zuckerman. In preparation. "Towards a Sociology of Valuation: Convergence, Divergence, and Synthesis." *Annual Review of Sociology.*

Langfeldt, Liv. 2001. "The Decision-Making Constraints and Processes of Grant Peer Review, and Their Effects on the Review Outcome." *Social Studies of Science* 31 (6): 820–841.

———. 2006. "The Policy Challenges of Peer Review: Managing Bias, Conflict of Interest, and Interdisciplinary Assessment." *Research Evaluation* 15 (1): 31–42.

Langhout, Regina Day, Francine Rosselli, and Jonathan Feinstein. 2007. "Assessing Classism in Academic Settings." *Review of Higher Education* 30 (2): 145–184.

Latour, Bruno. 1987. *Science in Action: How to Follow Scientists and Engineers through Society.* Cambridge: Harvard University Press.

———. 1988. *The Pasteurization of France.* Trans. Alan Sheridan and John Law. Cambridge: Harvard University Press.

Latour, Bruno, and Steve Woolgar. 1979. *Laboratory Life: The Social Construction of Scientific Facts.* Princeton: Princeton University Press.

Laudel, Grit. 2006. "The 'Quality Myth': Promoting and Hindering Conditions for Acquiring Research Funds." *Higher Education* 52:375–403.

Laudel, Grit, and Gloria Origgi. 2006. "Special Issue on the Assessment of Interdisciplinary Research." *Research Evaluation* 15 (1).

Leahey, Erin. 2008. "Methodological Memes and Mores: Toward a Sociology of Social Research." *Annual Review of Sociology* 34:33–53.

Lederman, Rena. 2006. "Introduction: Anxious Borders between Work and Life in a Time of Bureaucratic Ethics Regulation." *American Ethnologist* 33 (4): 477–481.

Leiter, Brian, ed. 2004. *The Future for Philosophy.* New York: Oxford University Press.

Lenoir, Timothy. 1993. "Discipline of Nature and the Nature of Disciplines." Pp. 77–78 in *Knowledges: Historical and Critical Studies in Disciplinarity*, ed. Ellen Messer-Davidow, David Shumway, and David Sylvan. Charlottesville: University of Virginia Press.

Lévi-Strauss, Claude. 1983. *Structural Anthropology*. Trans. Monique Layton. Chicago: University of Chicago Press.

Levinson, Jerold. 2002. "Hume's Standards of Taste: The Real Problem." *Journal of Aesthetics and Art Criticism* 60 (3): 227–238.

Lewis, Lionel. 1998. *Scaling the Ivory Tower: Merit and Its Limits in Academic Careers*. New Brunswick, N.J.: Transaction.

Liebert, Roland. 1976. *Disintegration and Political Action: The Changing Functions of City Governments in America*. New York: Academic Press.

———. 1982. "Productivity, Favor, and Grants among Scholars." *American Journal of Sociology* 83 (3): 664–673.

Lipset, Seymour M. 1979. *The First New Nation*. New York: Norton. (Orig. pub. 1963.)

Longino, Helen E. 2002. *The Fate of Knowledge*. Princeton: Princeton University Press.

Lukes, Steven. 1974. *Power: A Radical View*. London: Macmillan.

Lustick, Ian. 1997. "The Disciplines of Political Science: Studying the Culture of Rational Choice as a Case in Point." *PS—Political Science and Politics* 30 (2): 175–179.

Lynch, Michael. 1993. *Scientific Practice and Ordinary Action: Ethnomethodology and Social Studies of Science*. New York: Cambridge University Press.

MacKenzie, Donald, and Yuval Millo. 2003. "Constructing a Market, Performing Theory: The Historical Sociology of a Financial Derivatives Exchange." *American Journal of Sociology* 109 (10): 1907–1945.

Mallard, Grégoire. 2005. "Interpreters of the Literary Canon and Their Technical Instruments: The Case of Balzac Criticism." *American Sociological Review* 70 (6): 992–1010.

Mallard, Grégoire, Michèle Lamont, and Joshua Guetzkow. 2007. "Cognitive Contextualization, Epistemological Styles, and Peer Review in the Social Sciences and the Humanities." Cambridge: Harvard University, Department of Sociology.

———. 2009. "Fairness as Appropriateness: Negotiating Epistemological Differences in Peer Review." *Science, Technology and Human Values*.

Mansbridge, Jane J. 1983. *Beyond Adversary Democracy.* Chicago: University of Chicago Press.

Mansfield, Edward D., and Richard Sisson. 2004. *The Evolution of Political Knowledge: Theory and Inquiry in American Politics.* Columbus: Ohio State University Press.

Manzo, John. 1993. "Jurors' Narratives of Personal Experience in Deliberation Talk." *Text* 13 (3): 267–290.

March, James J., and Johan P. Olsen. 1976. *Ambiguity and Choice in Organizations.* Oslo, Norway: Universitetsforlaget.

Marcus, George E., and Michael M. Fischer. 1986. *Anthropology as Cultural Critique: An Experimental Moment in the Human Sciences.* Chicago: University of Chicago Press.

Martin, Brian, and Eveleen Richards. 1995. "Scientific Knowledge, Controversy, and Public Decision Making." Pp. 506–526 in *Handbook of Science and Technology,* ed. Sheila Jasanoff, Gerald E. Markel, James C. Paterson, and Trevor Pinch. Newbury Park, Calif.: Sage.

Martin, Emily. 1994. *Flexible Bodies: Tracking Immunity in American Culture from the Days of Polio to the Age of AIDS.* Boston: Beacon Press.

Maynard, Douglas W., and John Manzo. 1993. "On the Sociology of Justice: Theoretical Notes from an Actual Jury Deliberation." *Sociological Theory* 11 (2): 171–193.

McCartney, John. 1970. "On Being Scientific: Changing Styles of Presentation of Sociological Research." *American Sociologist* 5 (1): 30–35.

McPherson, Miller, Lynn Smith-Lovin, and James M. Cook. 2001. "Birds of a Feather: Homophily in Social Networks." *Annual Review of Sociology* 27:415–444.

Merton, Robert K. 1968. "The Matthew Effect in Science." *Science* 159:56–63.

———. 1972. "Insiders and Outsiders: A Chapter in the Sociology of Knowledge." *American Journal of Sociology* 78 (1): 9–47.

———. 1973. "Priorities in Scientific Discovery: A Chapter in the Sociology of Science." Pp. 286–324 in *The Sociology of Science: Theoretical and Empirical Investigations,* ed. Norman Storer. Chicago: University of Chicago Press. (Orig. pub. 1957.)

———. 1988. "The Matthew Effect in Science, II: Cumulative Advantage and the Symbolism of Intellectual Property." *Isis* 79:606.

———, ed. 1996. *On Social Structure and Science.* Chicago: University of Chicago Press.

Messer-Davidow, Ellen. 2002. *Disciplining Feminism: From Social Activism to Activist Discourse*. Durham, N.C.: Duke University Press.

Meyer, John. 1986. "Myths of Socialization and of Personality." Pp. 208–221 in *Reconstructing Individualism: Autonomy, Individuality, and the Self in Western Thought,* ed. Thomas C. Heller, Morton Sosan, David E. Welbery, Arnold I. Davidson, Ann Swidler, and Ian Watt. Stanford: Stanford University Press.

Meyer, John, Francisco Ramirez, David John Frank, and Evan Schofer. 2006. "Higher Education as an Institution." Stanford: Center on Democracy, Freeman Spogli Institute for International Studies, Stanford University.

Meyer, John, and Brian Rowan. 1977. "Institutionalized Organizations: Formal Structure as Myth and Ceremony." *American Journal of Sociology* 83 (2): 340–363.

Miles, Matthew B., and A. Michael Huberman. 1994. *Qualitative Data Analysis: A Sourcebook of New Methods*. Beverly Hills, Calif.: Sage.

Moser, Walter. 2001. "Posface: Pas d'euphorie! anatomie d'une crise." *Canadian Review of Comparative Literature* 26 (3–4): 193–210.

Mukerji, Chandra. 2007. "Cultural Genealogy: Method for a Historical Sociology of Culture or Cultural Sociology of History." *Cultural Sociology* 1 (1): 49–71.

Mulkay, Michael. 1976. "Norms and Ideology in Science." *Social Science Information* 15:627–656.

———. 1991. *Sociology of Science: A Sociological Pilgrimage*. Philadelphia: Open University Press.

Munch, Peter A. 1975. "'Sense' and 'Intention' in Max Weber's Theory of Social Action." *Sociological Inquiry* 45 (4): 59–65.

Musselin, Christine. 1996. "Les marchés du travail universitaires, comme économie de la qualité." *Revue Française de Sociologie* 37 (2): 189–208.

———. 2005. *Le marché des universitaires: France, Allemagne, Etats-Unis.* Paris: Presses de SciencesPo.

Nagel, Ernest. 1961. *The Structure of Science: Problems in the Logic of Scientific Explanation*. New York: Harcourt, Brace.

National Academy of Sciences. 2006. "Beyond Bias and Barriers: Fulfilling the Potential of Women in Academic Science and Engineering." Report prepared for the National Academies, Washington, D.C.

National Opinion Research Center. 2006. *Survey of Earned Doctorates, 2005.* Arlington, Va.: National Science Foundation.

National Science Foundation. 2004. "Report of the Workshop on Scientific Foundations of Qualitative Research." Report prepared for the National Science Foundation, Arlington, Va.

Nehamas, Alexander. 1998. "Trends in Recent American Philosophy." Pp. 227–242 in *American Academic Culture in Transformation*, ed. Thomas E. Bender and Carl E. Schorske. Princeton: Princeton University Press.

Novick, Peter. 1988. *That Noble Dream: The "Objectivity Question" and the American Historical Profession.* New York: Cambridge University Press.

Ortner, Sherry B. 2005. "Subjectivity as Cultural Critique." *Anthropological Theory* 5 (1): 31–52.

Pachucki, Mark, Sabrina Pendergrass, and Michèle Lamont. 2007. "Boundary Processes: Recent Theoretical Developments and New Contributions." *Poetics* 35 (6): 331–351.

Page, Scott E. 2007. *The Difference: How the Power of Diversity Creates Better Groups, Firms, Schools, and Societies.* Princeton: Princeton University Press.

Palumbo-Liu, David. 1995. *The Ethnic Canon: Histories, Institutions, and Interventions.* Minneapolis: University of Minnesota Press.

Perna, Laura W. 2001. "Sex and Race Differences in Faculty Tenure and Promotion." *Research in Higher Education* 42 (5): 541–567.

Perry, Merry G. 2006. "Feminism and Cultural Studies in Composition: Locating Women and Men in College Writing Courses." *Composition Forum* 15 (special issue "Composition and Location"): http://www.fau.edu/compositionforum/15/perryfeminism.php.

Polletta, Francesca, and M. Kai Ho. 2005. "Frames and Their Consequences." Pp. 187–214 in *Oxford Handbook of Contextual Political Studies*, ed. Robert E. Goodin and Charles Tilly. Oxford, Eng.: Oxford University Press.

Porter, Alan L., and Frederick A. Rossini. 1985. "Peer Review of Interdisciplinary Research Proposals." *Science, Technology, and Human Values* 10 (3): 33–38.

Porter, Theodore. 1999. "Quantification and the Accounting Ideal in Science." Pp. 394–406 in *The Science Studies Reader*, ed. Mario Biagioli. New York: Routledge.

Powell, Walter W. 1985. *Getting into Print: The Decision-Making Process in Scholarly Publishing.* Chicago: University of Chicago Press.

Putnam, Hilary. 1998. "A Half Century of Philosophy, Viewed from Within." Pp. 193–226 in *American Academic Culture in Transformation*, ed.

Thomas E. Bender and Carl E. Schorske. Princeton: Princeton University Press.

Ragin, Charles C. 1987. *The Comparative Method: Moving beyond Qualitative and Quantitative Strategies.* Berkeley: University of California Press.

———. 2000. *Fuzzy Set Social Science.* Chicago: University of Chicago Press.

Ravinet, Pauline. 2007. "La genèse et l'institutionalisation du processus de Boulogne." Ph.D. diss., Fondation Nationale des Sciences Politique (Sciences Po).

Readings, Bill. 1996. *The University in Ruins.* Cambridge: Harvard University Press.

Reskin, Barbara F. 2000. "The Proximate Causes of Employment Discrimination." *Contemporary Sociology* 29 (2): 319–328.

Reskin, Barbara F., and Debra B. McBrier. 2000. "Why Not Ascription? Organizations' Employment of Male and Female Managers." *American Sociological Review* 65 (2): 210–233.

Rhoten, Diana. 2003. "Final Report, National Science Foundation BCS-0129573: A Multi-Method Analysis of the Social and Technical Conditions for Interdisciplinary Collaboration." Report prepared for the National Science Foundation, Washington, D.C.

Ridgeway, Cecilia L. 1997. "Interaction and the Conservation of Gender Inequality: Considering Employment." *American Sociological Review* 62 (2): 218–235.

Rivera, Lauren. 2009. "Cultural Reproduction in the Labor Market: Homophily in Job Interviews." Paper presented in the Culture and Social Analysis Workshop, Department of Sociology, Harvard University, October 6.

Rosental, Claude. 2003. "Certifying Knowledge: The Sociology of a Logical Theorem in Artificial Intelligence." *American Sociological Review* 68 (4): 623–644.

———. 2008. *Weaving Self-Evidence: A Sociology of Logic.* Princeton: Princeton University Press.

Roska, Josipa, and Mitchell L. Stevens. 2007. "Diversity in Organizational Admission: Explaining the Success of Affirmative Action in U.S. Higher Education." Presented at the annual meeting Is Another World Possible? American Sociological Association, New York, August.

Rossi, Peter, and Howard Freeman. 1993. *Evaluation: A Systematic Approach.* New York: Sage.

Roy, Rustum. 1985. "Funding Science: The Real Defects of Peer Review and an Alternative to It." *Science, Technology, and Human Values* 10:73–81.

Rudenstine, Neil L. 2001. *Pointing Our Thoughts: Reflections on Harvard and Higher Education, 1991–2001.* Cambridge: Harvard University Press.

Sauder, Michael. 2006. "Third Parties and Status Systems: How the Structure of Status Systems Matter." *Theory & Society* 35:299–321.

Schiebinger, Londa L. 1999. *Has Feminism Changed Science?* Cambridge: Harvard University Press.

Scott, Joan M. 2001. "Women's History." Pp. 43–70 in *New Perspectives on Historical Writing,* 2d ed., ed. Peter Burke. University Park: Pennsylvania State University Press.

Sewell, William H., Jr. 2005. *Logics of History: Social Theory and Social Transformation.* Chicago: University of Chicago Press.

Shapin, Steven. 1994. *A Social History of Truth: Civility and Science in Seventeenth-Century England.* Chicago: University of Chicago Press.

Shapin, Steven, and Simon Schaeffer. 1985. *Leviathan and the Air Pump: Hobbes, Boyle, and the Experimental Life.* Princeton: Princeton University Press.

Shapiro, Ian. 2005. *The Flight from Reality in the Human Sciences.* Princeton: Princeton University Press.

Shapiro, Ian, Rogers M. Smith, and Tarek E. Masoud. 2004. *Problems and Methods in the Study of Politics.* New York: Cambridge University Press.

Shenhav, Yahouda A. 1986. "Dependence and Compliance in Academic Research Infrastructures." *Sociolocial Perspectives* 21 (1): 29–51.

Shumway, David R. 1997. "The Star System in Literary Studies." *PMLA: Publications of the Modern Language Association of America* 112 (1): 85–100.

Simon, Herbert. 1957. *Models of Man: Social and Rational.* New York: John Wiley and Sons.

Singleton, Royce A., and Bruce C. Straits. 1999. *Approaches to Social Research.* New York: Oxford University Press.

Skrentny, John D. 2002. *The Minority Rights Revolution.* Cambridge: Belknap Press of Harvard University Press.

Slaughter, Sheila, and Gary Rhoades. 2004. *Academic Capitalism and the New Economy.* Baltimore: John Hopkins University Press.

Smith, Daryl G., and José Moreno. 2006. "Hiring the Next Generation of Professors: Will Myths Remain Excuses?" *Chronicle of Higher Education* 53 (6): 64.

Smith, Dorothy E. 1990a. *The Conceptual Practices of Power: A Feminist Sociology of Knowledge*. Toronto: University of Toronto Press.

———. 1990b. "Women's Experience as a Radical Critique of Sociology" and "The Ideological Practice of Sociology." Pp. 1–57 in *The Conceptual Practices of Power: A Feminist Sociology of Knowledge*. Boston: Northeastern University Press.

Snow, Charles P. 1993. *The Two Cultures*. New York: Cambridge University Press.

Social Science Research Council. N.d. "Academic Fellowship Program Peer Review Process." Report prepared for the Social Science Research Council, New York.

Sonnert, Gerhard. 1995. "What Makes a Good Scientist? Determinants of Peer Evaluation among Biologists." *Social Studies of Science* 25:35–55.

———. 2002. *Ivory Bridges: Connecting Science and Society*. Cambridge: MIT Press.

Star, Susan Leigh. 1985. "Scientific Work and Uncertainty." *Social Studies of Science* 15:391–427.

Stark, Laura. 2007. "IRB Meetings by the Minute(s)." Presented at the Workshop on Knowledge Production and Evaluation in the Social Sciences, Russell Sage Foundation, New York.

Steinmetz, George. 2005. *The Politics of Method in the Human Sciences: Positivism and Its Epistemological Others*. Durham, N.C.: Duke University Press.

Stevens, Mitchell L. 2007. *Creating a Class: College Admissions and the Education of Elites*. Cambridge: Harvard University Press.

Stevens, Mitchell L., Elizabeth A. Armstrong, and Richard Arum. 2008. "Sieve, Incubator, Temple, Hub: Empirical and Theoretical Advances in the Sociology of Higher Education." *Annual Review of Sociology* 34: 127–151.

Stewart, Sharla. 2003. "Revolution from Within." *University of Chicago Magazine* 95 (5): 33–37.

Stinchcombe, Arthur L. 1990. *Information and Organizations*. Berkeley: University of California Press.

———. 2005. *The Logic of Social Research*. Chicago: University of Chicago Press.

Stout, Jeffrey. 2004. *Democracy and Tradition*. Princeton: Princeton University Press.

Strathern, Marilyn, ed. 2000. *Audit Cultures: Anthropological Studies in Accountability, Ethics, and the Academy.* London: Routledge.

Stuber, Jenny M. 2006. "Talk of Class: The Discursive Repertoires of White Working- and Upper-Middle-Class College Students." *Journal of Contemporary Ethnography* 35 (3): 285–318.

Szakolcai, Arpad. 1998. *Max Weber and Michel Foucault: Parallel Life-Works.* London: Routledge.

Tarrow, Sid. 2007. "Knowledge Struggles: Two Disciplines Processing Contention." Institute of Social Sciences, Cornell University, Ithaca, N.Y.

Thévenot, Laurent. 2006. *L'action au pluriel: Sociologie des régimes d'engagment.* Paris: La Découverte.

———. 2007a. "The Plurality of Cognitive Formats and Engagements: Moving between the Familiar and the Public." *European Journal of Social Theory* 10 (3): 409–423.

———. 2007b. "A Science of Life Together in the World." *European Journal of Social Theory* 10 (2): 233–244.

Tilly, Charles. 1984. *Big Structures, Large Processes, Huge Comparisons.* New York: Russell Sage.

———. 1998. *Durable Inequality.* Berkeley: University of California Press.

———. 2006. *Why?* Princeton: Princeton University Press.

Travis, G. D. L., and Harry M. Collins. 1991. "New Light on Old Boys: Cognitive and Institutional Particularism in the Peer Review System." *Science, Technology and Human Values* 16 (3): 322–341.

Trix, Frances, and Carolyn Psenka. 2003. "Exploring the Color of Glass: Letters of Recommendation for Female and Male Medical Faculty." *Discourse and Society* 14 (2): 191–220.

Tsay, Angela, Michèle Lamont, Andrew Abbott, and Joshua Guetzkow. 2003. "From Character to Intellect: Changing Conceptions of Merit in the Social Sciences and Humanities, 1951–1971." *Poetics* 31:23–49.

Turner, Mark. 1991. *Reading Minds: The Study of English in the Age of Cognitive Science.* Princeton: Princeton University Press.

Uzzi, Brian. 1999. "Embeddedness and the Making of Financial Capital: How Social Relations and Networks Benefit Firms Seeking Financing." *American Sociological Review* 64:481–505.

Walker, George, Chris Golde, Laura Jones, Andrea Conklin Bueschel, and Pat Hutchings. 2008. *The Formation of Scholars: Rethinking Doctoral Education for the Twenty-first Century.* San Francisco: Jossey-Bass.

Walzer, Michael. 1983. *Spheres of Justice: A Defense of Pluralism and Equality.* New York: Basic Books.

Weber, Max. 1978. *Economy and Society.* Berkeley: University of California Press. (Orig. pub. 1956.)

————. 1984. *Confucianism and Taoism.* Trans. M. Alter and J. Hunter. London: London School of Economics. (Orig. pub. 1913.)

Webster, Murray, Jr. 2003. "Working on Status Puzzles." Pp. 173–215 in *Power and Status, Advances in Group Processes,* ed. Shane R. Thye and John Skvoretz. New York: Elsevier/ JAI.

Weinberg, Alvin. 1963. "Criteria for Scientific Choice." *Minerva* 1 (2): 159–171.

Weingart, P. 2000. "Interdisciplinarity: The Paradoxical Discourse." Pp. 25–42 in *Practising Interdisciplinarity,* ed. P. Weingart and N. Stehr. Toronto: University of Toronto Press.

Weisbuch, Robert. 1999. "Why Women's Studies." *Woodrow Wilson National Fellowship Foundation Newsletter* (Fall): 4.

Wenneras, Christine, and Agnes Wold. 1997. "Nepotism and Sexism in Peer Review." *Nature* 387:341–343.

White, Harrison C., and Cynthia A. White. 1993. *Canvases and Careers: Institutional Change in the French Painting World.* Chicago: University of Chicago Press.

White, Jonathan. 2007. "A Political Bond in Europe." Ph.D. diss., European University Institute, Florence, Italy.

Whitley, Richard. 1984. *The Intellectual and Social Organization of the Sciences.* Oxford, Eng.: Clarendon Press.

Williams, Jeffrey J. 2004. "Here's the Problem with Being So 'Smart.'" *Chronicle of Higher Education* 51 (17): B16.

Williams, Joan. 2004. "Hitting the Maternal Wall." *Academe* 90 (6): 16–20.

Wilson, Logan. 1942. *The Academic Man.* New York: Oxford University Press.

Wimmer, Andreas, and Michèle Lamont. 2006. "Boundaries and Group Making: A Framework and a Research Agenda." Paper presented at the American Sociological Assocation's annual meeting, Montreal, August.

Worcester, Kenton. 2001. *The Social Science Research Council, 1923–1998.* New York: Social Science Research Council.

Zuckerman, Harriet, and Robert K. Merton. 1971. "Patterns of Evaluation in Science—Institutionalisation, Structure, and Functions of the Referee System." *Minerva* 9 (1): 66–100.

Acknowledgments

Nothing convinces me more of the collective character of knowledge production than finishing this book, which has been at the center of a great many conversations with friends and colleagues over the past several years.

My first thanks go to a few social scientists who helped me gain access to my research sites. Craig Calhoun, president of the Social Science Research Council, understood the interest of my research from the start, opened the door of SSRC, and contributed to enrolling other institutions. Stanley Katz, president emeritus of the American Council of Learned Societies and a former colleague at Princeton University, also played a crucial role, as did Robert Weisbuch and Judith Pinch of the Woodrow Wilson National Fellowship Foundation. I also thank the leaders of those participating organizations that requested anonymity, and the program officers with whom I worked.

The project would not have been possible without the goodwill of the many academics who agreed to be interviewed and observed. I am extremely grateful to each of you for your sense of adventure, generosity, and openness. I hope you will find your trust in me was deserved.

The start of the project was facilitated by a small grant from the University Committee for Research in the Social Sciences and the Humanities, Princeton University. The bulk of the research was supported by a grant from the National Science Foundation (SES-0096880). The Canadian Institute for Advanced Research also supported my time when I worked on the book. I want to acknowledge the special colleagueship of the CIFAR Successful Societies research group over these past five years, especially the input of Peter A. Hall, Natalie Zemon Davis, Bill Sewell, Ann Swidler, and Jonathan Arac on this particular project.

A first draft of the manuscript was written while I was a fellow at the Center for Advanced Study in the Behavioral Sciences, under a fellowship from the Andrew W. Mellon Foundation (grant no. 29800639). The book manuscript was completed while I held the Matina Horner Distinguished Professorship at the Radcliffe Institute for Advanced Study. As was the case at the CASBS, Radcliffe provided the ideal combination of intellectual stimulation and uninterrupted time I needed to work on this book. I want to single out the stimulating friendships that kept me going during these leaves. I thank particularly Jane Burbank, Fred Cooper, and Peter Gourevitch in Palo Alto, and Bruce Carruthers and Wendy Espeland at Radcliffe.

I have been very fortunate in being surrounded by a number of kindred spirits as I conceptualized the project, conducted interviews, and worked on the book manuscript. The most central presence was that of my colleagues, research assistants, and friends Joshua Guetzkow (now assistant professor at the University of Arizona) and Grégoire Mallard (now assistant professor at Northwestern University). Josh contributed to this project in all the various phases of the research. His judicious comments and his kindness enriched the process throughout. His substantive contributions, notably in the papers we coauthored, fed the argument of this book in a great many ways. The same holds for Grégoire (known as "Greg" in the United States), who, although he joined the project later than Josh, also made important contributions, notably in the construction of the typology of epistemological styles used in Chapter 5. At Harvard, another graduate student, Lauren Rivera, helped me in countless ways, as did several other assistants: Frederic Clark, Eva Dickerman, Joshua Wakeham, Luis Martos, Viktoria Slavinia, Janice Whang, and May Tobin-Hochstadt.

Other colleagues contributed directly to the project time and time again. At Princeton, my dialogues with Carl Schorske, notably around his work with Tom Bender concerning the transformation of the social sciences and the humanities, were very inspiring. My early thinking about the culture of excellence across disciplines was also enriched by conversations with John Borneman, Angela Creager, Bob Darnton, Tony Grafton, Rena Lederman, Liz Lunbeck, and Alexander Nehamas. Within sociology, Paul DiMaggio, Robert Wuthnow, Viviana Zelizer, and Marion Fourcade-Gourinchas were stimulating conversational partners around sociology of knowledge topics, while Chris Winship and Neil Gross played a similar role at Harvard. Beyond my department, Lisbeth Cohen, Peter Gallison, Howard Gardner, Ivan Gaskell, Sheila Jasanoff, Steve Shapin, Kay Shelemay, Gerhart Sonnert, and many others generously engaged my project. I want to underscore the particularly significant contributions of Jenny Mansbridge and Sandy Jencks, for their friendship throughout. My writing group, which includes Jenny as well as Ann Blair, Nancy Cott, Lani Guinier, Leah Price, and Harriet Ritvo, constituted the ideal interdisciplinary audience. So did my Radcliffe writing group, which was composed of John Diamond, Jane Kamenski, Peggy Miller, Leah Price, and Francesca Tribaletto.

Friends and colleagues from various disciplines played a crucial role by giving an essential "native" reader's reaction to my description of various disciplinary cultures in Chapter 3. I want to both acknowledge their generosity and exonerate them from all blame. They are, for anthropology, John Bowen, Don Brenneis and Nancy Schepper-Hughes; for philosophy, Rebecca Goldstein; for literary studies, Jonathan Arac, Homi Bhabha, and Leah Price; for history, Natalie Zemon Davis, Drew Faust and Bill Sewell; for political science, Suzanne Berger, Peter Hall, and Sid Tarrow; and for economics, David Cutler and Elhanan Helpman.

Conversations with a broader group of colleagues also enriched my thinking about the project. I am particularly grateful to colleagues who commented on the entire manuscript or on chapters: Steve Brint, Charles Camic, Bruce Carruthers, Wendy Espeland, Marion Fourcade, Marcel Fournier, Neil Gross, Josh Guetzkow, Annette Lareau, Grégoire Mallard, Jenny Mansbridge, Chandra Mukerji, Claude Rosenthal, Mitchell Stevens, Art Stinchcombe, Andreas Wimmer, and Chris Winship. I also benefited from exchanges with Julia Adams, Randall Collins, Nina Eliasoph, Irwin Feller, David Frank, Joan Fujimura, Patricia Gumport, Stanley Hegginbotham, Nathalie Heinich, Antoine Hennion, Warren Ilchman, Karin Knorr, Bruno Latour, Paul Lichterman, John Meyer, Kelly Moore, Christine Musselin, Francisco Ramirez, Susan Silbey, Peggy Somers, George Steinmetz, Laurent Thévenot, Diane Vaughan, Mark Ventresca, and Woody Powell. The book also greatly benefited from continuing exchanges with former graduate students who worked in the sociology of knowledge at Princeton: Sada Aksartova, Virag Molnar, Kyoko Sato, Anna Xiao Sun, and Laura Stark. At Harvard, the Culture and Social Analysis workshop also provided another ideal audience since 2003. I thank the graduate students who are regular workshop participants for their many contributions to my thinking on this and other topics: Alvaro Acuna-Santana, Chris Bail, Jovonne Bickerstaff, Jeff Denis, Crystal Fleming, Nathan Fosse, Joyce Liu, Mark Pachucki,

Sabrina Pendergrass, Lauren Rivera, Graziella Silva, and Jessica Welburn. I also thank the postdocs and the visiting graduate students and professors who joined the workshop for varying periods over the past few years, several of whom discussed the book with me: Gabi Abend, Janice Aurini, Katri Huutoniemi, Hunaida Ghanim, Fuyuki Kurasawa, Nasser Meer, Avi Shoshana, Sylvie Tissot, Alexis Tremoulinas, and Jonathan White.

Special thanks also go to Kathy Mooney, who so skillfully edited the book, and to my editor at Harvard University Press, Elizabeth Knoll, for her great enthusiasm for the project from the first time she learned about it. Also thanks to Adam Kissel, Dorothy Friendly, Mary Quigley, and especially Joe Cook, who did much more than providing technical help at various stages in the project.

Finally, I also thank my children, Gabrielle, Pierre, and Chloë, for offering diversion, entertainment, and love as I worked on the book. I first thought of dedicating this book to my youngest children, Pierre and Chloë, who were born as I was starting to conceptualize this project and reached the age of seven by the time I finished (these were well-spent years). The other natural choices might have been my colleagues (to oil the wheel of our collective deliberations) or my graduate students (to keep the flame alive). But in the end, I dedicate this book to my husband, Frank Dobbin, who is excellent in so many ways. With loving thanks for the past twenty-five years.

Index

Academic Revolution, The, 159–160
academic standards, 55; in English, 59,
69, 70–72, 75, 76–77, 104; in various
disciplines, 62–63, 103, 106, 159; in
philosophy, 66, 69; in history, 83–84,
85, 86, 103–104; in anthropology,
90, 92–93, 94; in political science,
99; in economics, 101–102. See also
evaluation; excellence
accuracy, 169
advocacy, 181
affirmative action, 64, 203, 224–235,
285n25
African American studies, 235
Age of the Democratic Revolution, The,
189–190
Akerloff, George, 164
Allen, Walter, 284n18
alliances of panelists, 120–121
American Association for University
Women, 218–219
American Council of Learned Societies

(ACLS), 13, 251; applicants to, 15;
grants by, 16, 25, 283n1; Humanities
Fellowship program, 24; evaluation
process, 27, 28–30, 167; and selection of panelists, 30–31; and diversity, 203, 212; and affirmative action,
224–225
American Philosophical Association
(APA), 66, 272n26
American Political Science Association
(APSA), 95–96, 237
American Political Science Review, 95
American Sociological Association
(ASA), 237, 274n42, 286n44
American Sociological Review, 11
Anderson, Benedict, 208
anonymity, 35
anthropology and anthropologists, 55,
56, 72, 93; and boundaries, 4, 88–91;
and "theory wars," 58–59; view of
other disciplines, 62–63; cultural,
74, 87–95, 274n44; identity crisis in,

anthropology *(continued)*
87–88; evaluative criteria in, 90;
anti-scientism in, 91; and multi-
sited research, 91–92; ethnography
in, 92–93; and notions of excellence,
94; and rational choice theory, 98; as
inward-looking discipline, 105
anti-positivism, 57
anti-reductionism, 184–185
anti-scientism, 91
area studies, 25–26
Asad, Talal, 274n47
assessment strategies, 241–242
attachments, theoretical, 54–55
attribution biases, 222
audacity, 195
audit culture, 281n18
authenticity, 161, 162, 195, 197–198, 199
autonomy, 32, 45, 66

balance, 32
belief, production of, 110
Bender, Thomas, 252
bias, 144, 246, 278n23; class-based,
191; gender, 221–224, 246; in-group,
222; ideological, 246; indirect,
285n38
Birmingham School, 230
blind review, 244
Boix Mansilla, Veronica, 284n15
Bologna Declaration, 243
Bologna Process, 243
Boltanski, Luc, 204, 266n60
boringness, 193
Borofsky, Robert, 274n44
boundary work, 88–91, 277n11
Bourdieu, Pierre, 18, 19–20, 36, 84,
180, 192, 223, 244, 261n15, 262n22,
275n2
Brenneis, Donald, 268n30

broad-mindedness, 132
bullshit, 162, 163, 280n6

Callon, Michel, 261n14
Camic, Charles, 184
canon formation, 70, 72
canon wars, 72–79, 272n28
canonical disciplines, 282n26
career, vision of, 197
career trajectories, academic, 38
chance, 153–155
character traits of panelists, 113
Chubin, Daryl, 262n37
citation counts, 262n30
clarity, 167–168, 185, 199
class, 192, 199, 221, 282nn30,31
Clemens, Elizabeth, 223–224
clientelism, 128, 157
Clifford, James, 89, 91
close reading, 72
coding scheme, 256
cognitive contextualization: defined, 6,
58; disciplinary, 57, 211; by panelists, 64–66, 106; and deprofessionalization, 73; and methodological
pluralism, 132–134, 142; and consistency, 144, 185
cognitive dimensions, 8
cognitive translations, 265n54
Cole, Jonathan, 261n15
Cole, Stephen, 261n15, 264n53
collegiality, 8, 113, 119–120, 138–141,
145, 244
Collins, Harry, 18, 265n54, 271n20
Collins, Randall, 36, 266n62
common good, 117
communication, discipline of, 87
competence, criteria of, 128–130
competition, 163
comprehensive style, 57, 174–176, 178

French theory, 179
Fuller, Sally Riggs, 285n23
funding panels, 12–16, 136. *See also individual panel names*

Galison, Peter, 261n13
"Garbage-can" model, 23–24
Gardner, Howard, 284n15
Garfinkel, Irving, 17, 280n11
gatekeepers, 12
Geertz, Clifford, 84, 87, 88, 89, 191–192
gender, 148, 149–150, 213, 231, 280n10, 284n19
gender bias, 221–224, 246
generalization, 57, 178, 186
generational differences, 79, 84–85
generosity, 137
Germany, 245
Glazer, Nathan, 285n25
global unification, 104
Goffman, Erving, 17, 20, 160, 275n2, 280nn4,11
gossip, 32, 144–145
Gould, Stephen Jay, 282n26
grading strategies, 39–41
graduate students, 25–26, 85, 91, 182, 227
Granovetter, Marc, 278n20
grants, 7, 15, 141
Green, Donald P., 274n50
Gross, Neil, 184, 230, 266n62
group dynamics, 49–50
group style, 260n12
Guetzkow, Joshua, 171–172
guidelines for review, lack of, 43–44
Guinier, Lani, 215

Habermas, Jürgen, 248
Hackett, Edward, 262n37
halo effect, 18, 164
Hartmann, Ilse, 264n53

Helpman, Elhanan, 100
high-balling, 123
hiring decisions, 249
history and historians, 55, 72, 73, 270n14; and craftsmanship, 4; and utilitarian epistemological style, 59; narrative vs. theory in, 63–64; and cultural studies, 74, 84, 230; as consensual discipline, 79–96, 103; vs. English, 80–81; empiricism in, 81; expanded pluralism of, 81–82; and funding of competitions, 82; as science, 82–83; and divisions around theory, 82–85; disciplinary fragmentation in, 83, 85–86; cultural vs. social, 84; and academic excellence, 86; and competition funding, 136; and originality, 172; and significance, 174; and comprehensive style, 175; and theory, 185; and elegance, 191; and subjectivity, 193; and evaluation criteria, 194; and diversity, 213–214; faculty numbers, 273n37
history from below, 81, 230
Hobbes, Thomas, 106
Homo Academicus, 244
homophily, 7–8, 20–21, 231, 247, 261n19, 278n22, 287n14
horse-trading, 121–125
humanism and humanities, 9, 169, 270n14, 282n26, 284n19; and grants, 15; polarizing stances of, 54; comprehensive epistemological style in, 57; and demographic patterns, 59; and interpretative skills, 61; and originality, 172; and significance, 174; and comprehensive style, 175; diffusion of theory in, 184; and elegance, 191; and subjectivity, 193; and diversity, 213; progressives in, 230; liberalism of, 236

Humanities Fellowship program, 13, 24

Hume, David, 176

humility, 195, 196, 199

hypothesis testing, 57

identity, 38, 200. *See also* self-concept of panelists

identity politics, 76, 278n23

idiosyncrasies, 6, 51, 128–132, 157, 247

Iggers, Georg, 81

impression management, 162

incommensurability of proposals, 42–43

inconsistency, 141–144

inequality, 180

influence, degrees of, 147

innovation, 154

inquiry beliefs, 54–55

insiderism, 15–17

institutional affiliation, 147

instrumental knowledge, 178–179, 180

intellectual similarity, 150–151

intelligence, signs of, 189–191

interactionism, symbolic, 17

interdisciplinarity, 14–15, 26, 48, 66, 202–205, 235, 242; cleavages in, 83, 85–86; of panelists, 114–115; of proposals, 139; evaluation of, 205–208

interestingness, 192–194

International Dissertation Field Research (IDRF) competition, 13, 24, 25, 27, 97, 229

interpersonal relations, 41, 45, 157

interpretive communities, 104

intersubjectivity, 4, 70, 94, 103

interviewing, 14, 253

Ivy League, 126, 147

jargon, 80, 92, 93, 185, 193

Jencks, Christopher, 159–160

job market, 81–82

journals, 3, 15, 158

judgment, 55, 111, 131

juries, 269n40

Keohane, Robert, 98

Keynes, John Maynard, 179

King, Gary, 98

Knorr-Cetina, Karin, 22, 264n48, 266n1

knowledge, 58, 63, 175, 180, 231

Kuhn, Thomas, 171

Lachs, John, 272n26

Ladd, Everett Carl, Jr., 230

Laitin, David, 274n50

Lakatos, Imre, 99

Langfeldt, Liv, 280n5, 283n14

Latour, Bruno, 17–18, 171, 194, 261n15, 264n48, 265n54

legitimacy, 31, 110, 137–145, 158, 228, 242–243, 247, 276n6, 277n10

legitimation crisis (English), 4, 70–79

letters of support, 163–165, 280nn7,10

limitations of study, 256–258

Lipset, Seymour Marin, 189, 230

listening, 116

localism, 245

location, institutional, 245

low-balling, 122, 123

MacKenzie, Donald, 261n14

Mallard, Grégoire, 171–172

Marcus, George, 89, 91

market ideology, 10

Marxism, 73, 179, 180

Masoud, Tarek, 96

mathematical formalism, 100–102

Matthew effect, 8, 18, 227, 246

meaning systems, 109

Her understg ant as defending its bondaries is odd isofar as all disc do bounday-wrle (Gieryn). What she doesn't point out is that the empl of her respondent reflects a "minon'ty descipline" POV - anthrop (more ofte than not) need to explain themsel to others insofar as th're in a soc science "space". Of cruse th'll be clarifying "what we do" + "what we don't do". If the ant is ⊕isr, then she will likly be doubly pressed to clarify; if humanist then th'll reinf. stereotypes abr "nihilis-ns — a — ns other soc sci.